Pragmatic Development in a Second Language

Gabriele Kasper
University of Hawai'i at Manoa

Kenneth R. Rose
City University of Hong Kong

Blackwell Publishing

© 2002 Language Learning Research Club, University of Michigan

Blackwell Publishing, Inc.
350 Main Street
Malden, MA 02148 USA

Blackwell Publishing, Ltd.
9600 Garsington
Oxford OX4 2XG
United Kingdom

ISBN 13: 978-0-63123-430-2
A CIP catalog record for this book is available
from the Library of Congress

Pragmatic Development in a Second Language

Language Learning Monograph Series

Richard Young, Editor
Alexander Z. Guiora, General Editor

Contents

Series Editor's Foreword

In the early days of the study of second language acquisition, scholars considered the activity of learning a second language as a single phenomenon. The nature of the linguistic forms to be acquired, their sequence of acquisition, and the contexts in which they were acquired were considered as part of the same problem, which was viewed as one at the intersection of linguistics and psychology. Since those early days the field of SLA has burgeoned, resulting in a far greater and more nuanced understanding of the language learning task and the learning processes that learners undergo, but along with greater understanding has come a division of the field that makes it increasingly difficult for scholars whose research focus is the acquisition of syntax to communicate meaningfully with those who attend to the social context of acquisition. This dichotomizing of the field of SLA is but one of the dichotomies that are at the root of much of Western thinking. Descartes gave us the mind-body duality, Saussure distinguished between *langue* and *parole*, and Chomsky sliced language knowledge neatly into competence and performance. But a consequence of this two-world view is that in language research, language is seen like the figure in a classical portrait painting, in which we view language as a central figure in a background of peripheral interest. Syntacticians, especially those working within the framework of Universal Grammar, attend to language as their central concern independently of the context in which language is produced, heard, or thought about. And sociolinguists focus on the context, believing that language structure responds to the social contexts in which it used.

Another dichotomy that we live by is one of method. Much psychological research into second language acquisition hews to a positivist epistemology in which psychological processes can be objectively described, while sociocultural theorists see language in a postmodernist light as part of lived experience that is essentially local. This epistemological split again results in largely incommensurable discourses of quantitative and qualitative research. The dichotomies in our field can be seen as a canyon, and those that work in just one of the approaches stand on one of the rims of the canyon. The canyon is wide and voices from one rim are not heard on the other.

Pragmatics, defined by David Crystal as "the study of language from the point of view of users, especially of the choices they make, the constraints they encounter in using language in social interaction and the effects their use of language has on other participants in the act of communication," certainly appears to be on the socio, postmodernist rim of the canyon. But the study of developmental pragmatics, as practiced by Gabi Kasper and Ken Rose in this book, is a discipline that challenges the divide and on some occasions jumps it as unexpectedly and as skillfully as Evel Knievel. Kasper and Rose believe that a cognitive processing perspective has demonstrated the greatest potential in explaining the facts of pragmatic development in a second language because unless learners consciously attend to the complex interaction between language use and social context they will hardly ever learn the pragmatics of a new language.

Another way in which Kasper and Rose jump the divide is in their insightful and innovative discussion of the relationship between the development of second language pragmatics and the acquisition of grammar. They consider two contradictory claims that have been made in this regard. Some scholars have claimed that second language speakers cannot learn pragmatics without the grammar to express it, while quite the reverse has been observed by other researchers: learners manage to be pragmatically appropriate without a command of the grammatical structures that native speakers expect. Kasper and Rose conclude that the apparent contradiction is due to the fact that different scholars have studied learners at different stages in their development, and the complex interaction between pragmatics and grammar is due to what functional linguists have recognized as different modes of communication at different stages of linguistic development: pragmatic and syntactic.

Kasper and Rose have themselves been at the center of research on interlanguage pragmatics for more than two decades and their knowledge of the research studies in the field is encyclopedic. It is this extensive knowledge of research practice that has enabled them to make one further leap across the disciplinary divide. They recognize the many sources of research methodology that pragmaticians adopted from across the social sciences, including descriptive linguistics, conversation analysis, interactional sociolinguistics, ethnographic microanalysis, language socialization, developmental pragmatics, cognitive and social psychology, discourse comprehension, and intercultural communication. They show that by embracing apparent differences in epistemology, pragmaticians have been able to develop a coherent picture of their field. Positivist research methodologies such as experiments and surveys supply researchers with a broad and general perspective on language in use, while interpretive methodologies such as ethnography and case studies provide us with indispensable and rich descriptions of social actors in unique social contexts.

Kasper and Rose's *Pragmatic Development in a Second Language* is the third volume in the Language Learning Monograph Series. The volumes in this series review recent findings and current theoretical positions, present new data and interpretations, and sketch interdisciplinary research programs. Volumes are authoritative statements by scholars who have led in the development of a particular line of interdisciplinary research and are intended to serve as a benchmark for interdisciplinary research in the years to come. Kasper and Rose's book provides a rich resource for current and future researchers interested in the fascinating field of interlanguage pragmatics.

Richard Young
University of Wisconsin–Madison

CHAPTER ONE

Introduction to Second Language Pragmatic Development

This book examines how nonnative speakers develop pragmatic ability in a nonprimary language. It shares with other publications on second or foreign language learning a focus on acquisitional processes, conditions, and sequential patterns. What makes this book different from most work in second language acquisition research is the learning object that we propose to investigate. Second language researchers have been studying nonnative speakers' pragmatic ability for more than two decades, resulting in a large and diverse international literature that takes more than average persistence to stay on top of. But for the most part, this impressive body of research addresses questions relating to nonnative speakers' comprehension and production of L2 pragmatic meanings, their interaction in different settings, and pragmatic aspects of foreign or second language writing. In other words, the pragmatics of nonnative speakers has predominantly been studied as an issue of second language use, not development. As Bardovi-Harlig (1999) acerbically observes, "Not only [is] interlanguage pragmatics not fundamentally acquisitional, but it [is], in fact, fundamentally not acquisitional" (p. 679). This is not a desirable state of affairs because the importance accorded to pragmatic ability surely must be met with a commensurate curiosity regarding the ways such ability develops, whether in order to better understand the different uses to which such ability is put, or to cultivate L2 pragmatic development as a domain within

1

second language acquisition research, or to establish a research basis for instruction in L2 pragmatics.

As an interdisciplinary research domain, pragmatics is so well institutionalized that the field does not need yet another definition. But we will dwell for a bit on what we treat as pragmatic phenomena, the learning of which therefore falls within the scope of this book. Delimiting what we consider pragmatics will also, we hope, forestall disappointment in readers who may have expected a different coverage, and whet the appetite of those who decide to follow us through the next eight chapters.

It is helpful to start with two much-cited definitions of the field and to develop the scope of pragmatic phenomena that we will consider from there. Mey (1993) defines pragmatics as "the societally necessary and consciously interactive dimension of the study of language" (p. 315). Instructively, Mey arrives at this definition at the conclusion of his 300-plus-page treatise on the topic, rather than supplying readers with an up-front assurance of what his book is all about. His definition does not identify any particular objects for study (the component view of pragmatics) but rather conceptualizes pragmatics as a *perspective* on the linguistic enterprise, as recommended by Verschueren (1987).

Crystal (1997) offers a compatible, but more specific, view when he delineates pragmatics as "the study of language from the point of view of *users*, especially of the *choices* they make, the *constraints* they encounter in using language in *social interaction* and the *effects* their use of language has on *other participants* in the *act of communication*" (p. 301, italics added). This definition alludes to the semiotic conceptualization of pragmatics in the theory of Charles Morris (1938), in which pragmatics describes one side of the semiotic triangle—the relation between the sign and its interpreters (users). Pragmatic meanings arise from choices between linguistic forms, such as using one discourse marker or particle over another, or opting for one linguistic format of a communicative act instead of a contextually possible alternative to convey illocutionary force or politeness. Speakers' and writers' choices, however, are not unconstrained but are governed by social conventions, which can be flexed to different, contextually varying degrees but only entirely set aside at the peril of losing claims to face, insider status, or sanity. These constraints are partly universal, partly activity- and genre-specific, and have to be worked out by language learners and other novices. Indeed, the tension between "choice" and "constraint" lends itself to a post-structuralist reinterpretation as the agency-structure dialectic, a view that has considerable currency in contemporary discourse-analytical and conversation-analytical practice.

The focus of pragmatics on social interaction can be understood in a narrow and a broad sense. In a narrow sense, social interaction refers to encounters in which at least two participants are co-present and engaged in a joint activity, either within the same temporal and spatial frame or within a shared temporal frame only, in which case the spatial displacement is compensated through electronic devices such as the telephone or Internet facilities. This is the sense in which interaction is defined in conversation analysis, where interaction is specified as "talk-in-interaction" and thereby distinguished from text. But in a wider sense, social interaction can usefully be extended to encompass all sorts of written and mixed forms of communication. For scholars of literature, it is a truism that no text is ever the first and that texts build on, respond to, synthesize, amalgamate, oppose—in short, interact with each other, a fact that has been theorized in such notions as intertextuality, dialogicity, hybridicity, symbiotic text, or literary sequences. The same interactivity can, of course, be postulated for the text producer, who is never the lone writer that she at times may imagine herself to be. Scholarly texts are a particularly clear case in point because without making due reference to other authors' work, academics do not even get published. In fact, the understanding of the entire research enterprise as cumulative strongly supports the view of scholarship as an interactive process. Tellingly, the interaction taking place in reading and responding to the work of others is now often referred to as "conversation," a metaphorical extension that clearly points to the shared give-and-take as a point of reference for both reading and speaking.

Consistent with the pragmatics-as-perspective view, not only orality, but literacy and the many hybrid modalities of language use, including the diverse and increasing forms of electronic communication, are included in the scope of the term. In fact, it is only by adopting a pragmatic perspective that the commonalities and particularities of different modes of language-mediated social activity can be compared and contrasted. Mey's and Crystal's emphasis on social interaction, as well as Thomas's (1995) description of pragmatics as "meaning in interaction," underscores the notion that pragmatics is not only concerned with the actions of the producing (speaking, writing) participant but also with the effect of such actions on their recipients. The effect—how recipients understand a particular action or sequence of actions—figures as an important issue in otherwise incompatible pragmatic theories, as evident in such speech act-theoretical notions as uptake and perlocutionary act and the conversation-analytical principle of analyzing meaning in interaction as the displayed hearing or treatment of the previous speaker's turn (or a part thereof) by the current speaker. This analytical scope extends not only to the addressee but to actors with different participation status, such as audience, bystanders, overhearers, and eavesdroppers (Goffman, 1981). The final criterial element in Crystal's definition specifies the "act of communication" as the core of pragmatics. From a component perspective, "act" serves as the focal unit of analysis, which is precisely the case in speech act theory and speech-act-based research. Though not necessarily as the central unit, "act" represents a level of analysis in Hymes's ethnography of communication, which distinguishes the levels of communicative situation, event, and act; and it equally constitutes the smallest unit of analysis in Sinclair and Coulthard's (1975) model of discourse. Other approaches to discourse and pragmatics emphasize the centrality of action rather than isolate specific communicative acts. Action as an analytical perspective is epitomized in conversation analysis, one of whose guiding questions is

"What action is X accomplishing by doing Y (where Y is some observable practice of interactional conduct)?"

The overarching interest in language use as action does not exclude from pragmaticians' analytical attention the linguistic forms or practices that implement actions. As we elaborate in Chapters 2 and 3, just as pragmatics draws on a variety of disciplines across the social sciences for its theories and research methods, so are ways of doing pragmatics informed by practitioners' disciplinary traditions. An analysis of prosody or modal particles may rely strongly on linguistic description; the comprehension of indirect speech acts may be conducted from the vantage point of cognitive processing models and implemented with psycholinguistic methodology; and identity construction in news interviews may be tackled from a microsociological perspective. But each of these research objects can also be examined from quite different disciplinary backgrounds and investigative orientations, as the research literature amply documents. Pragmatics as a perspective rather than as a set of components saves us and the reader the laundry-list approach to our domain of interest. Pragmatics-as-perspective has the advantage of being inclusive and open to study new research objects *as* pragmatics, without precluding them from being examined from a different angle as well.

As a domain within second language studies, pragmatics is usually referred to as interlanguage pragmatics, by analogy with interlanguage grammar, interlanguage phonology, and the interlanguage lexicon. This book is about interlanguage pragmatics, but not about the entire domain. Roughly, but adequately for the purpose, we can distinguish two sections within the wider domain of interlanguage pragmatics. As the study of second language *use*, interlanguage pragmatics examines how nonnative speakers comprehend and produce action in a target language. As the study of second language *learning*, interlanguage pragmatics investigates how L2 learners develop the ability to understand and perform action in a target language. This book focuses on the second, and, at the time of writing, considerably smaller subfield. Our topic, then, is second language learners' pragmatic development (or learning, or acquisition—we shall use these terms interchangeably throughout the book).

In a previous publication that had the express objective of moving interlanguage pragmatics within the scope of second language acquisition research, Kasper and Schmidt (1996) asked 14 questions about interlanguage pragmatics.

1. Are there universals of language underlying cross-linguistic variation, and if so, do they play a role in interlanguage pragmatics?

2. How can approximation to target language norms be measured?

3. Does the L1 influence the learning of a second language?

4. Is pragmatic development in a second language similar to first language learning?

5. Do children enjoy an advantage over adults in learning a second language?

6. Is there a natural route of development, as evidenced by difficulty, accuracy, acquisition orders, or discrete stages of development?

7. Does type of input make a difference?

8. Does instruction make a difference?

9. Do motivation and attitudes make a difference in level of acquisition?

10. Does personality play a role?

11. Does learners' gender play a role?

12. Does (must) perception or comprehension precede production in acquisition?

13. Does chunk learning (formulaic speech) play a role in acquisition?

14. What mechanisms drive development from stage to stage?

Most of these questions are addressed in the following chapters. In Chapter 2, we discuss several theoretical orientations that have been, or could be, fruitfully engaged to account for L2 pragmatic development. These include theories with an intra-psychological orientation (the acculturation model, cognitive processing models) and approaches that conceptualize L2 learning as social practice (sociocultural theory, language socialization, and interactional competence). In most instances, these theoretical positions have methodological corollaries or are associated with particular preferences for data collection and analysis.

In Chapter 3, we scrutinize the main methodological approaches deployed for examining how L2 pragmatics is learned. We briefly discuss the extent to which interlanguage pragmatics research draws its methodology from across the social sciences and consider longitudinal or cross-sectional designs. The remainder of the chapter divides the research approaches used in developmental interlanguage pragmatics into three parts. The first part examines spoken discourse as a source for pragmatics research and discusses three types of spoken discourse data: authentic discourse, elicited conversation and role play. The second part deals with different types of questionnaire: discourse completion, multiple-choice, and scaled-response questionnaires. The final part focuses on oral and written self-report: interviews, verbal protocols, and diaries. Chapter 3, then, discusses a range of methodological options in response to Kasper and Schmidt's Question 2: How can approximation to target language norms be measured?

Chapter 4 focuses on substantive findings from L2 developmental pragmatic research. This chapter serves as a companion to Chapter 2, which addresses the various theoretical orientations to account for pragmatic development in authentic learning environments. We begin with studies of the development of pragmatic comprehension, an area that has thus far received little attention. Following this, we turn our attention to the development of pragmatic production, dividing research into two main groups: pragmatic and discourse ability, and speech acts. We conclude the chapter with some discussion of the relationship between pragmatic transfer and development. To varying degrees, Chapter 4 takes up several of Kasper and Schmidt's questions: (3) Does the L1 influence the learning of a second language? (6) Is there a natural route of development, as evidenced by difficulty, accuracy, acquisition orders, or discrete stages of development? (13) Does chunk learning (formulaic speech) play a role in acquisition? And (14), what mechanisms drive development from stage to stage?

Chapter 5 reviews what the research literature has to say about the relationship of interlanguage pragmatic and grammatical development. After reviewing some recent studies that specifically addressed the issue, we reiterate Bardovi-Harlig's call to subject the relationship between pragmatics and grammar to renewed scrutiny. Next, we provide evidence for the primacy of pragmatics in interlanguage development. A central point in the argument is the range of pragmatic universals that adult second language learners draw on in developing L2 pragmatic ability (cf. Kasper and Schmidt's Question 1: Are there universals of language underlying cross-linguistic variation, and if so, do they play a role in interlanguage pragmatics?). Evidence for the primacy of pragmatics is contrasted with studies documenting the opposite developmental pattern, namely, grammatical knowledge preceding its pragmatic deployment. Specifically, we comment on available grammatical knowledge that (a) is not put to pragmatic use, (b) enables non-target-like pragmatic use, and (c) is used in a way that is pragmalinguistically target-like but sociopragmatically non-target-like. Finally, we suggest how these seemingly contradictory findings may be reconciled.

Whereas Chapters 4 and 5 discuss, among other things, the knowledge and ability that adult learners bring to the task of acquiring L2 pragmatics and how they draw on L1 grammatical and pragmatic knowledge at different stages of L2 learning, Chapter 6 shifts focus to the role of the environment in pragmatic development. This chapter, then, is designated to address Kasper and Schmidt's Question 7: Does type of input make a difference? After considering the impact of duration of stay in the target community on pragmatic development, we examine learners' opportunities for participating and obtaining L2 pragmatic input in different types of ordinary and institutional discourse. One outcome of this discussion is that such opportunities and, indeed, the learning resulting from them are shaped both by learners' social category membership as constructed by members of the target community and by learners' own agency. We then turn to the language classroom as a context for learning L2 pragmatics under instructed but noninterventional conditions, observing that studies have arrived at quite opposite conclusions about the benefits and limitations of language teaching contexts for pragmatic development. In order to assess the potential of classroom arrangements and tasks for learning L2 pragmatics, it would seem critical to examine such arrangements as activities, that is, to analyze how participants transform organizational formats and tasks in their interactional engagements, as proposed by scholars working in a sociocultural framework. Lastly, we scrutinize research that compares the pragmatic ability of L2 learners in second and foreign language learning contexts, including the effect of study abroad on pragmatic development.

Whereas Chapter 6 considers opportunities for learning L2 pragmatics in authentic settings including classrooms, Chapter 7 examines how students acquire aspects of L2 pragmatics as a result of planned pedagogical action. It thus addresses Question 8 on Kasper and Schmidt's list: Does instruction make a difference? The rationale for examining the effects of instruction in pragmatics is underscored by Schmidt's (1993) contention that simple exposure to the target language is insufficient—pragmatic functions and relevant contextual factors are often not salient to learners and therefore not likely to be noticed despite prolonged exposure. Schmidt also notes that even the pragmatic development in a first language is facilitated by a range of strategies employed by caregivers to teach children the communicative practices of their social group, that is, children learning the pragmatics of their first language do so with more than mere exposure. Adults, on the other hand, tend to receive little feedback and sometimes lack relevant input for the learning of L2 pragmatics outside of instructional settings. Bardovi-Harlig (2001) makes a strong case for the necessity of instruction, documenting that second language learners who do not receive instruction in pragmatics differ significantly from native speakers in their pragmatic production and comprehension in the target language. Because instructed learning of second language pragmatics is a subcategory of instructed second language acquisition, we situate our discussion of interventional classroom research on instruction in pragmatics within the larger research domain. Topics examined include the learning targets, learner characteristics, and learning contexts represented in the small but growing body of research on the effects of instruction in second language pragmatics. Furthermore, three central questions relating to the effect of instruction in pragmatics are considered: whether pragmatics is teachable, whether instruction in pragmatics produces results that outpace exposure alone, and whether different instructional approaches yield different outcomes. Finally, we comment on some research design issues in studies on instruction in second language pragmatics.

Chapter 8 gives focus to a topic that has largely escaped scrutiny in interlanguage pragmatics research. Many aspects of pragmatics are inseparable not only from sociocultural practices and values but also from personal views, preferences, and style, which in turn may be related to learners' societal position and experience. Yet more often than not, in cross-cultural and interlanguage pragmatics research, individual variation is submerged in the aggregate. Whereas the study of individual differences has long been a recognized subfield of second language acquisition research, with its own research traditions and a voluminous literature, the role of individual differences in the acquisition of L2 pragmatics has rarely been addressed. This is a remarkable omission, considering that L2 pragmatic practices may provoke affective responses in L2 learners that are unlikely to have counterparts in learners' responses to L2 grammar. Chapter 8, then, examines the relationship between individual differences and the development of L2 pragmatics. Ellis's (1994) typology for categorizing individual difference research in SLA serves as a framework for classifying studies on individual differences in L2 pragmatic development. In examining the relationship between pragmatic learning and learners' social identity from a range of theoretical perspectives, we shift from conceptualizations of "learner" factors as individual traits and intrapsychological constructs to views of identity and self as socially and interactionally constructed. In so doing, the chapter addresses, but also goes beyond, the three pertinent questions from Kasper and Schmidt's list: (9) Do motivation and attitudes make a difference in level of acquisition? (10) Does personality play a role? and (11) Does learners' gender play a role?

Lastly, as an epilogue, Chapter 9 summarizes the outcomes of our discussions in the preceding chapters and closes by proposing several thematic areas for future investigation of L2 pragmatic development.

CHAPTER TWO

Theories of Second Language Pragmatic Development

Considering theoretical approaches to L2 pragmatic development is not a straightforward matter, because much of the research on the topic has been descriptive rather than motivated or guided by any particular theoretical orientation. In many cases, theoretical positions have been appealed to as post hoc explanations of findings rather than serving as the basis for the design and conduct of the study in question. It is true that speech act theory and politeness theory, for example, have frequently been invoked in setting the investigational target, but these (and other) theories apply to the *object* of the study, not the learning process. Recently, however, theory-guided research has been on the rise, such as studies adopting a sociocultural or language socialization perspective. In this chapter, we discuss a range of theoretical orientations that have been, or could be fruitfully, engaged to account for pragmatic development in authentic learning environments (i.e., in settings that have not been specifically arranged for research purposes; see Chapter 7 for theories in interventional pragmatics research). These include theories with an intra-personal orientation (i.e., the acculturation model, cognitive processing) and those adopting an inter-personal perspective, conceptualizing L2 pragmatic learning as social practice (i.e., sociocultural theory, language socialization, and interactional competence). Finally, we evaluate the merits of the five theories for explaining pragmatic development.

Descriptive Studies

With one notable exception to be discussed below, early studies on pragmatic development were descriptive rather than guided by theories of second language learning, and this remains a fair characterization of most developmental interlanguage pragmatics research to date. This is not to say that such studies are theory-free. They have engaged Gricean pragmatics to examine learners' comprehension of implicature (Bouton, 1992), Brown and Levinson's (1987) politeness theory to describe the acquisition of politeness strategies (Olshtain & Blum-Kulka, 1985), and theories accounting for listener alignment through the use of discourse particles (Sawyer, 1992). The majority of studies are grounded in speech act theory and its extension into empirically based models of the pragmalinguistics and sociopragmatics of different communicative acts, including requests (Achiba, 2002; Blum-Kulka & Olshtain, 1986; Ellis, 1992; Hassall, 1997; Hill, 1997; Rose, 2000; Svanes, 1992), apologies (Blum-Kulka & Olshtain, 1986; Rose, 2000; Trosborg, 1987), refusals (Houck & Gass, 1996; Robinson, 1992), suggestions and rejections (Bardovi-Harlig & Hartford, 1993a), invitations (Scarcella, 1979), complaints (Trosborg, 1995), and compliment responses (Rose, 2000). But the theorized objects in these studies are the learning targets, not the learning process. Even when theoretical explanations are provided to account for observed developmental patterns, these are offered as post hoc (and sometimes ad hoc) explanations rather than theoretical frameworks that motivated the study. To some extent, the absence of developmental theory follows from the research focus. The majority of cross-sectional interlanguage pragmatic studies (see Kasper & Rose, 1999, for review) were not designed with the same objective that cross-sectional formats usually serve in first and second language acquisition, that is, to project synchronic states of language performance (or knowledge) in learner groups with different language proficiency (sometimes age or target community residence) on a diachronic axis and thereby enable inferences about development over time. In most interlanguage pragmatic studies, L2 proficiency and length of residence are construed as independent variables that allow for the characterization of learners' pragmatic knowledge or performance at different developmental stages of their overall L2 proficiency or the duration of residence, but the central question is not *how* learners proceed from, say, a beginning stage to intermediate and advanced stages of pragmatic ability.

It is perhaps more surprising that even longitudinal studies are often not guided by an explicit theoretical model or framework to account for the observed developmental patterns. This probably reflects the fact that these are still early days for developmental interlanguage pragmatics. Although researchers do not usually comment on their choice to abstain from conducting acquisitional studies from an explicit theoretical perspective, they may deem a "research-then-theory" approach (Larsen-Freeman & Long, 1991, p. 224) more appropriate at a stage where descriptive accounts of pragmatic development are still scarce. The data driven approach to pragmatic development repeats the history of early second language acquisition research, a period in which establishing the descriptive facts of accuracy orders and acquisition orders of English morphemes took precedence over proposing theory-derived explanations of the observed orders (see Larsen-Freeman & Long, 1991, for review).

Because the body of research conducted under an explicit acquisitional theory is still small, we shall discuss theoretical perspectives that have been adopted to explain pragmatic development whether they served as the initial framework or were engaged as post hoc explanations of the research findings. The theories and constructs we will consider are the acculturation model, cognitive processing, sociocultural theory, language socialization, and interactional competence.

Theories and Constructs

The Acculturation Model

The first theoretical approach adopted to explain pragmatic development was Schumann's (1978) acculturation model. It may be helpful to recall the evidence and theoretical reasoning on which the model was first developed. In a longitudinal case study, Schumann observed how his research participant, Alberto, acquired English grammar. Alberto was a 33-year-old Costa Rican man working as an unskilled laborer in Cambridge, Massachusetts, on a 16-month visa and living in a neighborhood of Latin American immigrants. During the 10-month observational period, Alberto's interlanguage grammar developed only minimally. Schumann contended that Alberto's acquisition process could be understood as pidginization on the argument that it shared some of the typical characteristics of pidgin languages and the conditions for their emergence. As contact languages, pidgins typically develop when groups of speakers who do not share each other's languages need to communicate and the social situation prevents the normal process of second language acquisition. Since such speakers command at least one full-fledged language that they continue to use in their own speech communities, the range of communicative functions for which the pidgin is deployed is limited to transactional purposes. Corresponding to their functional restrictions, the formal structure of pidgins is simplified compared to their donor languages, including, among other things, few redundant morphological markers and syntactic transformations. Comparison of Alberto's interlanguage to several pidgins demonstrated similarities in Alberto's L2 English of such morphosyntactic features as the placement of the negative particle, word order in *yes/no* and *wh*-questions, several inflectional morphemes, and auxiliaries. According to some social-psychological theories of pidgin genesis, the functional, and hence formal, restrictions of pidgins originate in the social distance between pidgin users. Schumann further developed this hypothesis to account for the pidginized interlanguage of individual second language learners such as Alberto. He posited that the extended construct, called acculturation ("the social and psychological integration of the learner with the target language group"), was "a major causal variable in SLA" (Schumann, 1986, p. 379).

As a social-psychological model of second language acquisition, the acculturation model subsumes two factor groups comprising social and affective variables. The social variables include:

- The power relations between the groups of L2 learners and target language speakers (dominance, nondominance, subordination),
- The L2 group's integration pattern (assimilation, acculturation, preservation),
- The L2 group's relative enclosure,
- The L2 group's relative cohesiveness,
- The size of the L2 group,
- The cultural (in)congruence of the L2 and target groups,
- The mutual group attitudes, and
- The L2 group's intended duration of stay in the target language community (Schumann, 1978, 1986).

Because not all group contact situations can be unambiguously categorized according to these variables, Schumann argued that in addition to the *social* distance that individuals experience as group members, the learner's *psychological* distance to the target group needs to be taken into consideration. The affective factors include:

- Language shock, a psychoanalytic concept proposed by Stengal (1939) (not to be confused with the anthropological notion discussed by Agar, 1994),
- Culture shock—"the anxiety resulting from the disorientation encountered upon entering a new culture" (Schumann, 1978, p. 88),
- Integrative vs. instrumental motivation (Gardner & Lambert, 1972), and

- Ego permeability, a psychoanalytic construct proposed by Guiora (1972), roughly equivalent to empathy.

The values of the combined social variables describe the learner's social distance to the target community, while the values of the combined affective variables account for the learner's psychological distance to target language speakers. Low social and psychological distance is seen as equivalent to high acculturation, which predicts successful second language acquisition, and vice versa. Schumann (1986) suggested that "any learner can be placed on a continuum that ranges from social and psychological distance to social and psychological proximity with speakers of the target language, and . . . the learner will acquire the second language only to the degree that he acculturates" (p. 379). On Schumann's analysis, Alberto experienced high social and psychological distance to the Anglo community; his low acculturation was the main causal factor of his pidginized English interlanguage.

By a quirk of history, the first study of pragmatic development was designed to test the acculturation model. Schmidt (1983) conducted a case study of the Japanese painter Wes, an adult learner of English in Honolulu. Based on Wes's acculturation profile along the social and psychological dimensions included in the model, Schmidt predicted Wes's interlanguage development (see Chapter 8 for details). Fourteen out of sixteen social and psychological factors were predicted to have a facilitative effect on Wes's L2 acquisition. For the analysis of Wes's interlanguage performance, observed over a three-year period, Schmidt adopted Canale's (1983) framework of communicative competence. Results did not concur with the acculturation model's predictions. Wes's morphology developed insignificantly and he continued to rely strongly on formulaic expressions, an indication that his generative syntactic knowledge remained quite rudimentary. His pragmatic and sociolinguistic ability showed clear improvements, though non-target-like speech act realizations persisted or were first introduced as his pragmatic performance became more complex. The greatest progress was seen in Wes's oral discourse (interactional) competence, which intersected with the pragmatic component (see Chapter 4 for details). Likewise, his strategic competence (including repair and various communication strategies) was effective, although it is less clear from the report whether and how it developed during the observation period. Discussing the differential relationship between acculturation and the development of different components of communicative competence, Schmidt (1983) submits:

> It seems to me quite clear that Wes's failure to learn much of the grammatical component of his second language cannot be attributed to social distance factors, to lack of need of or interest in meaningful communication and interaction, to personality factors such as self-consciousness, or to poor attitude toward target language speakers. Low social distance, positive attitudes toward the second language community and high integrative motivation to use the second language for communication have led to a considerable increase in overall *communicative* competence but have had little effect on improved *grammatical* competence. I conclude, therefore, that the hypothesis that "the degree of acculturation toward the 'model' language group seems to be the primary consideration in attempting to account for the varied levels of *linguistic* achievement reached by second language learners" (Stauble 1978, p. 46, emphasis mine) is false. (Schmidt, 1983, p. 169)

Schumann (1986) accepted Schmidt's study as counterevidence to the acculturation model's claims. At the same time, Schmidt also demonstrated the model's value for explaining discourse-pragmatic development, which was outside its original purview. Schmidt's Wes study was a multiple "first" in second language acquisition research generally and interlanguage pragmatics specifically. It was the first study that expanded the prevalent focus of SLA research on interlanguage grammar to discourse-pragmatic and, not unrelated, strategic abilities. In his analysis of Wes's discourse competence, Schmidt (1983) introduced the notion of *conversational* or *interactional* competence, on the argument that "spoken discourse other than monologue is a cooperative effort by all parties to a conversation" (p. 156). With its data-collection period of three years, the Wes study remains one of the most prolonged longitudinal investigations in developmental interlanguage pragmatics. Within what Larsen-Freeman and Long (1991) called a "theory-then-research" approach to SLA, the study illustrates a causal-process form, described by Larsen-Freeman and Long (1991) as "traditionally, at least, the most valued in the nomothetic scientific tradition" (p. 224). It also impressively demonstrates that research in this tradition is not necessarily confined to controlled laboratory studies, large numbers of participants, and statistical data analysis, but can effectively be conducted in a qualitative longitudinal case-study format.

Thus far, the acculturation model has not been adapted to other studies of pragmatic development. Surely the model's fundamental assumption, namely, that second language learning is crucially linked to the learner's social position in the target community and interaction with members of the target group, is also recognized in other theories of SLA that ascribe a critical role in second language learning to social context. But unlike theories that have more recently been applied to SLA, the acculturation model is a causal model that conceptualizes the social dimension in L2 learning in social-psychological terms, as a complex independent variable that affects language learning, the dependent variable. In contrast, the theories that we will discuss later in this chapter do not conceive "the social" as a causal factor, separable from the L2 learning process and outcomes, but view the entire enterprise of second language learning as social practice. The acculturation model shares its psychological underpinning with cognitive models and constructs.

Cognitive Processing

The first explicit proposals to adapt cognitive-psychological theory to pragmatic development date back no further than the early 1990s. Two influential cognitive processing approaches proposed in SLA were extended by their authors to account for L2 pragmatic development: Schmidt's noticing hypothesis (Schmidt, 1993; Schmidt & Frota, 1986) and Bialystok's two-dimensional model of L2 proficiency development (1993, 1994). These two theoretical proposals address different stages of the learning process. The noticing hypothesis is concerned with the initial phase of input processing and the attentional conditions required for input (the L2 data available in the learner's environment) to become intake (the subset of the input that the learner appropriates to build the interlanguage). In order to distill intake from input and make it available for further processing, relevant input features have to be noticed, meaning they have to be registered under attention, or detected under awareness (Schmidt, 1995; cf. Tomlin & Villa, 1994; Truscott, 1998, for dissenting views; Schmidt, 2001, for further discussion). Furthermore, as Schmidt (2001) points out, global alertness to target language input is not sufficient, but attention has to be allocated to specific learning objects, that is, it "must be directed to whatever evidence is relevant for a particular learning domain . . . [and] must be particularly focused and not just global. . . . In order to acquire pragmatics, one must attend to both the linguistic forms of utterances and the relevant social and contextual features with which they are associated" (p. 30). Schmidt (1995) further distinguished noticing from understanding. Noticing is defined as the "conscious registration of the occurrence of some event," while understanding implies "the recognition of some general principle, rule, or pattern. Noticing refers to surface level phenomena and item learning, while understanding refers to deeper level(s) of abstraction related to (semantic, syntactic, or communicative) meaning, system learning" (p. 29). Whereas the noticing hypothesis accounts for initial input selection, the two-dimensional model explains the development of already available knowledge along the dimensions of analyzed representation and control of processing. Bialystok's model contends that children's primary learning task in pragmatics is to develop analytic representations of pragmalinguistic and sociopragmatic knowledge, whereas adult L2 learners mainly have to acquire processing control over already existing representations. This is not to say that adults do not have to acquire new representations. Anglo-European learners of Japanese have to learn sociopragmatic categories such as *uchi* (in group) and *soto* (out group), sociolinguistic distinctions such as different speech levels, and pragmalinguistic categories such as donative verbs. Although the complexity of the pragmatic and sociolinguistic categories and attendant linguistic forms for which adult L2 learners have to establish new representations can be considerable, unlike children acquiring their first language, adults have the advantage of building on a rich foundation of available pragmatic knowledge when learning the pragmatics of another language (see Chapter 5 for pragmatic universals). Since the noticing hypothesis and the two-dimensional model address different phases of the L2 learning process, they are not in competition but rather complement each other.

There are no acquisitional studies outside of research on instructional intervention that have tested whether the two-dimensional model or the noticing hypothesis successfully predict L2 pragmatic learning, but both proposals have been engaged in theoretical frameworks for investigating pragmatic development and as post hoc explanations of research findings. Hassall (1997) interprets the results of his study on L2 Indonesian in terms of Bialystok's (1993) model. He notes that

> The important role for successful transfer of L1 pragmatic knowledge and/or reliance on universal pragmatic knowledge in [Bahasa Indonesian] requesting by these Australian learners supports Bialystok's (1993) claim that for adult L2 learners, the task of forming representations of pragmatic knowledge is already largely accomplished, such that the most important task facing them is the development of control over attention in selecting knowledge when appropriate. (p. 287)

The first prediction of the two-dimensional model—that for adult learners "the task of forming representations of pragmatic knowledge is already largely accomplished"—is also in agreement with

Koike's (p. 286) observation that "pragmatic competence in inter-language does not have to develop *conceptually* in a developmental continuum from simple/basic to the elaborate/complex forms" (italics in original). The second prediction—that an adult's learning task in pragmatics is primarily to gain control over effective allocation of attentional resources—has been related to observations about learners' speech production and conversational skills. Examples include the prosodic composition of learners' utterances and their conversational responses. Some of the EFL learners in Kasper (1981) and the learners of Bahasa Indonesian in Hassall (1997) produced their utterances in short intonation contours as in extracts (2.1)–(2.3).

(2.1) Someone has taken the learner's library seat

NNS: you _**wou**ldn't (.) be _**angry** (.) if you er come _**back** and you _**see** that there's **some**_thing (.) er that there's somebody _other

(_ = rising intonation; (.) = micro pause. Adapted from Kasper, 1981, p. 162)

(2.2) Asking to try a cassette in a store

NNS: Saya (.) saya mau (.) uh (.) mendengar (.) uh (.)
I (.) I want (.) uh (.) to hear (.) uh (.)
kaset (.) Iwan Fals.
a cassette (.) Iwan Fals.

(Hassall, 1997, p. 136f.)

(2.3) Ordering a drink in a restaurant

NNS: Saya (.) saya harus (.) uh (.) membeli (.)
I (.) I must (.) uh (.) buy (.)
sebotol bir juga (.)sekarang.
a bottle of beer too (.)now.

(Hassall, 1997, p. 136f.)

In terms of Levelt's model of speech production (1989), these data suggest that the learners have their requests mapped out in their Conceptualizer when they take their turn, but that the linguistic material required to implement their speech act is not yet available for fast and effortless recall from the Formulator. For these learners, accessing the linguistic forms requires much attention and can be accomplished only in an incremental, one-segment-at-a-time procedure, resulting in a dysfluent, choppy speech style.

Processing difficulties can also affect sequencing constraints on speech act strategies. Hassall (1997) observed that in response to the interlocutor's request for specification, the learners of Bahasa Indonesian tended to repeat the initial want statement, as in extract (2.4).

> (2.4) Buying a movie ticket
>
> 1 NNS: Uh (.) saya (.) uh mau (.) uh (.) karcis (.)
>   *Uh (.) I (.) uh want (.) uh (.) (a) ticket(s) (.)*
>   untuk duduk (.) uh (.) di tengah (.)
>   *to sit (.) um (.) In the middle-front(.)*
>   depan bioskop? ya.
>   *of the cinema, okay?*
> 2 NS: He eh-
>   *Uh huh.*
> 3 NNS: Ada (.) Ada ongkosnya
>   *What's (.) what's the cost?*
>   (.)
> 4 NS: Uh (.) tiga ribu lima ratus.
>   *Um (.) three thousand five hundred.*
> 5 NNS: Oke (.) uh (.) says mau (.) uh (.) satu (.) satu
>   *Okay (.) uh (.) I want (.) uh (.) one (.) one*
>   karcis (.) ya?
>   *ticket (.) yes?*

(Adapted from Hassall, 1997, p. 140f.)

The second *want* statement in turn 5 repeats information that had already been established in turn 1; it thus aligns poorly with the preceding turn. The native speaker group in Hassall's study used elliptic goal statements for follow-up requests, which in this case could be *Satu, Pak* 'One, father' (*pak* = respectful address term for older men). The learners' problem in producing cohesive responses did not seem to be how to construct elliptic turns but to attend to the contingently evolving interaction and designing their contributions in a sequentially appropriate fash-ion (Hassall, 1997; House, 1996; Kasper, 1981, 1984; Stemmer, 1981; Trosborg, 1995). House (1996) made a parallel observation about poorly aligned responses in advanced German EFL learn-ers' interactions. She, too, argued that the inappropriate response turns indicate insufficiently developed control of processing.

Because their processing control is not yet well developed, learners may strive to reduce their processing load in utterance production. Both Hassall (1997) and DuFon (1999) observed that the learners of Indonesian in their studies made their conversa-tional participation more manageable in various ways. Instructive examples concern learners' choice of address terms, a complex undertaking because of the large variety of address terms in Indonesian and the intricate rules for their use (DuFon, 1999). In order to manage this demanding sociolinguistic task, the learners in both studies had recourse to three different production strate-gies (in the sense of organizing goal-related action, not necessarily suggesting intentionality or even awareness). The first was to avoid terms of address. In contrast to native speakers of Indone-sian, who liberally "scattered" respectful kinship terms through-out their requests to higher status interlocutors (Hassall, 1997), the learners in both studies used address terms sparingly during ongoing interaction, even though in DuFon's study, they com-mented on the target practice in their self-report diaries. This contrast between noticing and action suggests that pragmatic awareness and processing control may be unrelated dimensions. The next strategy was to use one address term for all addressees. Some learners overgeneralized a particular personal pronoun, *kamu* or *anda*, as all-purpose address terms, thus reducing the burden of matching the sociolinguistic speaker-addressee rela-tionship with the appropriate address form. The psycholinguistic gains learners made in facilitating their utterance production were offset by the sociolinguistic effects of this simplification strategy, because in Indonesian interaction, *kamu* is only accept-able in addressing familiar peers, and the indiscriminate use of *anda* is perceived as impolite when addressed to higher status co-participants and as constructing too much social distance with familiar status equal interlocutors. A similar simplification strategy, and one that had equally undesired social consequences, was observed in the use of L2 Japanese. Although in target language practice, speech styles are selected relative to interlocutor status, some learners of Japanese chose *desu/masu* style regardless of their co-participant (e.g., Siegal, 1994, 1996), very likely a teaching-induced overgeneralization. The third strategy adopted by the learners of Indonesian was to use address terms in conjunction with formulaic expressions, such as alerters in requests. Since formulaic routines are stored and retrieved as chunks, their production demands less attentional resources than producing freely constructed utterances. Consequently, adding address terms to routines requires less processing control than inserting them into or between nonformulaic utterance segments (DuFon, 1999).

At a more general level, not yet sufficiently developed control of processing can account for a phenomenon that has been observed in many interlanguage pragmatic studies (Hassall, 1997; Kasper, 1981; Trosborg, 1995), that is, less proficient learners' tendency to design their utterances according to a pragmatic priority list of sorts. In speech act terms, illocutionary and propositional goals appear to range uppermost, whereas such concerns as politeness marking through selection among various pragmalinguistic options are less central. This is not to say that beginning learners are not aware of the need to speak politely—quite to the contrary, learners use such parenthetical forms as *please* and its equivalents in other target languages from early on. But as we will discuss further in Chapter 4, even when their interlanguage lexicon and grammar contain material deployable for internal speech act modification (Blum-Kulka, House, & Kasper, 1989), learners often do not use this material for such pragmalinguistic functions. Internal modification through grammaticalized material requires a highly developed control of processing. Before learners have reached the necessary levels of control, they select fewer politeness markers, and the politeness markers they do choose demand less attention to produce.

It should be noted that most of the studies reporting (even advanced) learners' difficulty with conversational fluency and discursive skills have two things in common: they examined *foreign* language learners and used *open role plays* for data collection. Both factors may well contribute to the findings. First, foreign language classroom learning, no matter how communicative and learner-centered, may just not provide sufficient conversational practice, making it difficult for learners to develop the processing control in utterance comprehension and production required for effective participation in conversation. Second, role plays can be quite taxing even for fluent speakers because in the absence of an external situating context, participants have to create and sustain an imagined speech situation. These extra demands on learners' processing capacities may result in an under-representation of their discourse abilities, an effect that may be compounded in the case of foreign language learners (Kasper & Rose, forthcoming). However, the participants in DuFon's (1999) and Siegal's (1994, 1996) studies were sojourning learners of Indonesian and Japanese, respectively, who were immersed in the host community during the period of the study. The discourse data were recordings of authentic interactions involving the learners and diverse target language speakers as co-participants. It thus seems that for beginning and intermediate learners, and even for the more advanced learners of Japanese, developing control of processing in interlanguage pragmatics can be a challenging process across learning contexts and task environments.

Turning to the noticing hypothesis, Schmidt (1995) applied his distinction between noticing and understanding to pragmatics as follows.

> In pragmatics, awareness that on a particular occasion someone says to their interlocutor something like, "I'm terribly sorry to bother you, but if you have time could you look at this problem?" is a matter of noticing. Relating the various forms used to their strategic deployment in the

> service of politeness and recognizing their co-occurrence with elements of context such as social distance, power, level of imposition and so on, are all matters of understanding. (p. 30)

DuFon (1999) found evidence for the noticing hypothesis in her study on the acquisition of politeness in L2 Indonesian. What her six participants noticed depended partly on a feature's pragmatic salience (Errington, 1988). All learners commented extensively in their journals on address terms and greetings but not on experience questions, which DuFon (1999, p. 167, 2000, p. 77) defined as "queries concerning whether one has engaged in an activity (e.g., play gamelan, ski, eat), observed or participated in an event (e.g., attend the concert, arrive in Singapore), sensed a particular feeling (e.g., hunger, satisfaction) or achieved some other state (e.g., know, have)." These questions and the responses to them are particularly interesting to study because sociocultural and grammatical knowledge are closely intertwined in their use. Extract (2.5), occurring between a native (worker) and nonnative speaker of Indonesian (Keith), illustrates such an exchange.

(2.5) Experience question

Keith: Anda sudah pernah keluar Sumbawa?
Have you ever gone outside of Sumbawa?
Worker: Belum.
Not yet.

(DuFon, 2000, p. 86)

If it is possible that the event addressed in the question will happen in the future, the question is phrased with *sudah (pernah)*, and the unmarked negative response to it is *belum*, as in extract (2.5). A negative response excluding future occurrence, *tidak*, is possible but highly marked because it indexes that the questioners' presupposition was wrong. Learners thus have to figure out what constitutes culturally expected events or experiences and make their grammatical choices accordingly—a compelling example of how L2-specific sociopragmatic knowledge is required in order to choose the correct grammatical forms. In their journals, the learners did not devote any metapragmatic reflection to experience questions, but DuFon (1999, 2000) reports that in interaction, native speakers made the correct use of negative responses salient for the learners through modeling, expansions, translations, backchanneling, and requests for confirmation. In the case of answers to experience questions, the native speakers did not shy away from focusing the learners' attention on form, presumably because they perceived learners' incorrect uses of negative responses as grammatical errors, which they deemed open to correction without posing a threat to the learners' face. The learners also asked questions about the use of negative markers, thus demonstrating that they did attend to and reflect on these forms, even though they did not comment on them in their journals. All of this metalinguistic activity was to the learners' great benefit, as they progressed toward more native-like uses of negative responses to experience questions during the two months of their stay in Indonesia.

The learners' acquisition of address terms illustrates well that noticing is a necessary but not a sufficient condition for pragmatic learning. All six learners commented in their diaries on the many different terms of address used in Indonesian. On the level of noticing, there seems to have been little difference between them. Yet one learner, Kyle, persisted in using *anda* in a rather undiscerning fashion, apparently without realizing that addressing higher status interlocutors with *anda* is quite rude. Charlene, on the other hand, took great care to discover the sociolinguistic regularities that govern the intricate system of Indonesian address terms. She put effort into understanding and made use of what she had understood in her own communicative practice. Charlene noticed the gap between her own selection of address terms and those of Indonesian speakers and made efforts to close it; Kyle noticed the gap and left it at that. To explain such individual differences, one has to look beyond cognitive processing. DuFon (1999) notes that Kyle mainly seemed concerned about feeling comfortable, which for him implied that social differences between him and his interlocutors were minimized. Charlene, however, showed great concern for displaying proper "respect," and using target-like address terms was one important way for her to accomplish this. As studies by Norton (Norton, 2000; Peirce, 1995) and Siegal (1996) on learner subjectivity suggest, learners' personal values may influence how much effort they expend on understanding L2 pragmatic and sociolinguistic practices and to what extent they converge to native speaker use. Whether learners' social orientations and attitudinal dispositions also affect what pragmatic information they notice is not clear from the research reports, but there is good reason to assume this to be the case. Recent studies addressing the relationship between motivation and learning have found links between motivational variables and learners' strategies of focusing and sustaining attention to properties of the target language (Schmidt, 2001, p. 9). For the learning of pragmatics, this finding suggests that highly "motivated" learners—in one or more of the many senses of the term—may be more inclined to notice pragmatic particles and other indexical material with little referential value and low perceptual salience but important pragmatic meanings. The connections between motivation, attention, and pragmatic development are taken up in Chapter 8.

The examples from the literature discussed in this section suggest that cognitive models and constructs have significant explanatory potential for understanding pragmatic development. Thus far, cognitive-processing theory has primarily been adopted as a theoretical framework in interventional classroom research on instruction in pragmatics, the topic of Chapter 7. In the observational studies reported in this section, cognitive-processing approaches were either subsumed under a different primary theory, such as language socialization in DuFon (1999), or they served as post hoc explanations. Quite likely, the role of cognitive-processing theory in developmental interlanguage pragmatics is related to the predominance of experimental research in cognitive psychology. Although it is possible to identify instances of noticing in nonexperimental data, such as in learner diaries (Schmidt & Frota, 1986; DuFon, 1999), determining the conditions for noticing and its learning effects outside controlled experimental settings is difficult, if not impossible, because the "coarse temporal granularity" (Tomlin & Villa, 1994, p. 185) of diaries does not permit recording the split-second attentional activity typical of online processing. To understand in detail the role of attention in input processing and speech production requires microanalytic study of online cognitive activity, and the traditional setting for such studies, the controlled laboratory experiment, remains one key venue for such research. An alternative possibility is to microanalyze interaction in natural settings, as we will discuss later in this chapter.

More recent developmental studies outside of experimental classroom research have adopted theoretical approaches that conceptualize language learning in interaction as socially situated activity. Of course, the orientation toward social dimensions in SLA is by no means new. In her book *Issues in Second Language Acquisition*, published in 1987, Beebe wrote "the formerly common footnote acknowledging the possible influence of social factors [on SLA] is no longer acceptable as analysis" (p. 43). This remark prefaced her discussion of "Five sociolinguistic approaches to second language acquisition": variationist sociolinguistics, the dynamic paradigm, communicative competence, accommodation theory, and the socioeducational model. In their book *Second Language Learning Theories*, Mitchell and Myles (1998) devoted a separate chapter to Vygotsky's sociocultural psychology of cognitive development, followed by a chapter on four sociolinguistic perspectives on SLA: the ethnography of communication, variation in L2 use, pidginization and acculturation, and second language socialization. In his recent appraisal of socio-linguistic approaches to SLA, Young (1999) gave prominence to three theoretical proposals to account for variable L2 use and development: discourse domains (Douglas & Selinker, 1985), co-construction (Jacoby & Ochs, 1995), and interactional competence (Hall, 1995b). While some of the theoretical perspectives that have found their way into SLA are of recent origin, others were imported during SLA's early days in the late 1960s and 1970s.

In the plethora of variously hyphenated social theories, "social" means quite different things. Some theories emphasize the substantive dimension of "social": for instance, conveying, appropriating, resisting, or sharing social values, assessments, norms, beliefs, and participating in social practices. This emphasis is particularly pronounced in the ethnography of communication, the notions of communicative and interactional competence, language socialization, theories of social identity, and more recent concepts such as communities of practice. But "social" can also be understood in a formalist sense, by abstracting from the concrete, historical, cultural, and political circumstances in which people live their lives. What remains after stripping "social" from all those dimensions is interaction. Some theories of social cognition, such as collaborative theory (see Wilkes-Gibbs, 1997, for review), examine the joint construction of knowledge as emerging in collaborative action under laboratory conditions. Conversation analysis, particularly in its early days, abstracted from the content of the conversation and its extra-discoursal context, focusing the analysis on the interactional mechanisms by which participants conduct their talk exchanges in an orderly fashion. Likewise, in SLA, the interaction hypothesis attends to the interactional modifications by which input is crunched, output pushed, and attention focused. There is no interest whatsoever in the substance of so-called meaning negotiation, or what participation in the interaction means to the learners. Of the more recent approaches that focus on language learning as social practice, we shall consider those that have been engaged in developmental interlanguage pragmatics as defined in Chapter 1. Studies that have adopted these approaches can be categorized as theory-driven, in the sense of being conducted from the perspective of a coherent theoretical framework.

Sociocultural Theory

In the introduction to the West German edition of Vygotsky's *Thinking and Speaking* of 1964—30 years after the work's first publication and two years after its first English edition (Hanfmann & Vakar, 1962)—the editor Thomas Luckmann remarks on the "rediscovery" of Vygotsky by "Western" psychologists, sociologists, and ethnologists of language. With the notable exception of an early study by Frawley and Lantolf (1984), it took another 30 years for second language acquisition researchers to discover Vygotsky's sociocultural theory and appropriate it for the study of second language learning (Lantolf, 1994; Lantolf & Appel, 1994b). It is hardly by chance that the upsurge of interest in the works of Soviet psychologists (e.g., L. S. Vygotsky, A. N. Leont'ev, S. L. Rubinstejn, A. R. Lurija, and A. A. Leont'ev) and scholars of literature and linguistics (e.g., M. M. Bakhtin and V. N. Volosinov) coincided with the collapse of the Soviet Union. In SLA and second language pedagogy, the discovery of sociocultural theory and activity theory occurred at a time when increased (though not new) attention was given to the social foundation of language learning.

The ontological and epistemological differences between cognitive-processing theories and the interaction hypothesis of SLA (Long, 1996), on the one hand, and sociocultural theory, on the other, have been extensively discussed in the literature, especially in the work of Lantolf and colleagues (e.g., Dunn & Lantolf, 1998; Frawley & Lantolf, 1984; Lantolf, 1994; Lantolf, 2000a, 2000b; Lantolf & Appel, 1994b) and more recently by Hall (e.g., Hall & Verplaetse, 2000) and Ohta (e.g., 2001b). From the perspective of L2 pragmatic development, it is noteworthy that SLA research under the interaction hypothesis has typically asked how interaction and the cognitive processes afforded through particular interactional arrangements contribute to learners' acquisition of *grammar*. In contrast, sociocultural studies of SLA do not conceive of interaction as just a means for acquiring morphosyntax and lexis. In analogy to the double function of language as means for communication and a tool for thinking, interaction is viewed as a tool for L2 learning and as a competency in its own right. The single most fundamental tenet of sociocultural theory is that human cognition is mediated in various ways— through tools, semiotic systems (especially language), and social interaction. Importantly, social interaction, itself mediated by language, is seen neither as the "context" of learning, for it is inseparable from the learning process, nor as a feeding mechanism for input and propeller of output, as the interaction hypothesis has it. Rather, social interaction between children and adults, or novices and experts more generally, *is* learning or, as Vygotsky's puts it, "cultural development." One of the most well-known quotes from Vygotsky's (1981) writings expresses his view on the relationship between social interaction and the development of the higher cognitive functions:

> Any function in the child's cultural development appears twice, on two planes. First it appears on the social plane, and then on the psychological plane. First it appears between people as an interpsychological category, and then within the child as an intrapsychological category. (p. 163)

Since according to Vygotsky, the higher cognitive functions have their origin in social relationships, examining novices in interaction with expert participants affords a view on the microgenesis of cognitive processes. This theoretical assumption has significant methodological consequences for the study of L2 pragmatic development, as we will see shortly. Through an expert's assistance, novices are enabled to accomplish tasks that they would not be capable of performing independently. The differential between autonomous and collaborative task accomplishment is famously called the zone of proximal development—"the site where social forms of mediation develop" (Lantolf, 2000a, p. 16). Recent developments in social theories of learning have contributed to sociocultural theory notions of differential types of participation and apprenticeship (e.g., Lave & Wenger, 1991; Rogoff, 1990; Wenger, 1998).

A significant development of Vygotskyan psychology was seen when A. N. Leont'ev (1981), together with a group of then Soviet psychologists, proposed a theory of activity that has since become a cornerstone of sociocultural theory. An activity is a functional category that integrates external and cognitive aspects of action. Within an activity (as the superordinate category), three levels of analysis can be distinguished: activity (as subordinate category), action, and operation. Activities (as the highest level of analysis) are identified by their motives and the objects toward which they are addressed, actions are defined as goal-directed such that different goals result in different actions, and operations are recognizable by the material, semiotic, and interactional means by which they are produced, including the social circumstances of their production (Wertsch, 1981b). As Lantolf and Appel (1994a) note,

> The level of motive answers why something is done, the level of goal answers what is done, and the level of operations answers how it is done. The link between socioculturally defined motives and concrete actions and operations is provided by semiotic systems, of which language is the most powerful and pervasive. (p. 22)

The tenet that semiotic (especially linguistic) mediation not only facilitates activities but constitutes them in the first place is a familiar assumption to pragmaticians. In fact, some German accounts of pragmatics include activity theory among the contributing approaches (e.g., Schlieben-Lange, 1974). The units of analysis proposed by activity theory are particularly compatible with the units of analysis in speech-act-based pragmatics, where activity can be seen as roughly corresponding to an actor's sociopragmatic assessment, action to the illocutionary act, and operation to the linguistic resources by which the action is implemented, whereby all three levels are both shaped by and operate on the concrete historical and sociocultural circumstances of the speech situation and unfolding interaction. Moreover, since activity theory and sociocultural theory generally adopt a genetic approach to explain psychological phenomena, they also offer a developmental category that is translatable into analysis. The notion of microgenesis (Wertsch & Stone, 1978) refers to "grasp[ing] the process in flight" (Vygotsky, 1978, p. 68), that is, it enables researchers to observe how new abilities emerge while learners are engaged in an activity. The analytical corollary of microgenesis is a microanalytic approach to the examination of interactions in which learners are involved, whether as focal or peripheral participants.

From our brief sketch of sociocultural theory, it follows that adapting a sociocultural framework to the development of discourse, pragmatic, and sociolinguistic ability in a second or foreign language has a number of methodological implications. First, because activity theory holds that activities are dialectically related to the sociohistorically structured environments in which they take place, great priority is given to observing learners in authentic settings rather than in laboratories. Socioculturalists by no means exclude laboratories as contexts for psychological research, but the laboratory has to be co-analyzed as a social context of the ongoing activity. In L2 sociocultural research, authentic classrooms and other social settings that are not arranged for research purposes are typical research venues. Second, because social interaction plays a prominent role as a locus of learning, particular focus is given to the interactions in which learners participate: how learning happens through collaboration is a central research issue. Third, implementing the genetic approach on different levels of analysis, sociocultural studies are often longitudinally designed in order to observe development over time. But even where a single-moment design is adopted, researchers will trace the microgenesis of L2 knowledge and skills in situ. In either case, microanalysis of interactions in which learners participate affords the analytical tool by which microgenesis and development over time become apparent.

Among the sociocultural studies of L2 pragmatic learning, Shea (1994) is exceptional because he examined interactions between *advanced* nonnative speakers in a *second* language context *outside* the classroom, analyzing authentic conversations between advanced Japanese ESL speakers and their North American, native English-speaking interlocutors along two dimensions, called "perspective" and "production." "Perspective" refers to the negotiated degree of intersubjectivity (i.e., the extent to which participants establish a shared referential focus), while "production" refers to participants' "interactional authority," their control over the floor and patterns of solicitation and uptake (p. 364). The two dimensions configure into four interactional patterns:

- Incongruous perspective and asymmetric production (in the interaction between Jiro, an undergraduate junior, and his academic advisor in an advising session),
- Incongruous perspective and symmetric production (in the interaction between Fumiko, a first-year graduate student, consulting with a professor about her thesis research),
- Congruent perspective and asymmetric production (in the interaction among Kazuko, a post doc, and her colleagues at dinner), and
- Congruent perspective and symmetric production (in the interaction between Kazuko and Lilly, a lab technician, over lunch).

In his comments on the maximally contrasting patterns, Shea observes on Jiro's interaction with his advisor:

> In the advisement session, Jiro is severely reduced as a speaker. He is prevented from expressing his ideas when he is restricted to passively confirming what his advisor says to him. There is little opportunity for him to express his opinion, to hold the floor, or speak with authority. What he does say carries little weight, eliciting minimal recognition and response. (p. 378)

By contrast, the lunch conversation between Kazuko, a post doctoral researcher in chemistry, and Lilly, a lab assistant, has completely different interactional characteristics:

> Within the jointly attended, symmetrically balanced participation developed in the lunch conversation, Lilly's response served to positively structure Kazuko's participation, supporting and extending her discourse. Kazuko's ideas are elicited, sustained, and developed within Lilly's engaged response. Her ideas . . . are built up interactively over a series of turns through successive comments that add various details and extend implications as they are drawn out by Lilly's questions. . . . In other words, Kazuko's proficiency as a NNS is extended in

> the collaboration beyond her "individual" competency. Lilly's engagement provides a scaffold which supports and amplifies Kazuko's talk. In an important sense, Kazuko's discourse is not solely her own but is collaboratively constructed within this dialogic relationship. (p. 377)

On Shea's analysis, the four participation structures provide differential opportunity spaces for learners' development of conversational ability. Engaging Vygotsky's notion of the zone of proximal development and Rogoff's guided participation (1990), Shea notes that "the quality of conversational participation can be seen as a critical locus for the development of second language proficiency (even for advanced speakers) because the native speaker's response is a critical means of constructing the nonnative speaker's discourse" (p. 378). This observation has far-reaching implications for second language teaching and assessment. As will be discussed below, the interlocutor's role in shaping learners' contributions to the discourse affects the learning opportunities afforded by different instructional arrangements. The literature on language proficiency interviews documents that interviewer styles shape candidates' performance in these test formats (McNamara, 1997a; Young & He, 1998). In a similar vein, Swain (2001) argues that in small group testing, "performance is not solo performance, but rests on a joint construction by the participating individuals" (p. 278).

Most sociocultural work on, or including, the development of L2 pragmatics has concentrated on classroom interactions involving beginning foreign language learners. We will focus on two important observations from this research. The first observation relates to differentially configured pair or small group work. One popular concern among students and teachers is that in groups or pairs of students with unequal L2 proficiency, only the weaker student will benefit. Studies by Ohta provide evidence to the contrary. Ohta (1995) examined how students of Japanese as a foreign language (JFL) at different proficiency levels used polite Japanese request strategies in a role play activity. Both the stronger and the weaker learner brought their interactional skills to bear on the activity and shifted expert-novice roles during interaction. It was not the case that only the weaker learner profited from the activity at the cost of the stronger partner. Also, unlike previous studies, there was no evidence of learners picking up each other's errors; rather, they assisted each other in reaching more advanced levels of communicative ability. The peer interaction enabled target language use beyond each individual learner's current pragmatic ability. Ohta's findings transcend those of Shea (1994) in an important sense. Shea's observation that native speaker interlocutors can open up of zones of proximal development for learners falls squarely into Vygotsky's definition of the ZPD, according to which assisted performance requires a *more* competent interactional partner. However, through collaborative, task-structured effort, both participants can take on alternating roles as expert and novice in the same task. A parallel finding was reported by Donato (1994) in his study of collaborative planning by three learners of French as a foreign language, showing that the learners assisted each other through collective scaffolding. Ohta's and Donato's studies demonstrate that it does not take individual superior L2 competence to guide other learners' performance, but that through collaboration as one form of mediation, learners can contribute building blocks to each other's individual knowledge. This revision of the requirements for assisted performance has obvious implications for second language learning theory and educational practice. Sociocultural analyses of peer interaction have contributed important insights into the opportunities for L2 learning afforded by learner-learner collaboration. In order to examine actual development of communicative ability, Brooks, Donato, and McGlone (1997) emphasize the need for longitudinal study. As they note,

> it is only by viewing learner performance across multiple opportunities to engage in similar tasks and by attending to task-related talk that we even begin to capture the development of the learners' communicative confidence and competence. A developmental perspective on language

learning is, therefore, critical to understanding the potential benefits of collaboration on task performance. (p. 530)

The second major finding concerns the learning opportunities in the teacher-fronted Initiation-Response-Follow-up (IRF)
structured classroom. The literature on pragmatic learning in the
L2 classroom is unequivocal in its verdict: the IRF routine is an
unproductive interactional format for the learning of pragmatics
and discourse (Kasper, 2001; cf. Chapter 6 for more discussion).
For instance, Hall (1995a) examined how topic development and
management were interactively constructed in teacher-fronted
speaking practice. She concluded that students were not provided
opportunities to develop the complex interactional, linguistic and
cognitive knowledge required in ordinary conversation. Likewise,
Ohta (1995) found that teacher-fronted exchanges provided a
narrower interaction potential for students learning to perform
requests in Japanese than collaborative peer activities. However,
Hall's and Ohta's more recent studies suggest that the IRF's bad
reputation may not be entirely justified. In a subsequent paper,
Hall (1998) examined more closely how the same teacher as in her
1995 study interacted with four students during IRF-structured
speaking practice in a Spanish-as-foreign-language classroom.
She identified qualitatively different patterns of teacher-student
interaction based on the participant status that the teacher assigned to the students: two students were accorded status as
primary players, the other two as supporting staff. To the primary
players, the teacher displayed more attention, treated their contributions as knowledgeable and relevant, and gave them more
rights to participation. The supporting staff received less teacher
attention, and their participatory rights were increasingly cur-
tailed as the semester progressed. Hall suggests that the students'
differential participation opportunities in the same teacher-
fronted exchange structure may affect their development of interactional ability in Spanish, noting that "it was not the IRF
exchange *per se* that limited learning here. Rather, it was both the
amount and qualitative nature of the opportunities for participation in the exchange that the teacher made available to each of the

students" (p. 308). Quite similarly, Antón (1999) concludes from her study on teacher-learner interaction in first-year French and Italian classes that "teachers, through dialogue, can lead learners to become highly involved in the negotiation of meaning, linguistic form, and rules for classroom behavior during classroom activities" (p. 314).

While Hall's (1998) and Antón's (1999) studies indicate that the specific implementation of the IRF pattern warrants closer investigation, Ohta (2001a) suggests that for evaluating the potential for L2 learning in the IRF, the learning target may be a decisive factor. An important feature of conversational ability in Japanese is to act as an active listener and orient to the current speaker's contribution by providing listener responses (Ohta, 2001b, pp. 181ff.). In classroom discourse, a prime locus for a listener response is the third turn in the IRF exchange—the follow-up turn. While the follow-up turn may include an evaluation, such as *hai* (yes) or *ii desu ne* (good/well done), it can also contain a comprehension token such as *mm* or *un* (uh-huh) or *aa soo desu ka* (is that so), or an assessment token such as *omoshiroi desu ne* (how interesting). The evaluative responses are typical of pedagogical discourse, but the comprehension signals and assessments are very common in conversation outside the classroom. In Ohta's corpus, 97% of the follow-up turns in the IRF routine were taken by the teacher. Since listener responses typically occur in this discourse slot, the students were not provided much opportunity to use listener responses productively during IRF, but they were massively exposed to the teacher's listener responses as peripheral participants (Lave & Wenger, 1991). As Ohta demonstrates, it is in peer interaction that students had most occasion to produce listener responses, but their peripheral participation in the IRF routine—supported by the teachers' explicit guidance to use response tokens—enabled students to gradually develop their productive use of assessments and alignments in peer activities. Even though few studies adopting a sociocultural framework have specifically examined the development of discourse-pragmatic competence, Ohta (2001a, 2001b) and Hall (1995a, 1998) have been able to show how differently structured classroom activities promote and obstruct pragmatic learning and how it develops (or does not develop) over time. The researchers accomplished this remarkable task by combining sociocultural theory with microanalysis. The theoretical link that enables this connection is the notion of microgenesis.

Although the history and disciplinary origin of sociocultural theory is quite different from that of language socialization, both perspectives emphasize the developmental roles of interaction and assisted performance in concrete sociohistorical contexts. In fact, sociocultural theory is one of the theoretical foundations of language socialization, to which we now turn.

Language Socialization

Language socialization was proposed by its founding mothers as a linguistic-anthropological perspective on developmental psychology (Schieffelin & Ochs, 1986). As an interdisciplinary approach to the joint processes of enculturation and language acquisition, it draws on sociology, psychology, linguistics, and anthropology, specifically on the ethnography of communication, symbolic interactionism, phenomenology, and sociocultural theory. Language socialization has been defined as "the process whereby children and other novices are socialized through language, part of such socialization being a socialization to use language meaningfully, appropriately, and effectively" (Ochs, 1996, p. 408). In this perspective, then, language plays a dual role in that it constitutes both the means and a central goal of socialization. Particular focus is given to the linguistic resources and interactional practices that inform novices about statuses and roles in their social group and the recognition and expression of affect. The locus of language socialization is concrete activities in which novices participate with experts—in the case of children, with peers, older siblings, or adults—and in which they attain, through language use in interaction, sociocultural knowledge of specific activities and contexts as well as those of the wider society. Although language socialization as an approach to the development of cultural and communicative competence originated from the study of children, it also encompasses the socialization processes that novices to any community participate in, whether as members of a wider group who join a new community of practice (Wenger, 1998), such as a workplace, educational program, or sports club, or second and foreign language learners of any age group. Accordingly, language socialization is seen as a lifelong process through which social groups and individuals transform themselves and each other by taking on alternating expert and novice roles. Finally, language socialization is no one-way street: the novice is not a passive recipient but takes an active part, which may include contesting and resisting socialization goals and "counter" socializing the expert.

Of particular interest in our context is Schieffelin and Ochs's (1986) distinction between language socialization and developmental pragmatics. Developmental pragmatics examines how children acquire different aspects of communicative competence, such as conversational participation and organization, understanding and producing speech acts, politeness, genre-specific discourse, and indexicality. These communicative abilities can be, and have been, objects of investigation from a language socialization perspective as well. The difference between developmental pragmatics and language socialization as approaches to the acquisition of communicative competence is one of scope and perspective, not research object. For developmental pragmatics, the relevant data are the discourses that children and their co-participants are engaged in, collected either in naturalistic settings such as the children's home or kindergarten, or in the laboratory, and interviews with parents or other caregivers. Apart from investigating discourse in naturalistic settings (rather than under laboratory conditions), language socialization research casts its net wider by adopting as a goal "the linking of microanalytic analysis of children's discourse to more general ethnographic accounts of cultural beliefs and practices of the families, social groups, or communities into which children are socialized" (Schieffelin &

Ochs, 1986, p. 168). The micro-macro link emphasized by Schieffelin and Ochs requires a comparative account of communicative practices, such as comparing interactions among children and between children and caregivers with those of adults in a variety of activities and contexts. Unlike developmental pragmatics, which takes a narrower focus on children's acquisition of linguistic action and interaction in social contexts, language socialization research subscribes to a broader, more holistic, culturally contextualized and interpreted view. But the comparative perspective also distinguishes language socialization from sociocultural theory, which, although conceptualizing mind and language as shaped in sociohistorically situated interaction, concerns itself with the processes and phases through which the higher cognitive functions develop, rather than with the relationship of linguistic and cultural practices. Although the language socialization perspective integrates sociocultural theory as one of its theoretical foundations, its orientation is distinctly anthropological, rather than psychological or psycholinguistic.

Since language socialization comprises "socialization through the use of language" and "socialization to use language" (Schieffelin & Ochs, 1986, p. 163), all aspects of language use in local contexts are potential candidates for investigation. However, particular attention has been given to the socializing role of indexicals, that is, linguistic resources that derive their meaning from conventional associations of linguistic forms with dimensions of context. Ochs (1996) contends that "a basic tenet of language socialization research is that *socialization is in part a process of assigning situational, i.e., indexical, meanings* (e.g., temporal, spatial, social identity, social act, social activity, affective or epistemic meaning) to particular forms (e.g., interrogative forms, diminutive affixes, raised pitch and the like)" (p. 411, italics in original). By definition, indexicals (or deictic expressions, Levinson, 1983) are pragmatic phenomena because their use is inseparable from speakers' (or writers') *ego-hic-nunc origo* (Bühler, 1934), or the speech situation. In second language socialization studies, an indexical category that has been studied extensively as a resource to socialize affective and epistemic stance is sentence-final particles in Japanese. As we noted above, Ohta has demonstrated in several studies (1994, 1999, 2001a, 2001b) how JFL students are socialized in classroom interaction to display attentive listening through *ne*-marked responses. Yoshimi (1999), analyzing JSL learners' use of *ne* in conversations with native speakers, showed how the learners' use of the particle was influenced by different, L1-based epistemic constraints and stances of "sharedness." Indexicals that convey epistemic stance were one of the socialization objects in DuFon's (1999, 2000) study on negative markers in experience questions. Inasmuch as the use of these markers is constrained by cultural presuppositions, their choice in native-nonnative interaction also indexes cultural expectations and values.

Social status can be conveyed through participation structures and speaking rights, but also through choices of deictic expressions. L2 socialization studies have examined several status-indexing linguistic forms and practices, such as choices of address terms (DuFon, 1999), speech levels (Lim, 1996), the choice and realization of speech acts (Falsgraf & Majors, 1995; Poole, 1992), and interactional routines (Kanagy, 1999a). In second or foreign language teaching settings, it has been shown how teachers socialize students into culturally varying status relationships through status-indexing practices. Teachers' directives can be designed so as to downplay or emphasize status differences between them and their students. Research on ESL and JFL classes provides contrasting evidence in this regard. Poole (1992) found that the ESL teachers in her study solicited suggestions (e.g., *How should we fix this room*) and mitigated directives through the choice of inclusive pronouns and verb forms (e.g., *Let's do our journals*). In the ESL setting, teachers thus avoided overt displays of the status difference between teacher and students. In contrast, Falsgraf and Majors (1995) observed that teacher directives in JFL immersion classes and elementary school classes in Japan were significantly more direct than those in English-medium classes. While the high directness style reflects the teachers' authority and the status differential between teachers and students, it also characterizes the relationship between teachers and young students as close and informal. In Lim's (1996) study of beginning college JFL classes, teachers commented on first-year students' inappropriately casual demeanor when talking to the instructor, such as using plain instead of *desu/masu* style, inappropriately assertive prosody, and inappropriate content of their contributions. Teachers would correct and model the status-congruent linguistic choices for the students, which appeared to bear fruit, as one instructor described second-year students as "more well-behaved" (p. 60), that is, conforming to what for the teachers counts as appropriate student demeanor in Japanese classrooms. As Lim's data show, teachers and beginning students relied on different cultural models of the student-teacher relationship: the students constructed a casual relationship that de-emphasized de facto existing status differentials; the JFL teachers, on the other hand, required that students recognize the teacher's higher status through the use of suitably deferential linguistic forms and non-verbal conduct and avoidance of disrespectful remarks.

Studies on foreign language socialization in classroom settings also demonstrate that the teachers' socialization goals are informed by social and pragmatic norms of the target culture. The ESL teachers in Poole's (1992) study transferred the goals and interactional patterns from child socialization by white middle-class American caregivers to their interaction with adult ESL students through such practices as expert accommodation of novice incompetence, crediting novices with task accomplishment, and avoiding overt displays of status differentials. In Lim's (1996) study of beginning JFL classes, teachers aimed to instill in students an appropriate status-congruent mode of interaction with the teacher, a sense of responsibility for the entire group, and displays of diligence and conformity as desirable classroom behavior. Lim's findings show that socialization goals for adult L2 learners—even *foreign* language students rather than second language learners—can reflect cultural orientations and practices in the target society and caretakers' and teachers' socializing interaction with young children in Japan.

As we have seen, language socialization research pays special attention to indexical expressions and discourse practices that convey sociocultural messages. In order to specify the focal research object more precisely, such subcategories as "pragmatic socialization" (Blum-Kulka, 1997) and "discourse socialization" (Duff, 1996; Morita, 2000) have been introduced. Blum-Kulka (1997) defines as pragmatic socialization "the ways in which children are socialized to use language in context in socially and culturally appropriate ways" (p. 3), including learning how to use "the local cultural rules regulating conversation, such as the choice of topics, rules of turn-taking, modes of storytelling, and rules of politeness" (p. 12). Discourse socialization refers to the interactional processes by which novices learn how to participate in discourse-mediated activities, while the discourse practices, at the same time, embody information about institutional and societal organization and values. The second function of discourse organization is particularly evident in central activities within a larger setting. This is well illustrated by Duff's (1996) and Morita's (2000) studies, both of which selected as their focal activity a central speech event within different educational institutions and wider sociocultural contexts. As part of an extensive ethnographic study on late immersion in secondary schools in Hungary, Duff (1995, 1996) compared two types of student presentations, the traditional *felelés* (recitation), practiced in nonimmersion programs, and the "Western-style" student lecture, a common activity in dual-language schools. While the practices of conducting the student presentations were somewhat in flux and varied from school to school, they also displayed some striking commonalities that distinguished them from the traditional recitation. For the *felelés*, the presenter and topic were selected by the teacher, the student had to deliver a solo performance without support by classmates or prepared written material, and her performance was graded for fluency, mastery of the appropriate academic register, and content. Whereas the *felelés* thus served as an exam, the student presentation was assessed informally and predominantly served as a discussion starter. Students would volunteer and propose topics in the session before the presentation, and support by reference material, prepared notes, and interaction with the class was allowed during the presentation. Students' greater control and responsibility in the oral presentation was seen to reflect a societal reorientation toward more participatory Western models of social organization. Duff notes that "the *feleles* is not only a rich locus for language socialization . . . but also a micro-level crystallization of macro-level changes and tensions pervasive in the school community and beyond" (p. 409). Moving upward in the education system, Morita (2000) examined graduate students' discourse socialization in two courses in an MA TESL program at a Canadian university. Just as in Duff's study, the focal speech event was students' oral class presentations (referred to as oral academic presentations, OAP), one of several recurrent activities that Morita described as "important not only for the successful completion of their courses and programs but also for their disciplinary enculturation and apprenticeship into academic discourses and cultures" (p. 280). Occasions for discourse socialization were identified in presenters' communication of epistemic stance, strategies of audience engagement, and collaboration with different participants. The course instructors emphasized that presenters were expected to critically discuss a chosen article and link it to their own teaching experience and practice rather than merely summarizing and displaying understanding of the text. They explicitly taught students how to conduct an OAP by providing directions and model presentations. Thus, students developed discourse competence in OAPs both through instruction and participation in the speech event.

Our last observation begs the question whether pragmatic and discourse socialization is predominantly implicit or explicit. While for the most part, language socialization appears to occur through novices' participation in recurrent communicative practices, in some aspects of pragmatics, explicit socialization is strongly in evidence. Explicit pragmatic socialization reflects metapragmatic awareness of pragmatic practices that are salient and important to the party who invokes the pragmatic norm. In her study of dinner table conversations in Jewish American, American Israeli, and Israeli families, Blum-Kulka (1997) found that both adults and children regularly engaged in metapragmatic discourse. The Jewish American families especially paid considerable attention to violations of the Gricean maxims and to discourse management, as in the following exchange between Marvin (age 8), Daniel (age 6), and their parents.

> (2.6) Whose turn is it?
>
> Marvin: Can I say something? Is it my turn?
> Mother: I don't know.
> Daniel: *No!* You have to wait until I finish!
> Marvin: [whining] You had a long turn, so there.
> Daniel: You had a longer one!
> Marvin: No, I didn't.
> Daniel: Yes, you did.
> Father: Daniel, are you finished saying what you were saying?
>
> (Blum-Kulka, 1997, p. 184)

As this rather passionate exchange (which goes on for another 29 turns) demonstrates, the children have successfully acquired the rules for conversational participation extant not only in the intimacy of the family dinner but in informal interactions throughout the white North American middle class. In Blum-Kulka's words, "Fair turn allocation and the censure of untimely interruptions seem to represent the discourse corollary of American ideals of individual rights and equal opportunity for all" (p. 184).

It might be assumed that outside of educational contexts, only children have the benefit of explicit language socialization. However, DuFon (1999) reports several occasions for explicit language socialization in the Indonesian study abroad program. During the initial orientation to the program, the adult learners of Indonesian were explicitly instructed to *pamit,* or ask for permission, every time before leaving their host family's house. Further into the program, the learners were corrected when they made wrong choices of the negative marker, and a rare correction of address term use by an upset recipient was also reported. Yet for the most part, language socialization in the many noninstructional settings in Indonesia was implicit, occurring through learners' participation in activities with members of the target community. Classrooms are a more likely environment for explicit language socialization of adult learners, as evident from Morita's (2000) study. As a metalinguistic activity par excellence, second and foreign language teaching is especially prone to explicit pragmatic socialization through metapragmatic comments. Ohta (2001b) reports how the JFL teachers in her study explicitly reminded students of providing third-turn responses during peer activities. Teachers would sometimes interrupt the pair work, reminding students to *ne o tsukatte kudasai kakunin* (Please use *ne* to confirm) and *minasan itte kudasai yo aa soo desu ka* (Everyone please say "oh really?") (pp. 196–197). In the Japanese immersion kindergarten investigated by Kanagy (1999b) in a series of studies, the interactional routines *aisatsu* (greeting), *shusseki* (attendance), and *jiko-shookai* (personal introduction) were metapragmatically announced by the teachers, as in extract (2.7).

> (2.7) Morning routines in a Japanese immersion kindergarten
>
> T: Hai, asa no aisatsu o shimasu. Rei.
> *OK, we will have our morning greeting. Bow.*
>
> T: Hai, jaa shusseki o torimasu. (name)-san/kun
> *OK, (I) will take attendance. (name)*
>
> T: Ja:, namae o kite.
> *OK, ask his name.*

(Kanagy, 1999a, pp. 1470f.)

But whether in the classroom or outside, most language socialization occurs implicitly, either through the learners' repeated participation in target discourse practices, or through participation and various strategies by which the more competent co-participant makes the pragmatic information salient to the learner. We have already seen that through the IRF routine, the JFL teachers in Ohta's (2001b) corpus provided a virtual input flood of listener responses to their students. In her JFL study, Lim (1996) observed how teachers socialized students to appropriate classroom behavior. Students were expected to comport themselves as members of the class community, not just as individual students. One strategy of fostering group-orientedness was the teachers' displays of intolerance to students' tardiness. Apart from direct reprimands, one teacher in Lim's study reacted to two students who walked in late as in extract (2.8).

(2.8) Late for class

Teacher: *Irasshaimase.   Futari sama desu ka?*
              Please come in. Will it be [a table] for two?
Students: ((a few chuckle))

(Lim, 1996, p. 69)

The teacher adopted here the voice of a restaurant hostess, using the conventional greeting formula complete with honorific. Even though the irony was lost on the two latecomers, the chuckling by their classmates suggests that some did get the message. A different teacher reported the following method of discouraging tardiness: latecomers were not allowed to take their seat before having apologized in two ways—first, standing in front of the teacher and saying *osokunatte mooshiwake arimasen* (I am late and I have no excuse) while bowing, then making the rounds and apologizing with a bow to each of their classmates individually. Meanwhile, the teacher continued the class, without making allowances to the tardy student or to the students who were being apologized to. It goes without saying that the techniques by which these teachers socialized students to group-orientedness in the JFL classroom may be quite idiosyncratic, yet the socialization goal is widely accepted among JFL educators. The main point here is that teachers employ various techniques to make socialization goals salient for students, without using explicit metacomments.

It is worth noting that one of the teachers in Lim's study who put particular emphasis on appropriate JFL classroom conduct was a North American nonnative speaker of Japanese. This brings up an issue specific to L2 language socialization, namely, the role of native-nonnativeness in these socialization contexts. As Lim's study shows, in order to apprentice students to target practices, teachers do not need to be natives of the target community. Rather, the critical qualification is that teachers themselves have been sufficiently socialized to L2 pragmatic practices, that they can comfortably draw on those practices as part of their communicative and cultural repertoire, and that their metapragmatic awareness enables them to support students' learning of L2 pragmatics effectively. As has been noted for second and foreign language education generally (e.g., Rampton, 1990), language teachers have to be experts in the target language rather than native speakers of it. Likewise, L2 language socialization, an integral aspect of L2 teaching, relies on teachers' cultural, pragmatic, and interactional expertise in L2 but is not conditional on native speaker status. Conversely, Morita's (2000) study demonstrates that graduate students, whether native or nonnative, have to develop discourse competence in academic genres. Although the nonnative students in her study commented on linguistic, sociocultural, and psychological difficulties they experienced with the presentations (p. 298), they deployed such compensatory strategies as extra-careful preparation and presentation aids, which made their presentations very effective. As Morita notes, "the NS-NNS distinction alone did not determine how successful a student would be in performing an OAP; in this regard NSs varied as widely as NNSs did" (p. 300). This research finding, which echoes the informal observations of many instructors of linguistically diverse student groups, speaks to the notion of language socialization as a process in which novices to any setting participate, irrespective of membership in other social categories. Still, from the perspective of interlanguage pragmatics, L2 learners' socialization to educational settings or other social contexts in the target community at large remains of particular interest. We would like to know, for instance, what factors contribute to the differential success of nonnative graduate students in mastering academic genres, whether oral or written. Further studies under a discourse socialization approach should be enlightening on this complex issue.

We shall conclude our discussion of language socialization as an approach to L2 pragmatic and discourse development with a few remarks on method. As noted above, language socialization research in its original conceptualization has a strong leaning toward anthropological concerns and, consequently, is comparatively oriented. Language socialization studies of nonnative speakers frequently adopt a comparative perspective as well. Examples of comparative research outside of educational settings are Blum-Kulka's (1997) study of pragmatic socialization during dinners in American, Israeli, and American-Israeli families and DuFon's (1999) investigation, which compared how address terms, greetings, and experience questions were used in discourse among native speakers of Indonesian and in interactions with learners of Indonesian. Within educational settings, Falsgraf and Majors (1995) compared teacher directives in JFL immersion classes, elementary school classes in Japan, and English-medium classes, Poole (1992) examined how ESL teachers interacted with adult L2 learners, compared to child first language socialization by white middle-class American caregivers, and Duff (1996) compared two speech events in an educational setting, the *felelé́s* and the student lecture. But even where no explicit comparison between target practices in different contexts is made, L2 language socialization research with a developmental focus on novices' apprenticeship to a particular setting is often nonetheless comparative, although on a diachronic rather than synchronic axis. Examples are studies by Pallotti (2001) of a child's increasing participation in kindergarten activities, Kanagy (1999a) of preschool children's learning to perform interactional routines, Willett (1995) of four children's "becoming fourth graders," and Ohta (1999) of two college JFL students' development of listener responses.

Consistent with its anthropological orientation, language socialization research on children learning their first language and culture is closely tied to ethnographic methodology. Pragmatic and discourse socialization studies of second and foreign language learners, however, have engaged a variety of research methods, including ethnographic studies (DuFon, 1999), ethnographies of communication focusing on a particular speech event both inside (Duff, 1995, 1996; Morita, 2000) and outside the classroom (Blum-Kulka, 1997), and discourse-analytical L2 classroom research (Falsgraf & Majors, 1995; Kanagy, 1999a; Lim, 1996; Ohta, 1999; Pallotti, 2001; Poole, 1992). Watson-Gegeo and Nielsen (in press), although conceding that language socialization studies can be conducted from a number of methodological vantage points, nevertheless privilege ethnography as the most appropriate approach to language socialization. Their position is understandable in historical perspective, for in the original language socialization framework, developed in research on the interactional processes by which children are apprenticed to the linguistic and cultural practices of their native community, language socialization as a theoretical perspective had its methodological counterpart in ethnography (e.g., Ochs, 1986; Schieffelin, 1990; Watson-Gegeo, 1992; Watson-Gegeo & Gegeo, 1986). However, one of the influential early studies, Clancy's (1986) investigation of language socialization in Japanese as a first language, falls methodologically in the tradition of longitudinal case-study research, a classic approach to first language acquisition. It is also true that the ethnographic studies on second language pragmatic and discourse socialization have clearly demonstrated the strength of an ethnographic approach for L2 language socialization research. But language socialization studies adopting a microanalytic perspective on second and foreign language classroom interaction have also proven effective and insightful. As the language socialization studies conducted in JFL classrooms show, settings for foreign language education sometimes constitute their own cultural world, or community of practice, set apart from the world outside the classroom—and perhaps even from that of the target community. Distinguishing between the "cultural" and the "situational," as Watson-Gegeo and Nielsen (in press) recommend, may therefore be difficult to implement in such settings.

In language socialization research, as well as in sociocultural theory, social interaction is theorized as the central process through which learning is mediated. The last theoretical approach to discourse-pragmatic development we will consider is interactional ability itself.

Interactional Competence as Goal and Process

The notion *interactional competence* emerged simultaneously in different social sciences. In microsociological perspective, Heritage and Atkinson (1984) defined the focal objective of conversation analysis as "the description and explication of the competences that ordinary speakers use and rely on in participating in intelligible, socially organized interaction. At its most basic, this objective is one of describing the procedures by which conversationalists produce their own behavior and understand and deal with the behavior of others" (p. 1). In his foundational text for interactional sociolinguistics, Gumperz (1982) redefined communicative competence in interactional terms as the

> knowledge of linguistic and related communicative conventions that speakers must have to sustain and create conversational cooperation. . . . Once established, such conventions come to serve as communicative resources which, by channeling inferences along certain lines, facilitate communication and enable individuals to build on shared understandings which eliminate the need for lengthy explanations. (p. 209)

Unlike conversation analysts, whose traditional investigative object is talk-in-interaction among competent adult members of the same wider speech community as that of the analyst, Gumperz's work on interethnic communication led him to comment not only on interactional competence as an already available ability but also on the conditions by which it may be acquired.

> The knowledge is of a kind that cannot be easily acquired through reading or formal schooling. Face to face contact in situations which allow for maximal feedback is neces-

> sary. . . . In real life situations, learning of discourse
> strategies is most successful when outside conditions exist
> which force interlocutors to disregard breakdowns and
> stay in contact, or give the learner the benefit of the doubt.
> This is the case in mother-child interactions or in appren-
> ticeship situations at work. Ethnic and class solidarity are
> among such outside factors. (p. 209)

Gumperz adds that modern urban settings often do not provide
the kind of learning environment conducive to informal experien-
tial learning. More recently, he reiterated his skepticism over
learning contextualization conventions through direct instruction
(Gumperz, 1996).

In second language acquisition research, Schmidt (1983,
p. 156) introduced the concept of interactional competence to refer
to the oral, collaborative subset of discourse competence. Wes's
effective acquisition of interactional competence demonstrates
that adult L2 learners can achieve interactional ability successfully outside of instructional contexts when a supportive social
environment and the learners' own discursive style create favor-
able learning conditions, whereas Gumperz's work (e.g., 1982,
1992) points to the obstacles to successful development of interactional competence that immigrants often encounter in postcolo-
nial settings. In language testing, the construct of interactional
competence has been given particular attention and elaboration
in research on language proficiency interviews, an activity type
that discourse analysts in particular deem highly problematic. In
an early critical discussion, Kramsch (1986) pointed out that
"proficiency" as specified in the ACTFL/ETS Proficiency Guidelines (1986) and underlying the Oral Proficiency Interview as its
test form of choice for the assessment of speaking ability takes an
"oversimplified view on human interaction" and does not capture
the essential properties of interactional competence, such as collaboratively constructing a "sphere of inter-subjectivity" (p. 367).
Subsequently, data-based studies on language proficiency interviews as well as conceptual efforts sought to specify the construct
(e.g., Johnson, 2001; McNamara, 1997a; Young, 2002; Young & He,

1998). Drawing on the notion of co-construction (Jacoby & Ochs, 1995) and the socioculturally anchored concept of interactional practices (Hall, 1993, 1995b), He and Young (1998) theorize interactional competence as both an extension of communicative competence and crucially different from it. Unlike communicative competence, interactional competence is not an exclusively individual trait but jointly constructed by all participants and bound to the local social practice in which it is produced. Fortunately for the language teaching profession and language learners worldwide who depend on classroom learning for their development of interactional abilities, the dim prospect that Gumperz envisioned for the acquisition of interactional competence through formal instruction has given way to more optimistic views. Hall (1999) proposes a model for classroom practice that aims at developing students' interactional competence through guided participation and metapragmatic activities in which students "mindfully abstract, reflect upon, and speculate upon patterns of use" (p. 140). Likewise, under different theoretical frameworks, research on the effect of instruction in pragmatics recommends communicative tasks and awareness raising (see Chapter 7 for discussion). Studies collected in Hall and Verplaetse (2000) and Lantolf (2000b) report on opportunities for students to engage in varied, meaningful, and challenging classroom discourse practices, although exactly how students become progressively more interactionally competent is less apparent.

So far, we have considered interactional competence as a *goal* of L2 learning. This may appear to be somewhat off-topic in a chapter that discusses theories of pragmatic development. But as we have noted throughout this chapter, different theories of first and second language learning give interaction a prominent role as a process that *enables* L2 learning. When classroom L2 learners are engaged in meaningful, challenging, and cohesive interactional activities—and not all interactional classroom activities can be so characterized (Hall, 1995a)—they perform their current interactional competence in collaboration with peers or participation in IRF-structured classroom discourse and at the same time

develop their pragmatic, sociolinguistic, and interactional ability
(Hall & Verplaetse, 2000). In the notion of interactional competence, goals and processes of L2 learning are dialectically related.
Therefore, approaches to interactional competence have the potential to illuminate how pragmatic ability develops. One such
approach is conversation analysis, adopted by Markee (2000) to
examine how learners' interactional competence is involved in L2
learning. Markee was able to demonstrate that the students
learned vocabulary in the short term, but it remains to be investigated in future studies how pragmatic and interactional competence itself develops over time. Longitudinal interactional data
put under the conversation-analytic microscope should reveal
developments in learners' interactional engagements, but it remains to be seen how such observations can be theorized when the
approach does not include a learning component (Kasper, 1997).
With this problem in mind, we shall evaluate the merits of the five
theoretical orientations discussed in this chapter for understanding pragmatic development.

Explaining Pragmatic Development

Do acculturation theory, cognitive processing theory, sociocultural theory, language socialization, and the construct of interactional competence explain pragmatic development? The answer
depends to some extent on how "explain" is understood. Acculturation theory predicted a causal relationship between the learners'
social-affective disposition and L2 learning success or failure.
While more contemporary theories reject the view of acculturation
as a static, individual trait and instead emphasize agency and
subjectivity in a far more dynamic perspective (Peirce, 1995;
Siegal, 1994, 1996; Weedon, 1987), as theories to explain L2
development generally and pragmatic development specifically,
the old and the new proposals share one crucial property: they
theorize conditions for pragmatic development, both conditions of
social context and individual dispositions, but they do not specify
how pragmatic learning proceeds. Neither kind of theory makes

any predictions about stages of pragmatic development, nor explains why such stages are constituted in particular ways, or how learners move from one stage to the next. Sociocultural theory and language socialization research provide substantially stronger explanatory frameworks because they are both centrally concerned with development—the development of cognitive and linguistic ability in the case of sociocultural theory, and the joint development of cultural knowledge and language use in the case of language socialization research. From these perspectives, increasing communicative ability in L2 is associated with changes in participation status, as evident in learners' move from peripheral participation in interactive practices to assisted performance and eventually to autonomous accomplishments. In this process, interactional routines have been shown to play a crucial role because they occur in a repetitive and predictable fashion, project sequential trajectories, and embody culturally significant meanings (Kanagy, 1999a; Ohta, 2001b). Their structural properties facilitate novices' increasing participation in them, and as a routine becomes increasingly proceduralized in learners' interactional ability, it provides a vehicle for acquiring new conceptual, cultural, linguistic, and interactional knowledge. By linking the theoretical construct of microgenesis with microanalysis as analytical approach, researchers are able to observe in detail how interaction in zones of proximal development unfolds, how scaffolding is provided, and how students engage in different participation structures. If conducted over a sufficiently extensive observational period, microanalyzed data of learner interactions make visible developmental patterns of discourse-pragmatic ability, as demonstrated by Ohta (2001a, 2001b). Likewise, several studies have shown that L2 learners' pragmatic, discursive, and sociolinguistic development can successfully be examined in a language socialization framework (DuFon, 1999; Kanagy, 1999a; Ohta, 1999). As the approach to interactional competence with the longest research tradition and most rigorous analytical practices, conversation analysis has the virtue of providing precisely the microanalytic perspective and analytical tools required to describe learners' and their interlocutors' engagements in different activities with the necessary attention to linguistic, paralinguistic, and nonverbal detail. It affords a precise characterization of participants' orientations during the ongoing activity, their displays of comprehension and noncomprehension, the organization of turn-taking and repair, topic management, interactional alignments and disengagements, and their sequential accomplishment of actions. Conversation analysis is thus a prime candidate to examine learners' pragmatics in action, but can it account for pragmatic development? There is an obvious logical problem in adopting an approach to account for learning when nothing in that approach is made for the job. Although Markee (2000) did identify instances of lexical learning "at least in the short term" in his conversation-analyzed ESL classroom data, the jury is still out on the question of whether long-term learning of pragmatics can effectively be explained through conversation analysis.

Finally, then, cognitive-processing theory. With its long and enormously prolific research tradition, theoretical rigor, and methodological sophistication, information processing theories—as well as other cognitive-psychological theories that may replace the computer metaphor in due course—are well suited to examine important aspects of interlanguage pragmatic learning. Critiques of the predominant cognitive-processing views of second language learning have pointed out, quite rightly, that language learning is a form of social practice and has to be theorized and analyzed as such. In view of the massive evidence of socially distributed cognition and learning, they have made a valid and necessary point. But learning, including that of L2 pragmatics, also involves individual learners' minds and brains. While the Vygotskyan construct of internalization provides the theoretical link between the interpsychological and intrapsychological level of learning, how external sociointeractional processes are cognitively represented and restructured remains obscure. Furthermore, pragmatic transfer, although frequently attested in interlanguage pragmatic studies, has been skirted by other approaches thus far, whereas cognitive theories (e.g., Takahashi, 1995, 1996) have addressed transfer both as process and product phenomenon. Considering its demonstrated potential as a major theoretical foundation of second language learning, it is our prediction that cognitive theory will remain a key approach to explain interlanguage pragmatic development.

Chapter Summary

At the outset of this chapter, we noted that much research in L2 developmental pragmatics has, in fact, not been directly informed by theories of second language learning. Appeals have been regularly made to pragmatic and discourse theories in setting the target for analysis, but such accounts often theorize the object, not the process, of pragmatic learning. In many cases, theoretical positions have been invoked as post hoc explanations of findings rather than serving as the motivating force of a study. We then discussed in some detail five theoretical positions that have proven fruitful in explaining second language pragmatic development. These can broadly be divided into two groups: those with a primarily individual-psychological focus (the acculturation model and cognitive-processing models) and social practice theories (sociocultural theory, language socialization theory, and approaches to interactional competence). Each approach was illustrated by studies on second language discourse and pragmatics. Lastly, we discussed how capable each theory is to explain pragmatic development. In a research situation where the combined body of studies on pragmatic development is still quite small and that of investigations conducted from an explicit theory of L2 learning even smaller, studies conducted from a cognitive-processing perspective as well as from different or combined social practice approaches with an analytical focus on interactional engagements are promising candidates for explaining the many facets of L2 pragmatic learning.

CHAPTER THREE

Approaches to Developmental Pragmatics Research

In the previous chapter, we discussed a number of theories that have guided investigations of second language pragmatic development, noting that theoretical positions often have methodological corollaries or are associated with particular preferences for data collection and analysis. In this chapter, we will scrutinize the main methodological approaches deployed for examining how L2 pragmatics is learned. We will start by sketching some of the many ways in which interlanguage pragmatics research draws its methodology from across the social sciences. Following this, we address the pros and cons of longitudinal and cross-sectional designs in developmental research. The remainder of the chapter divides the research methods used in developmental interlanguage pragmatics into three parts. The first part, examining spoken discourse as a source for pragmatics research, distinguishes three types of spoken discourse data: authentic discourse, sociolinguistic interviews and conversation tasks, and role play. The second part is concerned with different types of questionnaire: discourse completion, multiple-choice, and scaled-response questionnaires. The final part focuses on diverse forms of oral and written self-report: interviews, verbal protocols, and diaries.

Methodological Resources From Across the Social Sciences

Studies of L2 pragmatic development typically inherit their methodology from either or both of two sources: from cross-cultural and interlanguage pragmatics research, which in turn relies on research methodology from different disciplines within the social sciences, or from relevant social sciences directly. Consequently, developmental L2 pragmatics research spans a wide scope of theories, research questions, and methodologies. Without going into detail, this section aims to give readers a taste of the range of methodological contributions that different social sciences have to offer.

Descriptive linguistic procedures are a methodological resource for *contrastive pragmatics*, analyzing and comparing the pragmatic meanings of linguistic forms, especially the conventions of means and form by which particular communicative acts are realized in different languages. Functional linguistic theories and methods for analysis provide the necessary foundation for exploring the grammar-pragmatics interface and examining the grammaticalization of pragmatic meaning, as in the case of modal particles and discourse markers (e.g., Traugott & Heine, 1991). Likewise, the interface of interaction and grammar, including prosody, has become of increasing concern to linguists who consider these two domains (to a large extent) mutually enabling and constraining (Ochs, Schegloff, & Thompson, 1996; Selting & Couper-Kuhlen, 2001). The interaction-grammar interface makes for a particularly attractive object of study in developmental perspective, at least from the vantage point of theories that accord interaction a privileged role in the development of second language ability.

Sociology has had a two-fold impact on the study of pragmatics, one direct and one indirect. The direct line from sociology to pragmatics is supplied by *conversation analysis* (e.g., Hutchby & Wooffitt, 1998), or the study of talk-in-interaction. Conversation analysis shares its constructivist foundation with ethnomethodology (Coulon, 1995), from which it derived and whose linguistically mediated incarnation it represents. As a microsociological approach, conversation analysis has the overall objective of illuminating how social order is interactionally constituted. It therefore examines in detail the procedures by which participants in talk exchanges display their orientations and understandings through sequentially organized action. The generic object of study is talk-in-interaction, made available for analysis through electronic records and detailed transcripts. Consistent with its ethnomethodological perspective, conversation analysis centers on social members' shared "methods" of producing meaning and intersubjectivity through their talk exchanges. Consequently, analysts suspend preconceived assumptions about social categories, power structures, norms, and values and abstain from speculating about participants' internal states as an interpretive resource. The radically emic analytical orientation parallels the phenomenological practice of "bracketing." Conversation analysis has recently been extended to talk exchanges including nonnative speakers, such as *lingua franca* talk in intercultural business encounters (Firth, 1996; Wagner & Firth, 1997) and educational settings (Markee, 2000; Mori, 2002). This extension is not unproblematic because analysts cannot presuppose that interactional "methods" are shared among participants. Turning to the second, more indirect link between sociology and pragmatics, quantitative and qualitative sociological research methodology has been imported to study the communicative practices of native and nonnative speakers from intra-cultural, cross-cultural, and intercultural perspectives. Methods used in survey research, such as questionnaires with different types of response measure (scales or multiple choice) and scheduled interviews (Babbie, 1990), as well as such qualitative procedures as different forms of observation, narrative interviews, and other types of self-report and text analysis (Silverman, 2001) have become standard components of pragmaticians' tool kit.

Linguistic anthropology (Duranti, 1997) shares with pragmatics its concern for the cultural meanings of interactionally and textually mediated activities within a speech community or more narrowly defined social group. Ethnographic research methodology, anthropology's methodological extension, offers a rich specification of principles and practices for theory-guided data collection and analysis. Particularly tailored to the study of communicative practices, the *ethnography of communication* provides a specialized ethnographic methodology that allows to examine communicative events at different levels of analysis (Saville-Troike, 1996). The main data sources in ethnographic research comprise observation, interviews, and artifacts (including documents). In ethnographies without a particular focus on communicative practices, the primary research instrument is the ethnographer, who participates in the community's daily activities, records observations in field notes, conducts interviews, and so forth. For ethnographies of communication, taking field notes from memory is inadequate because the finer details of communicative interaction are likely to escape the ethnographer's attention when they occur; and even if noticed, human memory does not permit exhaustive recall of the information in the sequence of its occurrence. Therefore, ethnographies of communication require audio- or video-taped interactions as their main data source, although traditional observational methods such as participation in community activities to varying extents and interviewing members remain important types of data (Duranti, 1997). The centrality of electronically recorded talk in different activities is particularly evident in two discourse approaches related to the ethnography of communication, *interactional sociolinguistics* and *ethnographic microanalysis*. Both of these approaches are microanalytic; thus, like conversation analysis, they rely on minutely transcribed discourse as the main object of analysis. Unlike the sociological approach, however, interactional sociolinguistics and ethnographic microanalysis are ethnographically oriented in that they draw into the analysis contextual information and cultural meanings that, together with the linguistic, paralinguistic, and nonverbal forms of expression, serve participants as resources for conversational inference. In fact, it is the hallmark of interactional sociolinguistics to explore the *indexical* relationships between communicative resources and their situated meanings as indicators of communicative acts, activities, social identity, and epistemic and affective stance (Ochs, 1996). *Ethnographic microanalysis* (Erickson, 1996) places considerably more emphasis on nonverbal aspects of interaction than either conversation analysis or interactional sociolinguistics, although especially in conversation analysis, the nonverbal dimension of interaction is increasingly recognized as an integral part of face-to-face encounters. Consequently, data collection requires videotaping, and the nonverbal components of the interaction must be systematically and minutely transcribed. Particular attention is given to the listener's role in talk exchanges, to listener-speaker coordination through the combination of paralinguistic, nonverbal, and linguistic features, and to the joint construction of social identity in ongoing encounters.

The three microanalytic approaches—conversation analysis, interactional sociolinguistics, and ethnographic microanalysis— have a common constructivist perspective and commitment to analyzing carefully transcribed talk exchanges. They differ in the emphasis given to the sequential organization of talk (conversation analysis), indexicality and conversational inference (interactional sociolinguistics), and nonverbal components of interaction (ethnographic microanalysis). As linguistic extensions of the ethnographic tradition, interactional sociolinguistics and ethnographic microanalysis are concerned with culture and context as constraining and constructed forces, and with the potential for conflict when participants' interpretive frames and interaction practices do not match. True to its sociological rather than anthropological origin, conversation analysis in its classical version eschews cultural and contextual interpretation and restricts legitimate data for analysis to talk exchanges between competent members of the analyst's speech community. However, conversation analysts coming from an anthropological tradition (Bilmes, 1996; Moerman, 1988) have demonstrated that in order to produce emically valid accounts, it may be indispensable to rely explicitly on cultural and contextual information. The combination of microanalysis with an ethnographic perspective makes interactional sociolinguistics and ethnographic microanalysis particularly powerful approaches for the analysis of intercultural interaction and has been especially fruitful in investigating intercultural gatekeeping encounters in a variety of institutional settings (Erickson, 1996; Gumperz, 1996).

Since the traditional purpose of ethnographic study is to account for a community's cultural practices and meanings, key participants and informants are typically competent adult members. In contrast, as a domain of study located at the crossroads between anthropology, developmental psychology, and sociolinguistics, *language socialization* research examines how children acquire the sociocultural practices of their community through interaction with adults and older children (see Chapter 2). Recently, language socialization theory has been expanded to child and adult second language learners. In fact, Ochs (1996) makes the point that any expert-novice interaction involves language socialization; unlike learning the morphosyntactic code of a first language, language socialization is thus a lifelong experience. Predominantly, language socialization studies follow ethnographic principles such as observation of naturally occurring interaction during sustained engagement in the community. Because they focus on communicative interaction in various activity types and particularly on the linguistic and discursive forms that are recurrently deployed to convey indexical meanings, the requirements for data are the same as in interactional sociolinguistics, that is, electronically recorded, authentic conversations and other situated talk exchanges, together with ethnographic information about social and institutional contexts and culturally salient dimensions in the social group.

Developmental pragmatics addresses the "acquisition of the knowledge necessary for the appropriate, effective, rule-governed employment of speech in interpersonal situations" (Ninio & Snow, 1996, p. 4), including the acquisition of communicative acts and their realization strategies, politeness, social marking, and conversational ability. As a branch of developmental psychology and first language acquisition research, developmental pragmatics shares the same fundamental research questions and methodologies as its foundational disciplines. Standard questions include the age of onset of a particular pragmatic skill, the processes by which such skills are acquired, factors influencing the speed and order of acquisition, and individual differences in the acquisition of pragmatic abilities. At the same time, since pragmatic ability is acquired in and shaped by specific sociocultural contexts, developmental pragmatics attends to sociocultural dimensions of children's pragmatic achievements. In this regard, developmental pragmatics differs from developmental psychology's focus on the acquisition of the formal linguistic system and aligns itself with such anthropological and sociological concerns as enculturation and social development. To some extent, developmental pragmatics overlaps with language socialization research; however, most developmental pragmatic studies retain a distinctly psychological orientation. Consequently, research methods include longitudinal or cross-sectional observations of interactions between children and caregivers in their home environment or in the laboratory, free or experimentally designed interaction including role play, and parent interviews. Unlike ethnographically informed approaches, developmental pragmatics has inherited from developmental psychology skepticism toward the use of observational, especially authentic, data because a child will not display her entire pragmatic repertoire during a brief observation session. The psychologist's response to this dilemma is to rely on elicited interaction in the controlled confines of the laboratory, whereas the ethnographer's solution is prolonged observation of children engaging in multiple interactions and activities in their community. On the other hand, developmental pragmaticians have found parents' interviews to be a valid source of information about the communicative acts their young children are able to perform, noting that parental reports correlate highly with independent observations (Ninio & Snow, 1996).

Moving still further away from sociocultural perspectives and closer to the center of psychological views on language in use, *cognitive psychology* (and *psycholinguistics*, one of its branches) has put several key pragmatic theories and constructs to empirical test. Originally inspired by Grice's (1975) cooperative principle and Searle's (1969) speech act theory, cognitive psychologists explore such issues as conventionality, politeness, indirectness, and other nonliteral types of language use (irony, sarcasm, metaphor, idioms, proverbs) from a processing perspective. An extensive series of studies on these issues has been conducted by Gibbs (see his 1994 book for a comprehensive synthesis). Rather than focusing on linguistic forms, pragmatics functions, and sociocultural meanings as *products*, as is typically the case in cross-cultural and interlanguage pragmatics research on speech act realization (Blum-Kulka, House, & Kasper, 1989), cognitive psychologists examine how pragmalinguistic and nonliteral semantic meaning is understood, produced, and represented by competent adult native speakers and what factors influence processing and representation. Consistent with a processing and representational perspective on language use and linguistic knowledge, experimental laboratory research is the main approach adopted by cognitive psychologists, including such standard practices as response time measurement and assessment of stimuli through multiple-choice questions or scaled responses. However, more ecologically valid procedures have also been adopted (see Clark & Schunk, 1980, for a classic study).

The pragmatic tradition in cognitive psychology sketched above provides an empirical foundation for philosophical and linguistic proposals about pragmatic meaning, which is largely confined to the utterance level or the relationship between utterances in contiguous turns. Another psychological approach to pragmatics addresses larger units of analysis. The study of *discourse comprehension* is concerned with recipients' (usually readers' rather than listeners') processing of intact pieces of text and can thus be seen as the psychological branch of discourse analysis. Investigators of discourse processes are interested in such issues as readers' strategies, sources and types of inferences, the role of different types of memory, and individual differences in discourse comprehension. Since working memory is heavily involved in discourse comprehension, one standard method for studying text processing is through verbal protocols, subjects' online verbalizations of their conscious thought processes. Verbal protocols are usually employed in conjunction with chronometric measures and compared to predictions derived from theories of discourse comprehension. Combining multiple techniques is regarded as indispensable in order to maximize the strength of each method and compensate for its drawbacks, such as incomplete reporting in verbal protocols. (See the articles in *Discourse Processes*, *21:3*, 1996.)

Social psychology, another major branch of psychology, has several related subfields that address pragmatic issues, among many others. *Social cognition* emphasizes the links between cognitive and social psychology. The fundamental mode of inquiry is an information-processing approach to the classic topics in social psychology, such as attribution, social judgment, self-construals, attitudes, persuasion, impression formation, and group relations. The cognitive perspective on these issues is reflected in the choices of research methodologies: whereas one prevalent method of investigation in social psychology is the large-scale survey, eliciting respondents' fairly stable, consciously considered, "off-line" views on the questions asked, social cognition research utilizes experimental procedures that can shed light on subjects' online processing of information, such as response time measurement, cued recall, word fragment completion, and recognition tests (Devine, Hamilton, & Ostrom, 1994). One issue of immediate relevance to pragmatics is the impact of context and linguistic politeness on memory. In a series of experiments in laboratory and naturalistic settings, Holtgraves (1997) established that politeness theory offers "a comprehensive framework for understanding how we produce and understand language in context" (p. 116). While the measures in experiments examining memory for conversation are recognition or recall tests, stimulus conditions include a variety of tasks, such as scenarios presented in written format, role plays, and semi-authentic interactions in which subjects are unaware of being involved in an experiment. Social cognition research mostly focuses on the formation of social knowledge and the impact of social context and linguistic forms on the memory in individuals. In other words, "social" refers to a property of the knowledge or context in which knowledge is established. In a different line of investigation, "social" refers to social interaction as the source of knowledge. Starting from the premise that "conversation is the fundamental site of language use" (p. 107), Clark and Wilkes-Gibbs (1992) investigated how interlocutors collaborate in establishing reference. Using abstract shapes (tangrams), direction giving, or other matching tasks, they examined how reference is interactionally established under different conditions of goals, knowledge distribution, and participants' roles as addressees or bystanders (Wilkes-Gibbs, 1997).

Communication research examines how people achieve social goals in interaction. Specifically, communication researchers seek to "(a) identify critical social goals such as gaining compliance, generating affinity, solving social conflict, and offering information; (b) specify . . . the strategies by which people can go about achieving these goals; and (c) determine predictors of strategy selection" (Wiemann & Daly, 1994, p. vii). As a theory to account for actors' management of multiple and often conflicting goals, politeness theory (Brown & Levinson, 1987) has attracted particular attention and has been submitted to various empirical tests. Research methods comprise the entire set of sociometric and psychometric procedures, including different forms of self-report obtained through surveys, interviews, and diaries; simulations, elicited social interaction under laboratory conditions, and postinteraction protocols. While the investigated goals and strategies are prime pragmatic categories, little attention has traditionally been given to the linguistic implementation of subjects' social action. However, some authors (e.g., Penman, 1990) emphasize the need for adopting a discourse-analytic approach to the study of face work in interaction.

Within the broader field of communication research, the study of *cross-cultural communication* (e.g., Gudykunst, 2000) examines similarities and differences in value orientations, affective dispositions, relationship management, and communicative style in members of two or more communities, referred to as "cultures." Data collection relies heavily on self-report by means of surveys and scheduled interviews and pays little attention to intra-cultural contextual variation. *Intercultural communication* research, by contrast, is concerned with establishing theories of interaction between members of different cultural communities. Most studies retain their distinctly psychological orientation by evidencing no concern for what participants actually say and do in intercultural encounters and thereby distinguish themselves sharply from the microanalytic sociolinguistic approaches discussed earlier. Consequently, various forms of self-report methodology prevail. One theory that emphasizes coordination in situated intercultural interaction and establishes an explicit link between sociolinguistics and social psychology is communication accommodation theory (e.g., Giles, Coupland, & Coupland, 1991). Practitioners of this approach have utilized such varied data collection procedures as combinations of matched guise with semantic differential scales, surveys, and observation of intercultural interaction in authentic contexts, often in institutional settings.

The distinctions made between the various offshoots of social psychology are somewhat arbitrary. Scholars with specializations in any one subfield often publish in the other fields and the parent discipline, resulting in much interchange in theories and research methodologies. In addition, the prevalent psychological orientation to issues of communication at the expense of attention to language in interaction has been problematized by some practitioners (e.g., Kellermann, 1992), who advocate incorporation of discourse-analytical approaches.

Cross-cultural pragmatics, the study of communicative practices in different speech communities, pursues overlapping and partly identical research goals as the social sciences and the specializations within them sketched above. Consequently, research methods range from participant or nonparticipant observation of authentic, socially situated interaction to survey-type methods eliciting open-ended responses to scenarios, or appropriacy judgments of contextualized pragmatic strategies. Methodological choices reflect not only compatibility with the research questions under study but also the investigator's onto-logical and epistemological commitment to a particular theoretical approach to pragmatics. Much research in pragmatics focuses on the communicative abilities and action of nonnative speakers, and the way their pragmatic knowledge and skills in a second language develop over time. *Interlanguage pragmatics*, the wider research domain of this book, shares a common interest with the larger discipline of *second language acquisition research*. Consequently, interlanguage pragmatics has inherited some of the methodologi-cal practices proposed for second language research. One such practice is to collect three sets of comparable data—linguistic performance in the target language, the learner's native language, and her interlanguage (Selinker, 1972). Comparison of the fea-ture(s) under investigation in these three data sets enables the researcher to identify learner-specific features—what the learner does differently from L2 native speakers—and possible influences from the learner's L1 on her interlanguage performance. (See Kasper, 1992, and Takahashi, 1996, on pragmatic transfer.) The comparative methodology has its problems in that it implicitly sets the L2 native speaker data as embodying a prescriptive norm against which the nonnative speakers' interlanguage performance is measured (see Chapter 7 for more discussion of norms in interlanguage pragmatics research).

As will be apparent from the research on second language pragmatic development that we will discuss in the upcoming chapters, interlanguage pragmaticians have liberally drawn on the intellectual resources offered by different social sciences and their specializations. For their investigative endeavors, in L2 developmental pragmatics as elsewhere, researchers choose the theoretical and methodological orientations they assess as most compatible with their research purposes, their disciplinary tradi-tions (which may include such institutional "constraints" as doc-toral advisor and committee preferences and getting published), and personal views. Some researchers find a tack that suits themselves and their specific interests best and pursue it without any reorientation over time; others are more intrigued by exploring—or supervising their graduate students' exploration of—the sociocultural dimensions of L2 pragmatic development from an ethnographic perspective in one study and the effectiveness of instructional options, based on cognitive theory, in another. As there is much to be learned from doing research on L2 pragmatic development from all of the perspectives outlined above, we hope that this book encourages high-quality research from a wide range of theoretical and methodological orientations.

While our focus in this book is on L2 pragmatic development, the social science resources sketched above have been found helpful in studies of interlanguage pragmatics generally, whether of an acquisitional orientation or not. What makes a study developmental—that is, permitting researchers to observe or enabling inferences about L2 pragmatic development—is not so much the choice of a particular method or methodological framework for collecting data but the overall organization of the study, which we refer to as its design (noting that, commonly, "design" is used interchangeably with "method"). "Developmental" designs have certain characteristics, to which we now turn.

Developmental Research Designs

In order to inform issues related to L2 pragmatic *development* (or development of any kind, for that matter), research must adopt a longitudinal or cross-sectional design, or a combination of the two. Longitudinal research involves the observation of the same participant(s) over an extended period. The most obvious advantage of a longitudinal design is that it allows for the direct observation of developmental patterns over time. Longitudinal studies from the L2 pragmatics literature include, for example, those on the acquisition of pragmatic and discourse ability discussed in Chapters 4 and 5: Schmidt's (1983) well-known study of Wes, Schmidt and Frota's (1986) account of Schmidt's acquisition of Brazilian Portuguese, Sawyer's (1992) study on the acquisition of the Japanese discourse particle *ne*, Ohta's (2001a) report of the acquisition of alignment expressions in Japanese, work reported in Kanagy and Igarashi (1997) and Kanagy (1999a) on how English-speaking kindergartners learn Japanese classroom inter-actional routines in an immersion environment, DuFon's (1999, 2000) research on the acquisition of politeness in Indonesian, and Rost-Roth's study (1999) of the learning of German modal parti-cles. Length of observation in these studies ranged from four months to four years. On the other hand, cross-sectional designs involve the collection of data from two (or more) cross-sections of a sample, based, for instance, on differences in level of proficiency in the target language. As such, cross-sectional designs do not allow for direct observation of developmental patterns, but they do have the potential to offer insight into development by extrapo-lating from differences observed across various cross-sections. Cross-sectional studies on L2 pragmatics include a number of the request studies also discussed in Chapter 4: Scarcella's (1979) study on the acquisition of requests in an ESL setting, and three request studies in EFL contexts—Trosborg (1995) in Denmark, Hill (1997) in Japan, and Rose (2000) in Hong Kong. Each of these studies involved students at two or more levels of proficiency, but other variables such as length of residence in the target language community (e.g., Olshtain & Blum-Kulka, 1985; see Chapter 6 for discussion) have also been used to differentiate learner groups.

As indicated above, both longitudinal and cross-sectional studies have something to offer to researchers interested in devel-opment, but each has some attendant shortcomings as well. In their classic text on educational research methods, Cohen, Man-ion, and Morrison (2000, pp. 174–180) provide an extensive list of the pros and cons of the two types of design. Their discussion of the strengths and weaknesses of longitudinal studies includes (but is not limited to) the following:

Strengths of longitudinal studies

- Useful for establishing causal relationships and for making reliable inferences.
- Shows how changing properties of individuals fit into systemic change.
- Separates real trends from chance occurrence.
- Useful for charting growth and development.
- Gathers data contemporaneously rather than retrospectively, thereby avoiding the problems of selective or false memory.
- Enables change to be analyzed at the individual/micro level.
- Individual-level data are more accurate than macro-level, cross-sectional data.
- Sampling error reduced as the study remains with the same sample over time.

Weaknesses of longitudinal studies

- Time-consuming—it takes a long time for the studies to be conducted and the results to emerge.
- Problems of sample mortality heighten over time and diminish initial representativeness.
- Control effects—repeated interviewing of the same sample influences their behavior.
- Problem of securing participants as it involves repeated contact.
- Data, being rich at an individual level, are typically complex to analyze.

In their assessment of cross-sectional studies, Cohen, Manion, and Morrison note (among others) the following strengths and weaknesses:

Strengths of cross-sectional studies

- Comparatively quick to conduct.
- Comparatively cheap to administer.
- Limited control effects as subjects only participate once.
- Stronger likelihood of participation as it is for a single time.
- Large samples enable inferential statistics to be used.

Weaknesses of cross-sectional studies

- Do not permit analysis of causal relationships.
- Unable to chart individual variations in development or changes, and their significance.
- Omission of a single variable can undermine the results significantly.
- Unable to chart changing social processes over time.
- Only permit analysis of overall, net change at the macro level through aggregated data.

The various strengths and weaknesses of longitudinal and cross-sectional studies could be the object of considerable discussion. For instance, the first "weakness" of cross-sectional studies is not generally recognized in developmental interlanguage pragmatics studies, or in second language acquisition research more generally, for that matter. Omission of variables is a familiar problem that can extend to participant variables, variables in the treatment or elicitation material (such as disregarding imposition as a factor represented in the instrument), or both. On the other hand, the complexities of analyzing longitudinal data are perhaps less daunting for pragmaticians, given the range of discourse, pragmatic, and sociolinguistic approaches referred to earlier in this chapter. While there is clearly much room for both longitudinal and cross-sectional designs in the study of developmental interlanguage pragmatics, a sequential or parallel research program, capitalizing on the strengths and compensating for the weaknesses of each format, remains on the wish list for future investigations at this time.

One additional point regarding research design is a useful clarification by Cook (1993), who argues for the introduction of a third term to describe research design. As he noted:

> [A] cross-sectional study . . . looks at different learners at different moments in time and establishes development by comparing these successive states in different people. . . . [Other studies] do not compare groups of learners at different cross-sectional levels to establish a series of developmental language states, but either lump all the learners

together in one group, or separate them by first language or criteria other than chronological development. . . . A further term, *single-moment* studies, needs to be coined to distinguish this approach from the true cross-sectional design. (Cook, 1993, p. 34, emphasis in original)

Cook also pointed out that many of the L2 morpheme studies were not truly cross-sectional and were thus unable to provide developmental information, as was attempted by equating accuracy orders with acquisition orders. It appears that much interlanguage pragmatics research has blurred the distinction between cross-sectional and single-moment research because many of the studies considered to be cross-sectional are in fact single-moment—they did not collect and compare data from learners at various levels of proficiency, but instead compared nonnative speakers to native speakers. This sort of research cannot shed light on development.

Moving on from basic design criteria required for a study to provide insight on development, we now consider the range of methodological options for data collection available for the study of L2 pragmatic development. We have grouped these into three categories: spoken interaction (authentic discourse, elicited conversation, and role play), questionnaires (DCTs, multiple-choice, and scaled-response), and oral and written self-report (interviews, diaries, and verbal protocols). Because of length constraints, our treatment of each method is rather abbreviated. Readers interested in more detailed accounts of research methods in interlanguage pragmatics are referred to Kasper and Rose (forthcoming).

Spoken Interaction

Authentic discourse, elicited conversation, and open role play share some fundamental properties: they are constituted through oral, interactive productions and therefore allow examination of a wide range of discourse features, and they enable investigators to observe the phenomena of interest, rather than relying on participants' self-reports. The obvious difference between the three types of spoken interaction is that authentic discourse is motivated and structured by participants' rather than by the researcher's goals, whereas elicited conversation and role play are brought into being for research purposes. From a sociolinguistic and pragmatic perspective, this underscores the fact that neither of the two elicited data types can ever be "the same" as authentic conversation since the overall purpose of an interaction is its most powerful structuring force. But contrary to the popular perception that "inauthentic" equals "invalid," interactions arranged for research purposes can be most useful sources of data if used judiciously.

Authentic Discourse

In interlanguage pragmatics research, authentic spoken discourse data have been collected by taking field notes and audio- or videotaping. Although the use of field notes has a time-honored tradition in anthropological research, the use of audio- and video-taping for the study of spoken discourse has decisive advantages; in fact, studies of extended speech events *require* electronic recording. Research on authentic speech events with nonnative speaker participants has predominantly focused on discourse in institutional settings, such as academic advising sessions (Bardovi-Harlig & Hartford, 1996), and oral proficiency interviews (Young & He, 1998). This choice is motivated by a number of factors. Institutional discourse lends itself well to demonstrating interrelation between text and context, for instance, how institutional structures influence communicative action and are reproduced by it. The relationship of communicative action and social power is thus particularly evident in institutional discourse. Compared to interpersonal conversation, institutional talk has the advantage of being more highly structured, routinized, and recurrent, a direct consequence of the purpose of the institution, role distribution between actors (institutional representative vs. client), and actors' goals. From a methodological perspective, this is greatly advantageous because the institutional patterning allows researchers to observe native and nonnative speakers in the same social roles, usually that of a client. In this way, studies of institutional discourse can have the advantage of including an in-built control group.

One obstacle to gathering extended authentic data can be to gain access to the research site. Institutional "gatekeepers" may be reluctant to allow any form of observation and be even less sympathetic to electronic recording. Such problems notwithstanding, the many published studies based on authentic video- or audiotaped discourse are encouraging: such data are possible to collect, and they are necessary. As microanalytic discourse studies amply demonstrate, interaction exhibits finely structured prosodic, temporal, sequential, and non-verbal details that escape even the well-trained observer and are impossible to fix in memory. There is thus a real danger that memorization and field note taking will result in recording salient and (un)expected facets of the interaction, at the expense of less salient but perhaps critical material. Field notes remain a valuable source of contextual information and are indispensable in ethnographic studies, yet they cannot replace electronic recordings (see Duranti, 1997, on practical suggestions for recording interaction). In fact, this not only is true for the study of extended speech events but may also apply to the investigation of individual speech acts. For instance, note taking has proven to be a productive method for studying compliments in different varieties of English because compliments are most frequently packaged as single-turn utterances with a simple, short, highly formulaic structure (e.g., Wolfson, 1989). If a study focuses on the content, syntactic structure, and lexical items in complimenting, note taking may indeed be effective. But if the object of inquiry is the complimenting *event* in its social and discourse context, including compliment responses and their uptake, electronically recorded data are of the essence because note taking from memory is bound to miss important interactional detail. Thus some of the most important insights on the management of compliment responses (Pomerantz, 1978) would not have been possible without microanalysis, afforded by audiotaped and carefully transcribed data.

Two studies from the L2 developmental pragmatics literature that relied on authentic discourse illustrate well the benefits of recorded data versus note taking. Schmidt's (1983) analysis of Wes's request development, which we discuss in the next chapter, was based on extensive field notes taken over the three-year observational period, unlike his analysis of Wes's narratives, which was based on a series of recorded monologues. The recorded monologues provided richer and more detailed data than was the case for Wes's requests, thus demonstrating the advantages of recorded data. A second study that illustrates this well is Bardovi-Harlig and Hartford's (1993a) work on suggestions and refusals, which relied on conversations between graduate students and their academic advisors audiotaped at intervals of seven to fourteen weeks. A brief selection from their data provides ample illustration of the benefits of recording spoken discourse.

(3.1) Transcript from recording of an academic advising session

S: [L530] is one?   Is a required   Can I waive for this?

A: The L530,   yes indeed.   [laugh]

S: Can I waive this course?

A: Ah ... on what basis ... would you waive it?

S: Uh, I think I have taken this course in the university. But I don't know whether they will be similar or not.

A: The best thing to do about that would be to talk to Professor Nobel and see   if what you have taken in the past

S: uh-huh   uh-huh

A: is comparable to what he does.   If he thinks it should be

S: um-hm

A: waived on the basis of what you've taken   then that's fine.

S: uh-huh
       okay

A: But if he doesn't   then you will ...

S: um-hm

A: have to take it.

S: So I have to wait and to choose these first.

(adapted from Bardovi-Harlig & Hartford, 1993a, p. 297)

The range of detail evident in even this short excerpt (e.g., back channel cues, overlapping speech) could have been provided only through some form of recording, audio or video. A note-taking approach would likely have been limited to the more salient aspects of learner production, such as the decidedly nonnative-like question "Can I waive for this?"

In discussions on how best to collect authentic conversational data, the observer's paradox (Labov, 1972) is often brought up: does the researcher's presence alter the normal course of the interaction, and is this effect exacerbated by a video camera? Based on rich experience with ethnographic studies, Duranti (1997) argues that the observer effect is usually temporary. The initial disturbance of routine transactions through the presence of an outsider and her video equipment tends to subside when the novelty effect has worn off and the routines have resumed. Routinized actions (for instance, teachers' and students' classroom practices) are highly overlearned and difficult to change; they will quickly re-emerge once the interaction is under way. However, the possible initial observer effect entails a warning against a hit-and-run approach to data collection. If the recording device and the observer have been present in the setting for some time prior to the data collection, participants are likely to get used to having them around. But in addition to potential problems such as gaining access and observer effects, authentic data may have other drawbacks. Depending on the research purpose, it may take an unreasonable amount of data to obtain sufficient quantities of the pragmatic feature under study—a particular speech act, for instance. And in some cases, authentic data may just not be an option, such as in studies of pragmatic transfer, where a range of data sets (i.e., the L1 data of native and nonnative groups, in addition to target language data from the learner group) needs to be compared. In cases like this, elicited conversations or role plays offer an alternative.

Elicited Conversation

The term *elicited conversation* refers to any conversation staged for the purpose of data collection. Unlike role plays, participants do not take on social roles different from their own; however, they assume discourse roles assigned by the researcher. We can distinguish two varieties of elicited conversation. In *conversation tasks*, participants are requested to converse about a topic or to jointly reach a particular goal determined by the researcher. Instructions can be as vague as asking participants to get to know each other (e.g., Scarcella, 1983; White, 1989) or prescribing specific tasks, such as addressing the interlocutor's troubles tellings (Kerekes, 1992). Data elicited through conversation tasks have been found useful to study various aspects of conversational management (Scarcella, 1983), for example, back channeling (White, 1989) and effects of pragmatic transfer in the use of discourse markers and strategies. Kerekes (1992) investigated if and how participants respond to troubles tellings by offering advice or expressions of sympathy. Her study thus focused on specific responding speech acts in troubles telling events. Billmyer's (1990a, 1990b) study on the effects of instruction in English compliments is another example from the developmental pragmatics literature that relied on data collected through conversations tasks. Her Japanese learners of ESL were paired with native English speakers for weekly "conversation partner" meetings that apparently extended beyond the aims of the research, but were guided by the researcher in terms of goals and content. As Billmyer (1990b) explains, participants "were asked to perform certain compliment-inducing tasks such as showing photos of their homes and family members, reporting on an accomplishment, visiting each other's homes, teaching each other a proverb in their native language, and showing a recently purchased item of apparel" (p. 35). Even though nothing prevents conversation tasks from including differentially symmetric or asymmetric participant configurations, the cited studies featured equal status encounters with fairly balanced participation structures, as far as one can tell from the reports.

In this regard, conversation tasks systematically differ from the other variety of elicited conversation, the *sociolinguistic interview*. As is true of any kind of interview, the sociolinguistic interview is an asymmetrical speech event in which "one party asks the questions and the other party gives the answers" (Schegloff, 1992, p. 118). Unlike conversation tasks, which are structured by the task at hand, *sociolinguistic interviews* often have a genre-specific structure, although hybrid varieties, where the interview transforms into a conversation, are also reported (Schiffrin, 1987). As part of the standard repertoire in sociolinguistic data collection (Labov, 1984), the interviewer asks informants about their life history, experiences, and attitudes. In Labov's original design, one important function of the sociolinguistic interview was to ask informants about highly emotional experiences under the assumption that such topics would trigger vernacular speech. In the sociolinguistic interviews conducted with nonnative speakers, this particular function of the interview has yet to be explored. Aspects of interlanguage pragmatics and discourse studied thus far include conversational management and repair (Færch & Kasper, 1982; Tao & Thompson, 1991) and the acquisition of the Japanese sentence-final particle *ne* (Sawyer, 1992). Tao and Thompson (1991) examined retroactive transfer in the back-channeling patterns of native speakers of Mandarin Chinese from their interlanguage English, whereas Sawyer (1992) compared learners' production of *ne* in four interviews, conducted over the period of one year, in order to determine developmental patterns in the use of the particle. Sawyer's (1992) study, one of the first on nonnative speakers' pragmatic development, raises an interesting design issue. As native speaker baseline data, Sawyer used the frequency of *ne* in the discourse contributions of the Japanese interviewer. This presents a potential validity problem because the asymmetrical structure of the interview positions interviewer and informant in different discourse roles and this asymmetry is very likely reflected in, and in fact co-constructed by, the use of *ne*. As a key discourse marker, *ne* has been shown to index epistemic and affective stance (Cook, 1992); as an indexical, its use is, by definition, highly context-sensitive. Therefore, comparisons to native speaker use of *ne* are made, it would seem important to compare native and nonnative speakers in the same discourse roles. In other words, baseline data could be obtained by conducting interviews with native speakers of Japanese that were otherwise comparable to the nonnative informants, allowing examination of the use of *ne* in native and nonnative informants' interview responses. Elicited conversations have the capacity to shed light on such discourse aspects as conversational organization and management, the expression of reference, modality, temporality, and aspect, task-specific communicative acts and narrative structure. But they are also limited in that they allow researchers to investigate only a fairly narrow range of communicative acts and activities and participant roles cannot be manipulated, as is the case with role plays.

Role Play

This limitation of elicited conversations is overcome in role plays, that is, simulations of communicative encounters based on role descriptions. Role plays can be defined as "a social or human activity in which participants 'take on' and 'act out' specified 'roles,' often within a predefined social framework or situational blueprint (a 'scenario')" (Crookall & Saunders, 1989, p. 15). Different types of role play can be distinguished according to participant involvement and extent of interaction. In spontaneous role plays, players retain their own identities. In mimetic-replicating role plays, they play the role of a visually presented model, while in mimetic-pretending role plays, actors assume a different identity (Kipper, 1988). Useful as these categories are as a first rough distinction, they are too broad to capture other potentially important variables that might affect the quality of role playing. For instance, a particular type of spontaneous role play is the idiographic role play, in which actors recall and role play specific, recent, and relevant extended interactions (Kern, 1991). The great advantage of this type of role play is that actors can rely on recent episodic memory, which will reduce the cognitive load associated with having to invent the action online.

Role plays also differ in the extent of the interaction. In interlanguage pragmatics, a distinction has been made between closed and open role plays (Kasper & Dahl, 1991). In closed role plays, the actors respond to the description of a situation and, depending on the communicative act under study, to an interlocutor's standardized initiation. Open role plays, on the other hand, specify the initial situation as well as each actor's role and goal(s) on individual role cards, but the course and outcome of the interaction are in no way predetermined. Unlike closed role plays, open role plays can evolve over many turns and different discourse phases. Communicative acts evolve over multiple turns and their sequential organization is contingent on the interlocutor's uptake. The conversational activity addresses interpersonal functions, such as politeness, and interactional functions, such as coordinating speaker and listener contributions through turn taking and back channeling. Open role plays thus allow researchers to observe those aspects of conversation that are fairly independent of particular contexts and goals but, unlike authentic discourse and elicited conversation, they also allow contexts and roles that are likely to elicit specific communicative events and acts—embedded in the role play as an activity in its own right. Moreover, through the role specifications, they also enable us to observe how context factors, such as power, distance, and degree of imposition in Brown and Levinson's (1987) politeness theory, influence the selection and realization of communicative acts and how the values of these factors may change through conversational negotiation. The rich potential of role plays is evident from their use in L2 developmental pragmatics research on communicative acts such as requests (Hassall, 1997; Scarcella, 1979; Trosborg, 1995), complaints (Trosborg, 1995), apologies (Trosborg, 1995), greetings (Omar, 1991), gambits (Wildner-Bassett, 1984, 1986), routine formulae (Tateyama, 2001; Tateyama, Kasper, Mui, Tay, & Thananart, 1997), pragmatic fluency (House, 1996), and interactionally appropriate responses to questions (Liddicoat & Crozet, 2001).

Because role plays tap into actors' interactional competence, they are, in principle, capable of producing a wide array of interactional conduct, but that fact is no guarantee that role plays provide valid representations of pragmatic practices in authentic contexts. Only a few studies have examined the validity of role play in interlanguage pragmatics. Eisenstein and Bodman's (1993) study of expression of gratitude by native and nonnative speakers of English sheds light on the effects of three data collection procedures: DCTs, open role plays, and field notes. All three data types yielded the same words and expressions, yet they differed in length and complexity. The DCT data were the shortest and least complex, the authentic data the longest and most complex, with the role play data coming in between. The oral data included more restatements of thanks and discussions about the received gift or service. Both role play and authentic data demonstrated that thanking is collaboratively constructed, involving the giver as much as the receiver. Other studies have compared role play and written DCTs. Margalef-Boada (1993) examined the production of refusals by native speakers of German, Spanish, and German learners of Spanish. The analysis showed the same content and range of semantic formulae in both conditions, with most of them occurring with roughly the same frequency. The main difference between the written responses and the oral interaction was the large number of semantic repetitions in the oral role play. Due to the interactive nature of the role play and the multiple turns over which the refusal event evolved, the role plays were naturally longer, "richer and more complex" (p. 153) than the written single-turn responses. However, in both conditions, participants produced less polite refusals than would be appropriate in an authentic setting, suggesting that the absence of social consequences may have relaxed their adherence to politeness norms. Sasaki (1998) investigated two communicative acts, requests and refusals, administering DCTs and role plays to Japanese EFL learners. Both methods elicited similar head acts and supportive moves for requests, and types and order of semantic formulae for refusals, but responses varied in length and content, with role play contributions featuring longer utterances and a greater variety of strategies. Edmondson and House (1991) found that nonnative speakers produced longer and more verbose utterances than native speakers on DCTs but not in role plays. The authors attribute this finding to learners either lacking or not having sufficient control over routine formulae. But in addition, the fictive world of the role play may affect learners differently from native speakers. Whereas in authentic interaction, participants' planning and execution of communicative action is supported by a rich social context, participants in a role play have to imagine their own and their co-actors' roles. Constructing and interpreting communicative intent can easily overstretch learners' social imagination and memory and thus reduce their capacity for online input processing and utterance planning. It is therefore possible that most types of role play under-represent learners' pragmatic ability.

Questionnaires

Compared to spoken interaction, investigating interlanguage pragmatics by means of questionnaires restricts the kinds of questions that researchers may ask. Excluded from investigation are precisely those pragmatic features that are specific to oral interactive discourse—any aspect related to the dynamics of a conversation, turn taking and the conversational mechanisms related to it, sequencing of action, speaker-listener coordination, features of speech production that may have pragmatic import, such as temporal variables, and all paralinguistic and nonverbal elements. Despite these limitations, however, different forms of questionnaire data are the most commonly used data types in interlanguage pragmatics. Unfortunately, in pragmatics research, questionnaires are sometimes treated as a quick fix for gathering data, not a commendable practice. Like any other research instrument, questionnaires should be chosen because they are the optimal data-gathering technique for the goals of the study (or one of several such instruments), not because they are "easier" or "faster" than other data-collection procedures. Questionnaires that are worth the paper they are printed on (or the bandwidth used in online administration) take considerable expertise and time to develop. While it may be true that when a good questionnaire is ready for use in data collection, the data can then be collected relatively quickly (as opposed to, say, lengthy periods of observation in an ethnographic study), the questionnaire design and evaluation process is not at all quick or easy. Fortunately, expert assistance is readily available in the numerous treatments of questionnaire design and development to which pragmaticians can turn (e.g., Converse & Presser, 1986; Fowler, 1995; Schwarz & Sudman, 1996). Here we discuss the three types of questionnaire most frequently used in pragmatics—DCTs, multiple-choice, and scaled-response—each of which differs from the others in the type of response it elicits. DCTs are open-ended in the sense that they require a participant-generated textual response that is coherent with the context specified in the stimulus item. Multiple-choice and scaled-response questionnaires, by contrast, provide fixed response alternatives from which the participant has to choose the most appropriate one.

Discourse Completion Tasks

A DCT item typically consists of a situational description followed by a brief dialogue, with (at least) one turn as an open slot to be completed by the participant (hence the term "discourse completion"). The specified context is designed to constrain the open turn(s) so that a specific communicative act is elicited. The example below, in which the exchange is terminated by a provided rejoinder, is taken from the (in)famous Cross-Cultural Speech Act Realization Project (CCSARP).

(3.2) DCT item to elicit an apology

At the College Teacher's office

A student has borrowed a book from her teacher, which she promised to return today. When meeting her teacher, however, she realizes that she forgot to bring it along.

Teacher: Miriam, I hope you brought the book I lent you.
Miriam: _____
Teacher: OK, but please remember it next week.

(Blum-Kulka, House, & Kasper, 1989, p. 14)

In addition to item designs as illustrated above, DCT formats vary in a number of ways, for instance, whether they include a first pair part or rejoinder, rejoinder type, or whether respondents have to provide both (or all) discourse contributions. Illustrating a format quite different from the CCSARP DCT, the following item from Rose and Ng's study of the effects of instruction in compliments and compliment responses does not provide a first pair part or a rejoinder, and requires the participant to provide two turns, which constitute two acts—a compliment and compliment response.

(3.3) DCT item to elicit a compliment and compliment response

Alex has an interview today for a part-time job with a large investment company, so he is wearing his best suit. What would you say to compliment him on his appearance? How do you think he would respond?

You: _____
Alex: _____

(adapted from Rose & Ng, 2001, pp. 153–154)

Yet another difference in DCT formats is whether the instructions include specific reference to opting out, that is, choosing *not* to perform the act in question, thus permitting the researcher to identify sociopragmatic differences in the appropriateness of communicative acts (Bonikowska, 1988).

Given their widespread use in the pragmatics literature, DCTs have been subjected to a good deal of methodological scrutiny. This research has tended to take one of two directions: the comparison of DCT data to data collected by other means (e.g., multiple choice, role play, or observation of authentic discourse), and the exploration of how specific design features (e.g., inclusion of rejoinder) might be the source of possible instrument effects.

The first study that explored the validity of DCTs was Beebe and Cummings (1996, first presented in 1985). They compared DCT and authentic refusals collected over the telephone, finding both similarities and also substantial differences between the two: the DCT data differed from the naturally occurring refusals of such features as amount of talk, actual wording, and range of semantic formulas used. Hartford and Bardovi-Harlig (1992) compared DCT and naturally occurring rejections produced by both native speakers and nonnative speakers of English. The naturally occurring rejections were drawn from their in-depth analysis of academic advising sessions discussed above. The DCT was designed to test three hypotheses: that native speaker rejections will be shorter, native speakers will prefer a smaller number of rejection strategies, and native speakers will not use "illegal content." All three hypotheses were supported. Differences between naturally occurring rejections and DCT rejections had to do primarily with variation in type and frequency of rejection strategies (i.e., semantic formulas). Rintell and Mitchell (1989) conducted a comparative study of written and oral DCTs (closed role plays) administered to native and nonnative speakers of English, and found that the two types of data differed in two ways: nonnative speaker oral responses were significantly longer than their written responses, and in some situations both native speakers and nonnative speakers were more direct on the DCT than in the closed role plays. Despite these differences, Rintell and Mitchell argued that "language elicited in this study is very similar whether collected in written or oral form" (p. 270). The effect of different delivery modes was also examined by Kuha (1997), who compared complaints elicited through a conventional paper-and-pencil DCT to complaints produced through use of a computerized interactive DCT format (IDCT). The two instrument formats were compared on three measures—response length, semantic formulas, and directness. Each of the ICDT turns was shorter than the one-turn DCT response, while the entire response length was greater in the ICDT. The use of semantic formulas also differed according to instrument, whereas the directness of problem statements was about equal, and repair was requested with more directness in the IDCT than the DCT, an outcome contrary to expectation.

As noted above, Eisenstein and Bodman's (1993) work on expressions of gratitude in English incorporated several data types, including authentic discourse, role plays, written and oral DCTs, and retrospective interviews. Their study thus provides an excellent example of method triangulation in pragmatics research. Although the focus of Eisenstein and Bodman's study was the negotiated nature of expressing gratitude, not method comparison, the authors did remark briefly on the various data types, noting that

> Role-plays and natural situations incorporated the same words and semantic formulas that appeared in the written data. In this sense then, our written data were representative of certain aspects of natural language use. . . . Yet the role-plays went beyond the written data by providing us with additional insights into the functions of thanking and responding to thanks as they exist in a conversational interaction. . . . [And] natural data was even richer and more revealing because it evidenced restatements of the same information using slightly different language and showed that the same function recurred over time. (Eisenstein & Bodman, 1993, p. 71)

Also employing multiple data-collection procedures, Turnbull (2001) assessed four data-elicitation techniques to determine how well each held up as a means of eliciting refusals to requests. Each technique was compared to naturally occurring speech. In the experimental technique, refusals were elicited over the phone by means of a scripted request, with the same scenario also used for written and oral DCTs, as well as role plays. Naturally occurring refusals also came from telephone calls, but these were unscripted. Results indicated that compared to the experimental condition, role plays and naturally occurring speech, DCTs yielded responses that were shorter and contained a smaller range of acts.

Several studies have compared DCT and multiple-choice responses in research on speech act production. Rose (1994) reports the results of two studies concerning the use of DCTs. In the first of these, an open-ended DCT to elicit requests was administered to Japanese (in Japanese) and American undergraduates. Contrary to the common perception that when compared to interaction in American English, Japanese interaction is often characterized by vagueness and indirectness (e.g., Clancy, 1986; Hinds, 1987; Lebra, 1976; L. Miller, 1994; Rose, 1996), Japanese requests were more direct than American requests, and where hints occurred, they were generally used more frequently by Americans. This prompted the second study, in which DCT responses were compared with responses from another group who completed a multiple-choice questionnaire (MCQ) consisting of the same request situations. Significant differences were found in most situations, with those completing the MCQ showing preferences for opting out and hinting, a finding that was replicated in a follow-up study by Rose and Ono (1995). Hinkel (1997) also reports similar findings from her comparison of speakers of Chinese and English.

Method effects have been observed not only between DCTs and other data-collection procedures, but also in variations of DCT formats. Bardovi-Harlig and Hartford (1993b) conducted a study that compared English native speaker and nonnative speaker rejections on two types of DCT: one that provided a description of the situation and a prompt (i.e., an opening conversational turn), and one that provided only a description of the situation. While native speaker differences across DCT type were rather minimal, nonnative speaker differences were in general noticeably greater, suggesting that the variations in DCT design seem to have produced greater response effects for nonnative speakers than for native speakers. Turning from the initial to the final structural element in the dialogue segment of DCTs, studies have also examined the effect of rejoinders. In the first of these, Rose (1992) administered two forms of a DCT that were identical except for inclusion of rejoinder. Although there were some slight differences between data collected by the two forms of the DCT, none of the differences were statistically significant. Johnston, Kasper, and Ross (1998) conducted a more complex analysis of the rejoinders and response effects, examining the effects of no rejoinder, preferred rejoinder, and dispreferred rejoinder, as well as the differential effects for speech act type (requests, apologies, and complaints), and differential effects for native speaker and nonnative speaker participants. Johnston et al. found effects for both inclusion of rejoinder and rejoinder type, and they also found that different speech act types were affected differently, as were different speech act realization strategies. Based on their findings, Johnston et al. question the comparability of data from studies that employed questionnaires with varying formats for inclusion of rejoinder or different rejoinder type. A third variable feature of DCTs concerns the amount of information provided in the situational description that prefaces the dialogue segment. Billmyer and Varghese (2000) compared the differential response effects of short descriptions and content-enriched descriptions on native speaker and nonnative speaker request realizations. No differences between versions were found for directness levels and internal modification of the head act, whereas the enhanced prompt elicited longer responses and more external modification. Very likely, the longer version prompted more external modification because the enhanced descriptions provided the justifications for the request that participants could readily incorporate in their response.

As the literature reviewed here shows, rather than speculating about DCT-specific response effects, studies have closely examined how DCT data differ from data collected through other methods, and how details of item design affect responses. They have also demonstrated that different populations may interact differently with various types of DCT format, indicating strongly that a specific instrument format has to be pretested for each population included in a study. Nevertheless, when carefully designed, DCTs provide useful information about speakers' *pragmalinguistic knowledge* of the strategies and linguistic forms by which communicative acts can be implemented, and about their *sociopragmatic knowledge* of the context factors under which particular strategic and linguistic choices are appropriate. Whether or not speakers use exactly the same strategies and forms in actual discourse is a different matter, but the questionnaire responses indicate what strategic and linguistic options are consonant with respondents' understandings of L2 pragmatic norms and what context factors influence their choices. In L2 developmental pragmatic research, we may be interested in finding how L2 learners' *knowledge* develops as opposed to development in *performance* under the much more demanding conditions of conversational encounters. For such research purposes, DCTs are an effective option, regardless of whether the data they yield are representative of face-to-face interaction.

Multiple-Choice Questions

Multiple choice is a versatile questionnaire format because it allows the researcher to elicit information on pragmatic production, pragmatic comprehension, and metapragmatic judgments at various stages of development in either longitudinal or cross-sectional research. As with DCTs, multiple-choice items specify the situational context and include a prompt for a response, but rather than leaving the response selection to the participant, they specify several response alternatives from which one must be chosen. As noted in the previous section, comparison of responses between DCTs and multiple-choice questionnaires has shown the multiple-choice responses to be more consistent with reports on preferences for pragmatic strategies in authentic settings, although no direct comparisons with authentic data were made. The reasons for these differences are far from being well understood, but they call for more research into the validity of both questionnaire types. From a cognitive perspective, the two questionnaire formats impose quite different processing demands on respondents, with the open-ended DCT representing a free-recall task and the closed format of the multiple choice falling into the category of recognition task (Schwarz & Hippler, 1991). Multiple-choice responses require that participants evaluate a small number of presented alternatives against their memory structures of compatible events, a much less demanding task than having to conduct a free-memory search and make an appropriate selection from a wide array of possible solutions. On the other hand, both multiple choice and DCTs can provide an opting-out option.

One example of the use of a multiple-choice format for the exploration of pragmatic production is the following item taken from Rose and Ono's (1995) study comparing requests in Japanese and English cited above.

(3.4) Multiple choice for pragmatic production

Today is Sunday. You are going to see your friend at the Umeda Station at noon. You are ready to leave home now, but you think you are probably going to be late if you walk to the nearest station. You see your father looking at a magazine in the living room. What would you say or do?

a. I would say, "Please drive me to the train station."
b. I would say, "Could you drive me to the station?"
c. I would say, "I'm meeting my friend at the Umeda Station, and I'm going to be late."
d. I would walk quickly to the station even though I expect to be late.

(Rose & Ono, 1995, pp. 220–221)

One problem that this item illustrates is the combination of directness levels with mitigation. On the one hand, alternative (a) would be quite unnatural without the politeness marker (or re-questive force indicator) please; on the other hand, inclusion of please makes it impossible to determine whether respondents opt for (a) because of the directness level, the politeness marker, or both. Similarly, the modal past could in option (b) reduces the force of the conventionally indirect request to a greater extent than the present tense can would. If the research goal is to identify direct-ness level preferences, it would seem mandatory either that response alternatives be not further mitigated or aggravated, or that they be modified in the same way. In example (3.4), it would be possible to change (b) to <u>Can you drive me to the station please?</u> However, it would be more difficult to modify (c) in the same way as (a) and (b).

In addition to being used to study pragmatic production, multiple-choice tasks are also a means of studying pragmatic comprehension. For instance, Bouton (1988, 1992, 1994a, 1994b) deployed a multiple-choice instrument in order to examine how advanced ESL learners understand conversational implicature, as illustrated in example (3.5).

> (3.5) Multiple choice item for testing pragmatic comprehension
>
> *Susan and Mei-ling are roommates and are getting ready to go to class together.*
>
> Mei-ling: Is it very cold out this morning?
> Susan: It's August.
>
> What is Susan saying?
> a.   It'll be nice and warm today. Don't worry.
> b.   Yes, even though it's August, it's very cold out.
> c.   It's so warm for this time of year that it seems like August.
> d.   Yes, we're sure having crazy weather, aren't we?
>
> (Bouton, 1988, p. 194)

In constructing multiple-choice tasks for examining pragmatic production and comprehension, the designer has to rely on previous research on the communicative act in question in order to make principled selections from the alternative responses. Relying on intuition to invent responses is not sufficient because pragmatic strategies might escape the researcher's attention. Valid sources from which to select response alternatives are speech act realization strategies collected through DCTs (Rose & Ono, 1995) or from spoken discourse (authentic or elicited) and free responses to comprehension questionnaires (Bouton, 1988).

Finally, a multiple-choice format can be used to shed light on respondents' metapragmatic knowledge, for instance, how they classify utterances in terms of speech act categories, and what elements in the utterance they use as interpretive resources. The example below is from Koike's (1989) study on learners' recognition of requests, apologies, and commands. Note that in this study, the stimuli were presented aurally so that learners were able to draw on prosodic information as contextualization cues.

(3.6) Multiple choice for speech act identification

Claudia: Oye, María, por favor, me gustaría ir al concierto esta noche pero no tengo dinero. Este artista es uno de mis favoritos. ¿Puedes prestarme cinco dólares? Puedo pagarte mañana, te lo prometo.

Oh, Maria, please I would like to go to the concert tonight but I don't have any money. This artist is one of my favorites. Can you lend me five dollars? I can pay you back tomorrow, I promise.

1. This is a(n)
    a. apology
    b. suggestion
    c. request
    d. command
2. What helped you understand?
    a. Certain words
       If so, name one: _____
    b. Intonation
    c. Every word was comprehensible to me
    d. Totally incomprehensible

(Koike, 1989, p. 289)

The versatility of the multiple-choice format makes it an attractive choice for a range of research goals, particularly when researchers are interested in categorical judgments as illustrated in extract (3.6). However, when the information sought is participants' graded assessments of such attributes as appropriateness or politeness, a scaled response format provides an effective option.

Scaled-Response Questionnaires

In addition to examining how learners assess strategies of communicative action and their linguistic realizations in terms of appropriateness, politeness, or other attributes, researchers may also want to know how learners evaluate the values and weights of the contextual variables that influence strategic and linguistic choices, such as participants' relative power, social distance, and the degree of imposition involved in a linguistic act. The first question raises a pragmalinguistic issue, derived from Hymes's theory of communicative competence. The second question poses a sociopragmatic problem, addressed in Brown and Levinson's politeness theory. And just as in formal linguistics, the most common method of obtaining metapragmatic assessments is by eliciting scaled category responses. Scaled-response items can be used in obtaining metapragmatic assessments for a range of purposes: as a research issue in its own right, as an additional resource to help interpret performance data, or as a preliminary step toward developing the instrument for the main study. This last function—the use of scaled-response items for instrument development—is particularly noteworthy because in studies using any kind of data-elicitation format (e.g., role plays, DCTs, multiple-choice), researchers need to know how respondents assess the context variables built into the stimulus situations. Such crucial information cannot be obtained by relying on the researcher's intuition. Sociopragmatic assessments of candidate contexts elicited during instrument development enable researchers to ground their item constructions empirically and thus to improve control over context variables. Without such careful preparation in designing instruments, results are difficult to interpret.

Scaled-response questionnaires have not been used as widely in studies on L2 pragmatic development as DCTs or multiple choice have been, but it is not the case that their use is unattested in this literature. One exemplary investigation in which the instrument for the main study was developed through a sequence of prestudies using sociopragmatic and pragmalinguistic assessments is Takahashi's (1995, 1996) investigation of pragmatic transferability. In their study of apologies produced by intermediate and advanced Japanese-speaking learners of ESL, Maeshiba, Yoshinaga, Kasper, and Ross (1996) employed a DCT together with a metapragmatic assessment questionnaire that collected learners' assessments of seven contextual factors: severity of offense, offender's obligation to apologize, likelihood for the apology to be accepted, offender's face loss, offended party's face loss, social distance, and social dominance. Assessments converged most on status, obligation to apologize, and likelihood of acceptance, and the least on offender's face loss, offended party's face loss, and social distance. Maeshiba et al. predicted that transfer of apology strategies (as inferred from the production data collected via DCT) could be based on similarities and differences in assessment of contextual variables, with positive transfer occurring with similar assessments, and negative transfer where assessments differed, and for the most part, these predictions were borne out. This study illustrates how scaled response instruments can be used in conjunction with a DCT to explore in a rather detailed fashion possible relationships between learner production (in this case, transfer from the L1) and a range of specific context features. As is evident from Maeshiba et al. (1996), scaled-response instruments presuppose that the constructs under study are known and well defined. When this is not the case, other types of self-report are preferable.

The example below, from Shimamura's (1993) study of Japanese EFL learners' use of supportive moves in requests, illustrates scales for both pragmalinguistic (Items 1–4) and sociopragmatic (Items 5–7) assessment.

(3.7) Sociopragmatic and pragmalinguistic assessment

Your friend from the mainland is visiting this weekend. You haven't seen her for a few years and this will be her first visit to Hawai'i, so you have decided to take her around the island. But your car broke down and you do not want to spend a lot of money renting a car. Then you remember that your classmate who lives in the neighborhood just bought

a new car last week. You decide to ask your classmate if
you can borrow her car for the weekend. You say . . .

1) Could I borrow your car this weekend if you're not using it?
   My car broke down. I'll return it with a full tank of gas.
   appropriate   not appropriate
              1__2__3__4__5

2) Could I borrow your car this weekend if you're not using it?
   My car broke down.
   appropriate   not appropriate
              1__2__3__4__5

3) My car broke down. Could I borrow your car this weekend
   if you're not using it?
   appropriate   not appropriate
              1__2__3__4__5

4) Could I borrow your car this weekend if you're not using it?
   appropriate   not appropriate
              1__2__3__4__5

5) Is it your right to make the request to your classmate in this
   situation?
   absolutely   not at all
              1__2__3__4__5

6) Is your classmate obliged to lend you her car in this situation?
   absolutely   not at all
              1__2__3__4__5

7) How likely is your classmate to lend you her car in this
   situation?
   very likely   very unlikely
              1__2__3__4__5

(Shimamura, 1993, p. 75)

In constructing scaled response instruments, it is essential
to heed the design principles specified in the sociometric and
psychometric literature (e.g., Bryman & Cramer, 2001; Miller &
Salkind, 2002). Informativeness, reliability, and validity will be
maximized if the following principles are followed. First, composite constructs (such as power or imposition) are unfolded into their

underlying dimensions (e.g., for imposition in apologizing: severity of offense, obligation to apologize, likelihood of acceptance of apology, offender's face loss). Second, each dimension is operationalized by at least two indicators (e.g., for severity of offense: "How serious is John's offense?" "How upset is Paul by John's damaging his car?" "How great is the damage done to Paul by John?" "How inconvenient is John's offense to Paul?" "How costly is John's offense to Paul?"). Third, rating scales are divided into five to seven steps. And finally, if the instrument is prepared in different languages, care must be taken that the stimulus material be cross-linguistically equivalent. This is achieved by back translation (Behling & Law, 2000).

Oral and Written Self-Report

Unlike studies on well-defined research objects and issues for which questionnaires may be an appropriate choice, exploratory research goals require modes of inquiry that are less predetermined. For this sort of research enterprise, forms of self-report that are more participant-directed, open-ended, and inclusive are necessary. The last three methods we discuss—narrative interviews, verbal protocols, and diaries—are forms of self-report data that exhibit these very characteristics, making them suitable for the investigation of new research issues or in-depth study of pragmetic development in particular settings.

Interviews

Exploratory research goals require open, inclusive, little predetermined modes of inquiry. But also for hypothesis-testing and triangulating purposes, researchers may prefer a dynamic, context-and respondent-sensitive procedure such as narrative self-reports. The most common procedure for obtaining such reports is the research interview. Briggs (1986) estimated that "90 percent of all social science investigations use interview data" (p. 1). Large-scale sociological surveys are mostly conducted as interviews. In

ethnographic research, interviews, together with participant observation, are a standard data-gathering procedure. But the scope
and frequency of their use is not matched by concomitant analysis
of just how interviews work and what kinds of data they produce.

In order to understand the structure and process of interviews, it is useful to consider them from discourse-pragmatic and
cognitive perspectives. Research interviews are a particular kind
of speech event. On the one hand, they share certain structural
characteristics with other types of interview that are common in
many but by no means all speech communities (Fiksdal, 1990). On
the other hand, research interviews include different varieties,
depending on such factors as medium (face-to-face, telephone,
electronic media), degree of prestructuring (open-ended vs. based
on an interview schedule), and length. Since the interplay of
context factors shapes interview interaction and outcomes, it has
to be taken into consideration in the analysis of interview data.
No matter how prestructured by an interview schedule, interviews
are ineluctably interactive, so rather than attempting to minimize
"interaction effects," research on interviews should explicate the
structure of interview interaction and how it is related to the data
produced by it. The most effective way of gathering such information is through microanalysis of interview discourse (Baker, 2001).
Given that the fundamental exchange structure of the interview
is the question-answer sequence (Schegloff, 1992; Wolfson, 1976),
the interviewee's answers will be "conditionally relevant"
(Schegloff & Sacks, 1973) on the interviewer's questions. Consequently, the view of interviews as "pipeline(s) for transmitting
knowledge" (Holstein & Gubrium, 1997, p. 113) and interview
answers as the sole product of the interviewee's mind is untenable
in light of the discourse-structural properties of the interview.
Interviews concerning informants' attitudes and their experiences
of past events are traditionally predicated on a static and passive
view of memory. Cognitive psychologists, by contrast, have insisted
since Bartlett (1932) that memory is constructive. Previously
encoded information interacts with more recently acquired memories, implicit theories, personal interests, and so forth (Pearson,

Ross, & Dawes, 1992). A cognitive perspective thus supports the view that interview answers are not immediate revelations of "facts" but cognitive and interactional constructions.

In pragmatics, "off-line" interviews (i.e., interviews not related to a specific immediately preceding activity) have served as initial exploration of a research issue, to triangulate the researcher's interpretation of authentic discourse data, as one among several data types in a multimethod approach, and as the main data source. Different types and applications of interviews in research on communicative acts can be illustrated by studies on compliments in American English by Knapp, Hopper, and Bell (1984) and by Miles (1994). Knapp et al. (1984) is a large-scale survey interview with partly closed-ended questions and brief responses, focusing primarily on the forms of compliments and compliment responses. Data were content-analyzed and frequencies reported. Miles (1994) is a qualitative study, based on observation of compliment exchanges occurring in authentic discourse for information about compliment forms and their distribution and on interviews for community members' emic views on the social meanings and functions of complimenting. Questions were open-ended and respondents engaged in extensive narratives and commentary. Data were analyzed interpretively, with particular attention to respondents' discourse. The report includes extensive quotes from interviewees' comments. These methodological differences resulted in major discrepancies in substantive outcomes. One such difference is the preferred response pattern identified in the two studies. According to the observational part of Miles's study, only 7% of the recipients expressed agreement with the compliment (e.g., "Yes, I like it, too" in response to a compliment on a new dress). In contrast, in Knapp et al. (1984), 46% of the compliment responses registered as agreements and only 16% were minimized (e.g., "It's not *that* pretty"). Further, Knapp et al.'s interview subjects reported without exception that they felt satisfied with the compliment experience, whereas Miles's interview participants reported feelings of embarrassment and face threat.

In order to investigate actual communicative practices—as opposed to what learners *believe* these practices to be—interviews are inappropriate because interview respondents' reports are affected by memory constraints and prescriptive orientations. The most appropriate method is observation, as the converging results of many observation-based studies on speech acts, discourse markers, routines, and other pragmatic objects demonstrate. However, interviews are useful and often indispensable when the research goal is to establish the cultural meanings that communicative practices have for community members, because such emic meanings can only be inferred from observation—that is, if we want to find out participants' views, we need to ask them directly rather than rely on observation alone. For the same reasons that make narrative interviews a procedure with unique potential for obtaining in-depth information about cultural meanings from "the native's" point of view, qualitative and ethnographic interviews hold substantial promise for investigating the meanings of L2 pragmatic practices in the understanding of L2 learners, and how such understandings may change over time.

Consonant with the multi-method approach of ethnographic research, several ethnographic studies examining the development of L2 learners' pragmatic ability have incorporated interviews as a data type (e.g., DuFon, 1999; Iino, 1996; Siegal, 1994). For instance, in DuFon's (1999) investigation of the acquisition of politeness in Indonesian, interviews served as one data source about community members' views of politeness:

> Teachers, tutors, program administrators, and [host] families were formally interviewed in order to get their evaluations of what constitutes polite behavior in Indonesian culture, what their expectations were regarding polite behavior by the learners, their impressions of individual learners in terms of their politeness in Indonesian and in terms of the progress they made or failed to make during the course of the program. (DuFon, 1999, pp. 133–134)

Among other purposes, such a use of interviews serves as an indirect indicator of learner's pragmatic development, which could provide useful information when employed alongside other data-collection types.

One important feature shared by such diverse interview genres as interviews prestructured by a detailed schedule (questionnaire) and open-ended, narrative interviews is that they purport to tap respondents' long-term memories of generalized knowledge states, attitudes, or past events. By contrast, another form of oral self-report is designed to provide information about participants' thoughts while they are engaged in a specific activity. Different forms of verbal report or think-aloud protocols will be considered.

Think-Aloud Protocols

One feature shared by interviews and diaries is that the self-reported data are elicited in isolation from the contexts in which the reported event occurs. Subjects retrieve pertinent information from long term memory in order to answer an interview question or submit a journal entry, but they are not currently engaged in an activity requiring online use of the information. In contrast, think-aloud protocols (TAP) are verbalizations of thought processes during engagement in a task. The expanded edition of Ericsson and Simon's (1984, 1993) seminal work *Proto col Analysis: Verbal Report as Data* not only provides the theoretical framework for predicting under which conditions verbal report should be a valid account of thought processes, but also when and why valid accounts cannot be expected. A simplified version of the theory goes as follows: Information processed in short-term memory while a participant is carrying out a task is reportable and veridical. Information not processed in short-term memory, such as perceptual processes, motor processes, and all automated processes, is not available for report. Veridical report is also possible immediately after task completion, when traces of the attended information are still in short-term memory. Once out of short-term memory, information will be lost or encoded in long-term memory, but storage in and retrieval from long-term memory always entails further processing. Therefore, the most valid reports are concurrent or immediately consecutive verbalizations. Delayed retrospective protocols may have only a tenuous relationship to the original attended information. In addition to type of information and recency of processing, the instruction to participants for verbalization is crucial. Prompts should request participants to say only what they are thinking. Participants should not be asked to describe, explain, or hypothesize because such requests will prompt different cognitive processes than those required by the task and will interfere with the task-related processes. Studies using verbal protocols in second language research have been reviewed in various places (e.g., Cohen, 1998; Gass & Mackey, 2000). Cohen (1996) and Gass and Mackey (2000) also review of the verbal report studies on interlanguage pragmatics. We will comment on three published studies by Robinson (1992), Cohen and Olshtain (1993), and Widjaja (1997) because they illustrate different types of verbal protocol and design issues.

Robinson's participants were asked to think aloud while completing a DCT on refusal. In accordance with Ericsson and Simon's (1993) prescriptions, instructions requested participants to verbalize whatever they were thinking while focusing on the task, in the language they were thinking in, and participants were given a practice session. Immediately after they finished the task, the tape-recorded think-aloud protocol was played back to participants in a retrospective interview. Coding categories were developed inductively from the protocols and an interrater reliability check was run on the coding of one entire protocol by three coders. Methodologically, one of the interesting outcomes of Robinson's study is the different information provided in the concurrent and consecutive reports. The concurrent reports were entirely task-focused, indicating what information in the stimulus participants attended to, their planning decisions, considerations of alternatives, the consulted pragmalinguistic and sociopragmatic knowledge, and the difficulties participants experienced in deciding on their response. In the consecutive reports, despite the stimulated recall, participants often had difficulties remembering their task-related thoughts, which was predictable since they completed the entire questionnaire before the retrospective interview. But in some cases, participants provided more complete reports than in the concurrent verbalization and very informative details about the reasoning underlying their planning decisions and the sources of the L1 and L2 pragmatic knowledge they drew on. For example, the following concurrent report sheds light on the response alternatives that the learner considered in refusing a classmate's request to borrow lecture notes because she once again overslept and missed class.

(3.8) Concurrent verbal report

Well um - for now I should s tell her that - I don't have it with me - and uh — um -um and so that she she will ask somebody else - hm — mm [*Researcher: What are you thinking?*] but um - she may ask again - what should I say - um - I cannot tell her that I - I I was absent from the class - I did attend - um - what I'm gonna say - it's really hard um - well - how can I refuse -mm - I can I can just - well I'll just tell her that I don't have it with me - and I have to - tell her that - my - my notes are - are not good - um - it's not sufficient for her - oh okay I I I should tell her that we - she should ask someone else - = um - well - I don't I have to ex explain that my notes are good - are not good =

('-' = micropause, '=' = pause while writing; Robinson, 1992, pp. 52–53)

Whereas the concurrent report proved useful in revealing options considered by this learner in formulating her refusal, the retrospective report below—prompted by the researcher's question "What was important about this situation?"—provides information on the learner's views of social relationships that guided her decision-making.

(3.9) Retrospective verbal report

Mm - well - I I I don't want to lend a lazy person uh my notes [laughs] [*Researcher: Hmm*] but like I said before it's also important to make other people happy - as long as I can do things for them - so - it's it's easy for me to um to to let other people use my notes -but since I have to refuse um - I just have to say that my notes are not good [*Researcher:Hmm*] yeah - or uh because in as long as uh - notes go um I - have a hard time no uh writing down what my professor says and stuff so I may need some help from someone so - as long as I can help I'd like to um - let the people use my no see my notes so that I can expect someone else to help me some other time.

(Robinson, 1992, p. 53)

As Robinson's study shows, the combined use of concurrent and retrospective verbal reports enables identification of the strategies that learners use in performing communicative acts—that is, the various options that learners consider in formulating a response—as well as the sociopragmatic information that they draw on in determining which response is most appropriate.

   In another study using think-aloud protocols, Cohen and Olshtain (1993) had advanced EFL learners interact in role plays with a native speaker of English. Each of the role plays was designed to elicit an apology, a complaint, or a request. After two role plays involving the same speech act, a retrospective interview was conducted, based on playback of the video-taped role plays. The retrospective interview was based on a schedule, including questions about the sources of the chosen linguistic material, utterance planning, and language of thinking. Coding categories reflected these questions. Widjaja (1997) examined how American and Taiwanese women refused American men's invitations to dates in three different contexts. Her study shared the main methodological features with Cohen and Olshtain (1993): a combination of video-taped open role play with a retrospective interview based on stimulated recall. Both the American and Taiwanese participants' retrospective comments demonstrated that the degree of social distance between the participant and her interlocutor was the decisive variable in choosing refusal strategies. The appropriacy of particular refusal strategies, on the other hand, was assessed very differently by the Taiwanese and American participants. A strong point in Widjaja's study is the inclusion of native speaker respondents. While presence or absence of native speakers is obviously mandated by the research questions addressed in a study, including native speakers is highly recommendable for verbal protocol research. As long as this line of investigation is as much in its infancy as it is in pragmatics, it is vital for researchers to understand what kinds of information native and nonnative participants attend to, what and how they report, and to what extent they experience concurrent verbalization as intrusive and retrospective reporting as overtaxing their memories. In the nonnative speaker group, close attention needs to be paid to respondents' L2 proficiency.

In verbal report studies involving nonnative speakers, the question arises in what language the verbal protocol should be delivered—the learners' L1, or the target language. Robinson's retrospective reports were elicited in participants' L2. Even though Robinson's respondents were explicitly instructed to use either Japanese or English during the concurrent think-aloud, they reported only in English, presumably out of courtesy to the researcher, who spoke no Japanese. Future studies must ensure that participants actually use whatever language comes to their minds during concurrent verbalization, to minimize the additional processing involved in recoding. For the same reason, immediate retrospection should be initiated in the language used during the think-aloud. Unless participants are advanced enough to think and speak effortlessly in the target language, it would seem advisable that the experimenter be bilingual in the L2 and participants' primary language of communication. A schematic decision to ask for reports in participants' native language would be psycholinguistically unsound because the native language may not be the language with the lowest activation threshold and thus may not be the language of thought.

A combination of authentic or simulated interaction with retrospective interviews is a common procedure in interactional sociolinguistics. For studies of miscommunication in interethnic encounters, Gumperz and Cook-Gumperz (1982) recommended commentary elicited through playback of a preceding recorded conversation as a technique for evaluating "how participants reflexively address the social activity that is being constituted by their ongoing talk" (p. 19). In the European Science Foundation project on second language acquisition by adult immigrants (Bremer et al., 1996), different types of authentic and simulated spoken discourse were supplemented by feedback sessions, which provided information about participants' understanding of the recorded interaction, their attitudes, intentions, and experience. In her study of cross-cultural gate-keeping interviews, Fiksdal (1990) examined the temporal organization and uncomfortable moments through microanalysis and focused playback. Participants first watched the video-taped interaction they participated in and provided any commentary they wished to make. In a second viewing, the researcher then stopped the tape and asked the participants for comments "at all moments that seemed uncomfortable because of the topic or because of specific comments of the subjects while viewing it; and . . . at all moments of postural change" (p. 66f.). The comments during the playback session provided a crucial source of information about participants' understanding and intent at those particular points in the discourse. In several respects, the use of retrospective interviews in interactional sociolinguistics and ethnographic microanalysis is more akin to analytic induction than to protocol analysis in the information-processing approach. (See Ericsson & Simon, 1998, and Smagorinsky, 1998, 2001, for a recent discussion, and Gass & Mackey, 2000, particularly for stimulated recall.)

Diaries

The least prestructured of all types of self-report is the diary. Diaries share with interviews their focus on past experiences and subjective theories while also permitting retrospective reports on specific attended information in the input or in the diarist's mind during an activity. They distinguish themselves from any other form of self-report in that they are—in the self-study variety at least—entirely participant-directed, since the diarist decides on

the substance, form, and timing of entries without being constrained by a particular task, response format, or social interaction. In second language research, diary studies date back to the
second half of the 1970s. The first review of the early studies from
a methodological perspective was offered by Bailey and Ochsner
(1983), and more recent updates include Bailey (1990), Peirce
(1994), and Schumann (1998). Diary studies are investigations
whose primary data are one or several persons' journal entries
about their experiences relating to the topic of the study. Because
diaries tell about the diarists' experiences and her interpretation
of them from an emic perspective in a holistic, open-ended fashion
and are kept during extended and often intensive engagement "in
the field," diary studies potentially meet some of the standard
criteria for qualitative interpretive research (Davis, 1995; Lazaraton, 1995). Because of the in-built emic perspective of personal
journals, diary studies in second language research have primarily
investigated individual differences, learner strategies, teachers'
and students' experiences of second language classroom learning
and teaching, and sojourners' and immigrants' perceptions of
second language learning and communication in particular social
and institutional contexts. Two types of diary study can be distinguished: the self-study, in which the diarist and the researcher are
the same person; and the commissioned diary study, in which the
researcher requests participants (often language learners or
teachers) to keep a journal that is then submitted to and analyzed
by the researcher (with or without participant collaboration).

Studies from the L2 developmental pragmatics literature
that rely on learner diaries as a main data source include one
published study (Cohen, 1997), one unpublished conference paper
(LoCastro, 1998), and one unpublished dissertation (DuFon, 1999).
One remarkable feature on which the three studies converge is
their focus on target languages other than English, two examining
pragmatic development in L2 Japanese and one in L2 Indonesian.
Cohen and LoCastro report on self-studies, whereas DuFon's investigation is based on commissioned diaries. Cohen (1997) reports his experience as a student in an accelerated course for

beginners in Japanese as a foreign language, providing information about a wide variety of aspects associated with the learning of L2 pragmatics, such as sociopragmatic and pragmalinguistic transfer from other languages, transfer avoidance, the difficulty of achieving control over routine formulae and selecting expressions with the appropriate formality level, and interactions of cultural and learning style factors. The outcomes of Cohen's learning experience dramatically highlight the discrepancy between successful classroom performance according to the syllabus and low ability to use the target language effectively in communication. LoCastro's (1998) main research question was how her social and cultural identity (as senior American faculty at a prestigious university in Tokyo) related to her development of Japanese pragmatics. Her social position within the sociocultural context of Japan proved to be the single most powerful constraint on her opportunities to acquire pragmatic ability in Japanese, both inside and outside her work context and even including the instruction in Japanese that she took on a regular basis. LoCastro's study provides further evidence for the need to incorporate a sociocultural perspective in theories of the development of L2 communicative competence. DuFon's (1999) study also commissioned diaries as one of its components. Participants were required to keep dialog journals (Peirce, 1994) according to specified guidelines. Once a week, group meetings were held to discuss issues brought up in the diaries. Results suggest that participants varied individually in the amount of their writing and the themes that preoccupied them, and that different pragmatic objects were differentially apt to appear in diary entries. In Chapter 2, we noted that L2 learners' social position in the target community and their participation in different societal domains and activities is increasingly recognized as a significant force in L2 learning. As a prime data source for learners' own perspective on their language learning experience, diary studies have a particularly rich potential for translating this theoretical orientation into research methodology.

For ease of exposition, this chapter has discussed each research method separately. But various combinations are possible and have been used in developmental interlanguage pragmatics research to good effect. For the most part, multi-method approaches are an important means to improve a study's validity (trustworthiness) and reliablity (dependability). As Denzin and Lincoln (2000) recommend, "the combination of multiple methodological practices, empirical methods, perspectives, and observers in a single study is best understood, then, as a strategy that adds rigor, breadth, complexity, richness, and depth to any inquiry" (p. 5), and add that Fielding and Fielding (1986) are particularly interesting for research on second language acquisition because they consider not only the theory and methodology of connecting different qualitative data sources but also of linking qualitative and quantitative data. Studies from the L2 developmental pragmatics literature that have relied on multiple methods range from the ethnographic work represented in Siegal (1994, 1995, 1996) and DuFon (1999, 2000) on one end of the spectrum to the classroom experimental research of Tateyama (2001) and Tateyama et. al. (1997) on the other. Siegal's study on the acquisition of Japanese by a group of "white women" was based on a range of data types including language learning journals, learner interviews, field observations, audio-taped learner-native speaker interactions, and relevant newspapers and magazine articles. DuFon's work on the acquisition of politeness in Indonesian in a study-abroad context collected data through use of participant observation, field notes, dialog journals, audio-and videorecordings of native speaker-learner interactions, interviews, questionnaires, and site documents. In Tateyama (2001) and Tateyama et al. (1997), multiple methods were put to use in measuring the effects of instruction, including written production, DCT, role plays, multiple choice, and interviews. As we note in Chapter 7, the bulk of studies on the effects of instruction in pragmatics relied on only one or two outcome measures, so Tateyama (2001) is exemplary in this regard.

Chapter Summary

This chapter has examined the main methodological approaches deployed in the L2 developmental pragmatics literature to date, starting with a condensed account of the wide range of methodological sources for research on developmental pragmatics (i.e., descriptive linguistics, conversation analysis, interactional sociolinguistics, ethnographic microanalysis, language socialization, developmental pragmatics, cognitive and social psychology, discourse comprehension, cross-cultural and intercultural communication, cross-cultural pragmatics, and interlanguage pragmatics). Following this, we addressed the issue of design requirements in developmental research, considering the relative strengths and weaknesses of longitudinal or cross-sectional designs. The remainder of the chapter divided the methods of data collection used in developmental interlanguage pragmatics into three parts. The first part concerned itself with spoken discourse as a source for pragmatics research and discussed three types of spoken discourse data: authentic discourse, sociolinguistic interviews and conversation tasks, and role play. The second part covered different types of questionnaire—DCTs, multiple-choice, and scaled-response questionnaires—and the final section focused on different types of oral and written self-report: interviews, verbal protocols, and diaries. Throughout our discussion, we noted the importance of appropriately matching research method to the task at hand, having a thorough understanding of what sort of information a particular approach can and cannot reasonably be expected to provide, and taking measures to critically explore the optimal implementation of whatever methods are chosen.

CHAPTER FOUR

Developmental Patterns in Second Language Pragmatics

Nearly two decades ago, Schmidt (1983) observed, "What is new, in fact just beginning, is systematic study of the actual acquisition of communicative abilities by nonnative speakers" (p. 138). While some progress has been made in the intervening years, it is also true that the body of research on the development of second language pragmatics is rather heavily outweighed by the proliferation of studies on pragmatic production in a second language. In fact, this imbalance has been acknowledged with such frequency in recent years that it is fast achieving cliché status. Given this state of affairs—and the developmental focus of this book—we will not discuss the production research here (for review, see Bardovi-Harlig, 2001; Rose, 2000), focusing instead on substantive findings from developmental research. This chapter, then, serves as a companion to Chapter 2, which addressed the various theoretical orientations that could be engaged to account for pragmatic development in authentic learning environments. We begin by discussing the development of pragmatic comprehension, an area that has thus far received little attention. Following this, we turn our attention to the development of pragmatic production, divided into two main categories of learning objects: various aspects of pragmatic and discourse ability, and speech acts. We conclude the chapter with some discussion of the relationship between pragmatic transfer and development.

Pragmatic Comprehension

Within the L2 developmental pragmatics literature, studies focusing on pragmatic comprehension are the least well represented, with only a handful of studies done to date. The research discussed here includes Carrell's (1981) early work attempting to identify a hierarchy of difficulty in comprehension of English requests, Bouton's (1988, 1992, 1994b) studies on the understanding of implicatures in English, Kerekes's (1992) study on perceptions of assertiveness in English, and Koike's (1996) research on the comprehension of suggestions in Spanish. Because each study focuses on very different aspects of pragmatic comprehension, we consider what each has to say about development separately.

Carrell (1981) conducted a cross-sectional study to determine whether certain English indirect requests were more difficult than others for learners of English, that is, whether there exists a hierarchy of difficulty in indirect requests. Learners at four proficiency levels were represented: low-intermediate, intermediate, high-intermediate, and advanced, all of whom were university students. Carrell chose a single request—to paint a circle blue—and drafted 10 different ways of realizing this request, each appearing in positive and negative forms (e.g., "Please color the circle blue" vs. "Please don't color the circle blue"). A number of requests were interpreted correctly regardless of proficiency (e.g., "Please color the circle blue," "I would love to see the circle colored blue," "The circle really needs to be painted blue," and "I'll be very happy if you make the circle blue"). A second set of requests revealed differences across proficiency, which often formed a rather clear cline, suggesting a possible hierarchy of difficulty. Requests in this second group were syntactically more complex, often incorporating interrogatives and negatives (e.g., "Must you make the circle blue?" "Why color the circle blue?" "Should you color the circle blue?" "Does the circle really need to be painted blue?" "You shouldn't color the circle blue," and "I'll be very happy unless you make the circle blue"). The fact that lower-proficiency learners had more difficulty interpreting requests stated as questions or involving some form of negation suggests that Carrell's study directly taps the interaction between grammar and pragmatics, which we treat at length in Chapter 5.

Bouton (1988, 1992, 1994b) has conducted a series of studies on the ability of university-level learners of ESL to interpret implicatures in American English. The participants in these studies were all rather advanced learners when the studies began, so this line of research covers only the latest stages of development in this area, not the entire developmental process. In fact, although by definition longitudinal, each of the studies Bouton has carried out involved data collection that more closely resembles a pretest-posttest design, that is, observations of learners' abilities to interpret implicature were made at two points in time only—a beginning and an end point—rather than at multiple points over the entire observation period, as is normally the case with longitudinal research. Thus his findings cannot illuminate the developmental *process* by identifying stages of development in the understanding of implicature. Nevertheless, because Bouton's two participant groups were observed for different lengths of time (four-and-a-half years, and 17 months), it is possible to speculate on possible stages of development (assuming that learners in both groups were at roughly the same levels of proficiency at the time of the first observation) by comparing the abilities of the two learner groups as measured at 17-month and four-and-a-half-year intervals.

In the first of his implicature studies, Bouton (1988) found that the participants' ability to interpret implicature initially fell well short of NS levels, particularly for relevance-based implicatures. These included implicature types such as general relevance-based implicatures (extract (4.1)) and a relevance-based implicature type Bouton refers to as "understated criticism" (extract (4.2)).

(4.1) Relevance implicature

When Abe got home, he found that his wife had to use a cane in order to walk.

Abe: What happened to your leg?
Wife: I went jogging today.

Another way the wife could have said the same thing is . . .

a. Today I finally got some exercise jogging.
b. I hurt it jogging.
c. It's nothing serious. Don't worry about it.
d. I hurt it doing something silly.

(4.2) Indirect criticism

Two teachers are talking about a student's term paper.

Mr. Ranger: Have you read Mark's term paper on modern pi-
       rates yet?
Mr. Ryan: Yes, I read it last night.
Mr. Ranger: What did you think of it?
Mr. Ryan: I thought it was well typed.

How did Mr. Ryan like Mark's paper?

a. He liked the paper; he thought it was good.
b. He thought it was certainly well typed.
c. He thought it was a good paper; he did like the form though not the content.
d. He didn't like it.

(Bouton, 1988, p. 59f.)

When first tested, only about half of NNSs selected correct interpretations for this sort of relevance-based implicature, but when tested again four-and-a-half years later, their scores for these implicature types were almost the same as those of NSs. There were, however, a number of additional items that continued to prove problematic for learners, even after a four-and-a-half-year stay in the United States. Concerning these items, Bouton (1988) notes that "no one type of implicature occurs in that set of items more often than any other. . . . Each of these items requires a certain knowledge of American culture and language that is independent of what is required by the others" (1988, p. 62). It appears, then, that items that caused learners difficulty did not reflect their lack of ability in interpreting implicature, but rather indicate areas of culture-specific (and perhaps rather arcane) knowledge they had yet to acquire. In a slightly different account of this study, Bouton (1994b) points out that when first tested, learners had difficulty with three implicature types (i.e., understated criticism, implicatures involving a sequence of events, and the infamous Pope Q implicature), but by the time of the second test (1992), these were no longer problematic. However, Bouton (1994b) reiterates that "the only items that were still causing trouble were related to *specific points of American culture* in the *substance* of the test item and not to the *type* of implicature involved, and in that sense, the problems caused by these items were arbitrary and idiosyncratic" (p. 163, italics in original).

Bouton's second set of participants completed the same implicature test, this time at a 17-month interval, and with rather different results. Although there was significant improvement in identifying the correct interpretation of various implicatures, unlike learners in the first study, learners in the second study had not achieved native-like comprehension of implicatures after 17 months. For these learners, four implicature types remained difficult: indirect criticism, sequence implicatures, the Pope Q, and irony. These findings are suggestive of a possible developmental sequence in the understanding of implicature, at least where the later stages of development are concerned. It is unfortunate that Bouton was unable to make interim observations in his two studies because such data would directly inform the developmental process. We can, however, say at this time that when provided with an acquisition-rich context and sufficient time, learners' ability to interpret implicatures in English rivals that of NSs, except in cases where learners lack culture-specific information, but this is not an implicature-related problem.

Bouton's research also speaks to the issue of the relationship between general language proficiency and pragmatic comprehension. In addition to his implicature comprehension test, Bouton administered a range of proficiency measures to his participants in both studies and found no significant correlation between proficiency and the ability to interpret implicature correctly. These findings support the claim that proficiency in L2 morphosyntax does not automatically bring with it proficiency in L2 pragmatics—that is, knowledge of morphosyntax may be necessary for pragmatics (and that is debatable), but it is certainly not sufficient (see Bardovi-Harlig, 2001; Chapter 5, for discussion). Another issue raised by Bouton's work is whether the rather long four-and-a-half-year interval learners in the first group seemed to require to reach native-like abilities to interpret implicature could be shortened by pedagogical intervention, a question Bouton (1994a) addresses directly, and one we cover in Chapter 7.

Rather than focus on the effective understanding of indirect responses, Kerekes (1992) examined differences in the way learners of ESL in the United States assessed the assertiveness of individuals whose speech contained a range of linguistic devices, with the aim of determining how learner ratings differed across three proficiency levels, and how learners factored gender into their assessments. Here are the features she was interested in (Kerekes, 1992, p. 19f.):

- Qualifiers (e.g., "It's *kind of* frustrating. I can't seem to, *y'know*, *kind of* organize my thoughts.")
- Tag questions using *isn't it* (e.g., "Yeah, it's on reserve in the library, *isn't it?*")
- Neutral statements (e.g., "On Thursday at 4 o'clock.")
- Strong assertions with *definitely* or *I'm sure* (e.g., "It was excellent. *I'm sure* you'd like it.")

Participants listened to short dialogues read by native speakers containing the target items, with speakers' gender varied so that both females and males used the forms in question. They were then asked to rate each of the speakers on an assertiveness scale. As expected, speech segments containing strong assertions received the highest ratings (followed by neutral statements, tag questions, and qualifiers), and women were rated as less assertive than men. An interesting pattern emerged for learner ratings of speech segments containing qualifiers and tag questions, that is, while there were no differences across levels in ratings of tag questions (in fact, all three levels produced ratings similar to those of NSs), ratings for qualifiers did differ significantly across levels, with those of the higher-proficiency group approximating NS ratings. Kerekes noted that the differences in perception of assertiveness across proficiency levels may have been due to "the salient position of tag questions, at the end of a sentence, as opposed to quantifiers, which, in the middle of sentences, are much less easily recalled. In this less salient position, qualifiers are therefore more difficult to discern than tag questions" (p. 28). It appears, then, that with increased proficiency, learners were more able to notice the effects of qualifiers, resulting in a more native-like perception of their level of assertiveness. As with Bouton's research discussed above, Kerekes's findings do not actually document development in pragmatic comprehension, but they do hint at a possible developmental sequence in comprehension in line with one of Slobin's (1973) operating principles for language acquisition, according to which learners attend first to the ends of utterances.

Changing target languages from ESL to Spanish as a foreign language, Koike (1996) examined how university students in their first, second, and third year of Spanish understood Spanish suggestions. After watching video-taped monologues produced by Spanish NSs, students had to identify the illocutionary act represented, and actually transcribe the speaker's last utterance (the speech act under study). Third-year students performed significantly better than those in the first two years in correctly identifying the speech act in question. One of the successful comprehension strategies employed by third-year students seemed to be their attention to certain words associated with various speech acts types, such as *por favor* (please) and *no tengo dinero* (I don't have any money) for requests, and *lo siento* (I'm sorry) and *accidente* (accident) for apologies. It would appear, then, that learners in their third year of Spanish had begun to develop the ability to identify the pragmalinguistic function of a range of basic vocabulary items—that is, they had begun to make the necessary form-function mappings—to enable them to correctly identify the illocutionary force of utterances incorporating those items. Note that this was true even for use of supportive moves (e.g., "I don't have any money"). The two lower groups were not able to discern the illocutionary force indicators. Unfortunately, there are methodological problems with Koike's study. She notes that although first- and second-year learners were monolingual NSs of American English, the third-year group included 32% Spanish-English bilinguals. Furthermore, Koike notes that many of the correct responses supplied by third-year learners were those of the bilingual members of the group. It would have been useful, then, to see whether between-group differences remained with the bilingual learners removed from the analysis, which Koike did not do.

The handful of studies on the development of L2 pragmatic comprehension does not describe, let alone explain, the process with any real specificity. Although each of the studies discussed hints at possible developmental stages or sequences, for example, difficulties in interpreting certain requests without the necessary grammatical competence, late-acquired implicature types, sentence-final assertiveness markers before those placed utterance internally, and the beginnings of form-function mapping necessary for the correct identification of speech act types, we await future research in this area to provide more substantial accounts of the development of pragmatic comprehension. Given that all of the studies we have cited in this section were cross-sectional, it is high time for some longitudinal research in this area, which would enable us to do more than, say, appeal to a hierarchy of difficulty to account for pragmatic development. We now turn to research on pragmatic and discourse ability, which provides a good deal more in the way of developmental insights.

Pragmatic and Discourse Ability

The development of pragmatic and discourse ability in a second language has fared better as a research topic than pragmatic comprehension. In this category we once again encounter Schmidt's (1983) well-known study of Wes's adventures in English, as well as Schmidt and Frota's (1986) account of Schmidt's acquisition of Brazilian Portuguese. Asian languages feature prominently in the rest of the group, for example, Sawyer's (1992) study on the acquisition of the Japanese discourse particle *ne*, Ohta's (2001a) report of the acquisition of alignment expressions in Japanese, work reported in Kanagy and Igarashi (1997) and Kanagy (1999a) on how English-speaking kindergartners acquire Japanese classroom interactional routines in an immersion environment, and DuFon's (1999, 2000) research on the acquisition of politeness in Indonesian. Without exception, the studies in this group are longitudinal, with observational periods ranging from four months to three years, and all involve beginning learners, thus making them ideal for the observation of development over time. In discussing the findings from this body of research, we will consider first general developmental trends observed across studies, followed by a more detailed accounting of research findings, and finally note some of the unresolved issues.

Most of the studies in this category reveal a marked tendency for learners to rely on unanalyzed formulae and repetition in the earliest stages of development, which gradually gives way to an expansion of the pragmatic repertoire characterized by analyzed, productive language use. Sawyer's (1992) study of the acquisition of *ne* provides one illustration of this developmental trend. While as a marker of epistemic and affective stance, *ne* is pervasive in Japanese discourse and therefore massively available in input outside of classrooms (cf. Ohta, 1994, for *ne* in teacher input, discussed in Chapter 6), the Japanese as a second language learners in Sawyer's study incorporated the particle only slowly into their interlanguage discourse. Compared to the interviewers' particle use, the learners used grammatical particles more frequently, whereas the interviewers' frequency of *ne*-marked utterances was four times that of the learners. Very likely, these differences were teaching-induced, since grammatical particles are traditionally taught as obligatory grammatical markers, whereas it is doubtful whether the grammatically inconsequential but interactionally necessary sentence-final *ne* was taught at all. Although Sawyer notes that the learners' progress in the use of the marker varied individually, a common sequence observed from the first to the fourth and last interview session was for learners to start with zero-marking, followed by the formulaic expression *soo desu ne* 'that's right' as a listener response, and gradually extending *ne*-marking to limited productive (non-formulaic) use. A related phenomenon that can accompany early reliance on unanalyzed formulas is the overgeneralization of one form to many functions, not all of which are appropriate. DuFon (1990, 2000) provides a good example of this. One area that DuFon examined was the acquisition of Indonesian address terms by her study-abroad participants. Indonesian has a wide range of address terms, each of which carries with it distinct politeness implications. Appropriate pronoun use, then, is a key part of Indonesian pragmatics, as indicated by a certain teacher of Indonesian DuFon mentions who actually refused to interact with foreigners who use *kamu* (the familiar "you"), rather than the more formal *anda*. DuFon notes that some beginning learners initially overgeneralized use of the more formal *anda*—including its use with the informal genitive suffix (*-mu*)—to contexts that called for the use of the informal pronoun *kamu*, thus sending a mixed social message.

Another way that the gradual move to productive use of analyzed form-function mappings shows itself is in a shift in the type of conversational contributions made by learners over time. This can be characterized as a move to higher level of involvement facilitated by grammatical as well as pragmatic development. One such case is the change in Schmidt's (Schmidt & Frota, 1986) conversational prowess in Brazilian Portuguese after just a five-month stay in Brazil. Analysis of recorded conversations between

Schmidt and his co-author (a NS of Brazilian Portuguese) revealed a decrease in use of repetition (self and other), confirmation and comprehension checks, clarification requests, requests for help, and minimal responses, with an attendant increase in the use of tag questions, statements, and back-channel responses. Excerpt (4.3) illustrates Schmidt's early conversational abilities:

(4.3) Schmidt's early conversational abilities

S: Como é que você se sentiu quando você sabia, soube, que vinha pro Brasil? Qual era sua idéia do Brasil?

How did you feel when you knew, knew that you were coming to Brazil? What was your idea of Brazil?

R: Um . . . no pensia, no pensia nada, no pensia que via a América Latina mas uh . . . porque eu sei e conheço Média Este e conheço também Asia . . . uh, Japon.

Um . . . I didn't think, I didn't think anything, didn't think I would go to Latin America but uh . . . because I know the Middle East and I know also Asia . . . uh Japan.

(S = Silvia Frota, R = Richard Schmidt. Schmidt & Frota, 1986, p. 262)

The exchange in (4.3) displays the question-answer structure commonly observed in native speaker–nonnative speaker discourse with learners of lower L2 ability. S self-repairs her original question by "pushing it down" to a syntactically less complex utterance. R constructs his answer turn incrementally through successively more complex self-repairs that recycle the previously produced turn-constructional units. His answer is limited to the telling of a past (cognitive) event and an account for that event, produced as two sets of parallel constructions. Both the telling and the account center on the repeated use of the (high-frequency) cognitive verbs *pensar* 'think' and *conhecer* 'know.' The answer turn includes no assessment of any kind. In comparison, in a later conversation, the participation structure had changed, and R's contributions became far more sophisticated (4.4):

(4.4) Schmidt's later conversational ability

S: É muito comum você ver um rapaz de 30 anos morando com
     pai e mãe.

     *It's very common for you to see a 30 year old guy living with
     father and mother.*

R: Ah, eu sei. Aos Estados Unidos se tem um rapaz de 25 anos
     ainda mora com os pais, ah . . . toda gente pensam que coisa
     estranha mas aqui, não, aqui talvez um cara de 25 anos mora
     sozinho a gente falam: uma coisa estranha.

     *Ah, I know. In the U.S. if there's a 25 year old guy [who] still
     lives with his parents, ah . . . everybody thinks that's a strange
     thing, but here no, here maybe a 25 year old guy lives alone
     and people say: a strange thing.*

S: É o opos . . .

     It's the oppo-

R: O oposto!

     The opposite!

(S = Silvia Frota, R = Richard Schmidt. Schmidt & Frota,
1986, p. 263)

The exchange in (4.4) is structured more like a casual conversation
than an interview. After a comment (rather than question) by S, R
takes a fairly long response turn, starting with an acknowledgement of S's comment ("Ah, eu sei") and proceeding not only to
compare common living arrangements for single men in the
United States and Brazil but also to comment on the contrasting
societal evaluations of such arrangements with great rhetorical
effectiveness. The sequence closes with an overlapping assessment, another common feature of ordinary interaction.

Similarly, although he was not able to comment on the
process of Wes's conversational development due to a lack of early
data, Schmidt (1983) notes that by the end of a three-year observational period, Wes was quite capable of engaging appropriately
in small talk, and also making use of back-channel cues differentially in Japanese and English, that is, he did not transfer to
English the generally more frequent and animated listener behav-

ior characteristic of Japanese conversation. Kanagy and Igarashi (1997) and Kanagy (1999a) report a similar developmental trend in their Japanese immersion kindergartners—over time, the use of formulaic speech decreased, use of voluntary expressions increased, and use of repetition decreased. Interestingly, they noted that the children were selective in what they chose to repeat, hypothesizing that input was more likely to be repeated when it was consistent with the children's pragmatic needs (e.g., use of attention getters, or asking for permission), and when it satisfied their desires for social interaction (e.g., short commands to stand or sit). A key finding was that "output gradually developed from the use of unanalyzed chunks which rely on cues with fixed verbal routines, to partially analyzed expressions used in an innovative way in new contexts" (Kanagy & Igarashi, 1997, p. 259), which sums up well what many studies have found.

Staying with learners of JFL, Ohta (2001a) is one of few researchers who have posited a developmental sequence for a pragmatic feature. Her one year longitudinal study looked at the development of Japanese expressions of acknowledgment, which indicate attentiveness, and alignment, which serve as markers of affective common ground. Given their importance in Japanese, they were well attested in the input Ohta's learners received from their teacher. Acknowledgment expressions observed included *un, mm* (uh huh), *hai, ee* (yes), *aa soo desu ka* (I see), and *soo desu ka* (oh really), while frequently used expressions of alignment included *soo desu ne* (it is, isn't it), *ii desu ne* (nice, great, good), and __ *desu ne* (that's __ isn't it). Ohta's participants were two American undergraduates—Candace and Rob—enrolled in a first-year JFL course. Ohta summarizes their progress at the end of the year in a chart listing the range of listener responses and frequency of use for the two participants (Table 4.1).

As the table indicates, both learners made progress over time, but Candace progressed further than Rob in her use of expressions of alignment. It is noteworthy, however, that Candace and Rob—despite differences in their use of acknowledgment and alignment expressions at the end of the six-month observational

Table 4.1

Progress by the End of the Academic Year in the Use of a Range of Listener Responses

	Un / Mm / hai	Ao soo desu ka	Soo desu ne	~desu ne
Rob	Uses *hai* occasionally	Uses spontaneously	Misuses for *Aa soo desu ka*	Uses only when scripted
Candace	Uses all three	Uses spontaneously	Uses as a hedge, not as a listener response	Uses spontaneously

Note. From "A Longitudinal Study of the Development of Expression of Alignment in Japanese as a Foreign Language," by A. S. Ohta, 2001, in K. R. Rose and G. Kasper (Eds.), *Pragmatics in Language Teaching*, p. 116. New York: Cambridge Iniversity Press.

period—appear to have followed a similar pattern of development, which led Ohta to posit a six-stage developmental sequence in the acquisition of alignment expressions by learners of Japanese.

Stage 1: Students ask and answer preformulated questions. There is no use of expressions of acknowledgement or alignment, in English or in Japanese, unless scripted. The follow-up turn of the IRF sequence is left unused, with speakers moving immediately, or after a pause, to a new initiation.

Stage 2: Students begin to use the follow-up turn for expression of acknowledgment, such as repetition of Japanese words and laughter. Use of Japanese minimal expressions of acknowledgment such as *hai* ['yes'] is rare. Alignment expressions are used only when scripted.

Stage 3: Students begin to use *Aa soo desu ka* ['Oh really?'] to show acknowledgment, particularly when prompted by the teacher, but occasional spontaneous use also emerges. Occasional use of the Japanese minimal response *hai* continues. Alignment expressions are used where scripted, and on a limited basis when prompted by the teacher.

Stage 4: Students use *Aa soo desu ka* with facility, beginning to use minimal expressions of acknowledgement beyond *hai*, such as *mm* and *un*, on occasion. Alignment expressions appear when prompted by the teacher.

Stage 5: Spontaneous use of a limited range of Japanese expressions of alignment emerges. Minimal response expressions occur more frequently. Expressions of alignment are limited to those commonly used by the teacher, with little or no creative expansion.

Stage 6: Students use a range of expressions of acknowledgment appropriately. Alignment expressions are used spontaneously, with greater lexical variety tailored to conversational content.

(Ohta, 2001a, p. 117)

The use of acknowledgment and alignment expressions observed by Ohta is reminiscent of findings from other studies discussed above—from early reliance on repetition and formula (in this case scripted for classroom use) to more productive use of these expressions that serve to mark a higher level of learner involvement in the interaction, as represented in Ohta's proposed developmental sequence.

Turning from Japanese to Indonesian as the target language, DuFon (1999, 2000) reported on the acquisition of the forms *belum* and *tidak*, two ways of responding negatively to experience questions in Indonesian that pose particular problems for learners because, as DuFon explains,

The two forms are similar in scope in that they both negate non-nominal predicates, but *tidak*, which means *no* or *not*, is stronger than *belum*, which means *not yet*. The contexts of use for which *belum* is preferred over *tidak* in Indonesian, however, are broader than those for which *not yet* is preferred over *no* in English, and *tidak* is considered pragmatically inappropriate in Indonesian in many contexts where *no* or *not* would be considered appropriate in English. Consequently, second language learners of Indonesian tend to overgeneralize the *tidak* form, using it in contexts where *belum* is more appropriate. (DuFon, 2000, p. 77)

In addition to similarity in the semantic and pragmatic scope of *belum* and *tidak*, the choice of either element is constrained by syntactic harmony, according to which the use of a particular form in the question projects either *belum* or *tidak* in the response turn. Native speakers at times produce syntactically unharmonious responses as a means of generating the implicature that the question has "implied an incorrect assumption about the possibility of a particular experience occurring" (DuFon, 2000, p. 86). While intermediate learners' negative responses to experience questions were for the most part as clear and syntactically harmonious as native speakers' responses, beginners' responses were usually unclear and unharmonious, thus generating unintended implicatures. She posits a developmental sequence for beginners that starts with use of English *no*, followed by use of *tidak* (marked with shaking of the head and, e.g., *huhuh*), and finally the irregular introduction of *belum*, but only after additional input in the form of clarification questions, correction, and confirmation requests. Use of *belum* by intermediate-level learners was almost native-like by the end of the program. The beginner's early reliance on *tidak* across a range of contexts also illustrates the issue of overgeneralization noted above, another prominent feature of early pragmatic development.

In addition to learners' tendency to rely at first on unanalyzed formulae and later generate more analyzed, productive speech, the studies discussed here also reveal some of the problems learners encounter as their pragmatic competence develops. Returning to Schmidt and Frota's (1986) account of Schmidt's acquisition of Brazilian Portuguese, we see how grammatical competence can interact with pragmatic development, sometimes limiting what learners are able to accomplish pragmatically (see Chapter 5). In Schmidt's case, one area of difficulty was responding to Brazilian Portuguese questions in the affirmative. It appears that a simple *yes* (i.e., *sim*) is not always an appropriate response because affirmative responses often require correct marking of verbs for person and number. Thus Schmidt's inability to supply the correct verb morphology also led to the production of pragmatically inappropriate responses to questions, a problem that cannot be remedied without the requisite grammatical competence.

Another problem DuFon encountered also has to do with barriers to pragmatic development, but these appear to stem more from individual learner characteristics than was the case for Schmidt's inappropriate responses to questions. DuFon (1999) found that the six learners of Indonesian changed their use of address terms over time, but they did not all follow the same development path. Two of the beginning learners initially overgeneralized use of the more formal *anda*, but only one eventually corrected this. Two other learners did not evidence any change in use of pronouns throughout the observation period, but while one relied on *anda*, the other relied almost exclusively on zero forms. Only two learners expanded their repertoire to include the familiar *kamu*. DuFon also noted that learners' journal entries showed more knowledge about address terms than was apparent from their production. Perhaps most revealing are the choices made by the two beginning learners—both expressed an awareness of their inappropriate use of address terms, but only one made the effort to remedy this. The other simply chose not to do so. This sort of interaction between pragmatic development and individual learner differences has to date received little attention in the literature (see Chapter 8).

The studies on the development of pragmatic and discourse ability that we have reviewed in this section are of particular interest because they are all longitudinal, and all involve beginning learners. This allows for development to be charted from its earliest stages. What we see across the studies is a tendency for learners to rely on routine formulas and repetition at first, which gradually gives way to an expansion of their pragmatic repertoire. We also see overgeneralization of one form for a range of functions, a potential source of pragmatic failure, as in the lack of syntactic harmony found in the use of negative markers by some beginning learners of Indonesian. As we will discuss in more detail in the following chapter, certain aspects of pragmatics that are closely related to proficiency in grammar are problematic for learners without the requisite knowledge of grammar, such as Schmidt's difficulty in acquiring the ability to respond in the affirmative to questions in Brazilian Portuguese. It is also clear, however, that even lower-proficiency learners are capable of controlling what might appear to be rather challenging aspects of target language pragmatics, such as Wes's ability to vary his back-channel behavior appropriately depending on whether he was speaking Japanese or English. An issue raised by DuFon's study—facilitated by her use of dialogue journals—is the possibility that learner's pragmatic knowledge may not be accurately represented in their production. DuFon's participants indicated more knowledge of Indonesian pronouns in their dialogue journals than was present in their production, but it is not clear how much of this gap was due to their conscious decision to avoid certain forms—as in the case of the less English-like greetings in the early stages—or whether other factors were involved. To answer such questions, in addition to collecting rich production data, we also need to probe learner knowledge.

Speech Acts

Studies of the development of speech acts in a second language are the best represented in the literature, with the bulk of work centering on English requests. Longitudinal request studies include Schmidt's (1983) work on Wes, Ellis's (1992) two-year study of the requests of two primary school children in the United Kingdom, and Achiba's (2002) account of her daughter's acquisition of English requests during their 17-month sojourn in Australia. Cross-sectional studies on English requests include Scarcella's (1979) work in an ESL context, as well as studies in a range of EFL contexts—Trosborg (1995) in Denmark, Hill (1997) in Japan, and Rose (2000) in Hong Kong. A number of studies have examined the development of other speech acts as well, including Bardovi-Harlig and Hartford's (1993a) longitudinal study of suggestions and refusals in an academic advising context, T. Takahashi and Beebe (1987) on the refusals of Japanese-speaking learners of English in Japan and the United States, and two studies of greetings—DuFon's longitudinal study of the development of Indonesian greetings and Omar's (1991) cross-sectional work on the acquisition of greetings of American learners of Kiswahili.

Requests

As was true for the development of pragmatic and discourse ability in a second language, the development of L2 requests can also be characterized generally as a move from reliance on routine formulas in the earliest stages of development to a gradual introduction of analyzed, productive language use. However, in the case of requests, a good deal more can be said about possible stages of development. Based on results from his longitudinal study of two beginning ESL learners' (whom Ellis refers to as J and R) request development in a classroom setting, Ellis (1992) proposes a three-stage developmental sequence for requests. In the first stage of request development, learners' utterances conveyed requestive intent through highly context-dependent, minimalist realizations, expressing the intended reference and illocution but no relational or social goals. In the second stage, requests were mainly performed by means of unanalyzed routines and imperatives. The third stage brought with it the unpacking of routine formulas that then become increasingly available for productive use, and more frequent use of conventional indirectness. A somewhat overlapping analysis is provided by Achiba (2002), the only other longitudinal study of which we are aware that involved a beginning learner, in this case Achiba's daughter, Yao. However, Yao seems to have been more than an absolute beginner when observation began, and she also appears to have developed her ability to request to a greater degree than J and R. Thus, Achiba's analysis actually posits four stages of development, with Yao's earliest requests (Achiba's first stage) more reminiscent of Ellis's second stage, and her second stage analogous to Ellis's third. Achiba's third and fourth stages—characterized by what Achiba calls pragmatic expansion and fine tuning—represent levels of development not observed in J and R. We discuss each of these proposed stages in turn.

As we will discuss in more detail in Chapter 5, Ellis's first stage of request development is well-documented in the literature and illustrates a pre-basic learner variety. In this stage, requestive intent is expressed through a "pragmatic mode," featuring highly context-dependent, minimalist realizations of illocutionary force, devoid of syntax. J and R's earliest requests were propositionally incomplete, including no more than *sir* as a request for the teacher to staple the student's card, or *big circle* as a request when the learner needed a cutout of a big circle, both of which illustrate well the entirely context-dependent nature of early requests. And once J and R began to produce propositionally complete requests, these were largely formulaic, making frequent use of imperatives, such as *leave it* and *give me*.

In Ellis's stage two (which is Achiba's stage one), requests are performed primarily through use of unanalyzed routines and continued reliance on imperatives, as the examples in (4.5) from Achiba's earliest observations of Yao's requests demonstrate:

(4.5) Yao's earliest requests

Look at the little baby. / Look at this picture.

Let's play the game. / Let's eat breakfast.

Do you want to play dolls? / Do you want to draw pictures?

Can I have this? / Can I have space?

Don't look. / Don't push it.

Clean up.

Keep going.

(Achiba, 2002)

Achiba points out that although unanalyzed formulas and imperatives were used most frequently at this stage, Yao also made use of the full range of strategies—direct, conventionally indirect, and even hints—displaying more variety than J and R. It would appear that Schmidt's (1983) observation of Wes also began at about Ellis's second stage of development because Wes's earliest recorded requests indicate a reliance on unanalyzed formulas and imperatives. However, like Yao, Wes's requests at this stage also included a wider range of strategies, including hints, in addition to the use of unanalyzed formulas and imperatives, as indicated in examples (4.6):

(4.6) Wes's early requests

Shall we go?

Can I have a banana spi . . . lit, please?

Please n you taking this suitcase.

This is all garbage ("Put it out").

Ah, I have two shirts upstairs ("Please get them while you're there").

(Schmidt, 1983, pp. 151–152)

It is interesting to consider why J's and R's requests at this stage were of a more restricted range than those of Wes or Yao. One possible explanation is that J and R, being absolute beginners, lacked the pragmalinguistic resources to produce more varied request forms. Another possible explanation is differences in learning context—while Wes and Yao had more varied opportunities for exposure to, and use of, the target language, and were also observed in a range of settings, it would appear that J's and R's exposure to and use of English might have been limited to the classroom, as was Ellis's observation of them. Yet another potential explanation is offered by Schmidt, who attributed Wes's early use of hints to the influence of Japanese, his—and Yao's—first language. Nevertheless, despite the more varied requests by Wes and Yao when compared to J and R, the second stage of development does appear to be dominated by formulaic requests and imperatives.

Ellis's third stage (which is Achiba's second stage) brings with it the unpacking of routine formulas that then become increasingly available for productive use, as well as more frequent use of conventional indirectness (with the concomitant decrease in directness), and the beginning of more frequent and varied mitigation of requests. For instance, Ellis notes that in this stage, J's and R's routinized conventionally-indirect ability questions were now used as flexible sentence frames, shifting in perspective between speaker (e.g., "Can *I* take book with me?") and hearer focus ("Can *you* pass me my pencil?"). J's and R's relational goals (i.e., politeness) were also beginning to be overtly marked in stage three, albeit with a restricted range of strategies. Achiba's stage two very closely matches Ellis's third stage, particularly with Yao's requests shifting from formulaic to productive (i.e., analyzed) request forms, as the following examples indicate:

(4.7) Yao's stage two requests

Can you pass the pencil please?

Can you do another one for me?

(Achiba, 2002)

Schmidt (1983) also notes that Wes's directives evidenced considerable development by the end of the three-year observation period. Among the changes he noted were the productive use of formulas, use of mitigated imperatives, and more elaboration, as the following examples illustrate:

(4.8) Wes's late requests

Shall we maybe go out for coffee now, or you want later?

OK, if you have time please send two handbag, but if you're too busy, forget it.

(Schmidt, 1983, p. 154)

These last examples from Wes strike us as a good deal more advanced than the achievements of J and R (at least at the time that Ellis stopped observing them), which indicates that Ellis's three stages do not extend to later development. Achiba's discussion of Yao's stage three and four requests provides more information on development.

The final two stages of Yao's request development were from about eight months to just under a year-and-a-half. Achiba characterizes stage three as one of pragmatic expansion, that is, the addition of many new forms to Yao's pragmalinguistic repertoire for requests. These included shifts in modality (e.g., from *can* to *could*), more frequent use of mitigation (especially supportive moves), and more complex syntax with (by then) fully-analyzed formulas, as seen in the following examples:

(4.9) Yao's stage three requests

Could I have another chocolate because my children - I have five children.

I don't know how to play this / can you - could you tell me how to play this?

Can I see it so I can copy it?

Can you help me to draw a donkey?

Can you put glue here and here?

(Achiba, 2002)

While noting that by this stage, Yao had already acquired most of the pragmalinguistic features of requesting observed in the final stage, Achiba argues that in stage four, Yao's requesting became considerably refined, particularly in her ability to fine-tune the force of her requests. Indicative of this refinement is Yao's expanded use of *could* as both an ability question and a (more subtle) suggestion.

(4.10) Yao's stage four requests

Could you please do that here and then I do the pants?

You could put some blu tack down there.

(Achiba, 2002)

Other noteworthy patterns observed are that Yao's use of conventionally indirect requests had more than doubled since the first stage, and by stage four had become the most frequent strategy used. And while hints were not used as frequently, after a slight drop in frequency from stage one to stage two, Yao's use of hints doubled with each stage. Two hinting strategies added in the final stage include "Is there any . . .?" and "Have you got . . .?", as shown below.

(4.11) Yao's use of hints

Is there any more white?

Mum have you got a lid?

(Achiba, 2002)

Taken together, then, the longitudinal studies (i.e., Achiba, 2002; Ellis, 1992; Schmidt, 1983) provide a good starting point for describing the development of requests in a second language, with Ellis's and Achiba's overlapping analyses combining into five developmental stages, summarized in Table 4.2. However, as with

Table 4.2

Five Stages of L2 Request Development (based on Achiba, 2002, and Ellis, 1992)

Stage	Characteristics	Examples
1: Pre-basic	Highly context-dependent, no syntax, no relational goals	"Me no blue", "Sir"
2: Formulaic	Reliance on unanalyzed formulas and imperatives	"Let's play the game", "Let's eat breakfast", "Don't look"
3: Unpacking	Formulas incorporated into productive language use, shift to conventional indirectness	"Can you pass the pencil please?", "Can you do another one for me?"
4: Pragmatic expansion	Addition of new forms to pragmalinguistic repertoire, increased use of mitigation, more complex syntax	"Could I have another chocolate because my children - I have five children.", "Can I see it so I can copy it?"
5: Fine-tuning	Fine-tuning of requestive force to participants, goals, and contexts	"You could put some blu tack down there", "Is there any more white?"

most longitudinal research, the database represented here is rather small—just four individuals in the case of L2 requests—so it is useful to examine what the cross-sectional request studies can contribute to this discussion.

Appeals to the cross-sectional research on L2 requests are useful because cross-sectional designs often involve significantly larger numbers of participants, making more robust generalizations possible, especially when findings from cross-sectional studies support those from longitudinal research. While none of the cross-sectional request studies represents the full range of developmental stages discussed above, several studies do offer evidence that confirms general developmental trends. Hill's (1997) study of the requests of learners of EFL at a Japanese university showed a marked decrease in the percentage of direct requests with increasing proficiency. The distribution of conventionally indirect requests followed the opposite pattern, with advanced learners' use of this strategy approaching NS levels. Rose (2000) also found that frequency of conventional indirectness increased with proficiency among Cantonese-speaking primary-school students in Hong Kong, and that directness was most frequent among the lowest proficiency group. Trosborg (1995) also found a preference for conventional indirectness in evidence across the three levels of Danish learners of EFL she examined, noting a slight shift from what she refers to as hearer-oriented (i.e., ability/willingness and suggestory formula) to what she calls speaker-based strategies (i.e., wishes and desires/needs) as proficiency increased. Interestingly, the use of direct requests actually increased with proficiency, while the reverse was true for hints, which runs directly counter to most studies. Trosborg suggests that the lower-proficiency learners avoided use of direct requests out of fear of sounding impolite, but it is not clear why advanced learners would not have had the same concerns. Overall, then, both longitudinal and cross-sectional research on L2 request development provides considerable evidence to support the five stages of development outlined above. Our discussion so far has focused on global strategies for requesting—two additional issues we will address are the development of mitigation in requesting, and insights from the L2 request studies concerning sociopragmatic development.

The learners in Ellis's (1992) study initially produced requests that were simple (i.e., usually consisting of a bare head act with little internal or external modification) and formulaic, but one of the first mitigating devices they introduced was *please*. This also was the case for Wes and Yao. However, it appears that *please* (particularly in early production) may best be considered a requestive marker rather than a politeness marker (see House, 1989),in which case its mitigating function might be lessened. Schmidt notes an elaboration of Wes's requests, but does not offer a detailed analysis of mitigating devices (i.e., when and how they were introduced). It is clear from the examples presented above, though, that Wes was able to use devices such as imposition minimizers (e.g., "OK, *if you have time* please send two handbag, but *if you're too busy, forget it*.") in a rather sophisticated manner. And, as noted above, Achiba found that Yao's use of mitigation increased over time, particularly during stages four and five when supportive moves became more frequent, as did the modal shift to *could* and *would* (although *can* and *will* were still far more frequent overall). Hill (1997) found that use of downgraders per request increased with proficiency, though the advanced group still fell short of native-speaker levels. He notes that because the Japanese NSs used considerably more internal modification than the native English speakers, the limited use of internal modification by the learners was probably not the result of first language influence. Trosborg (1995) also reported a general increase in internal and external modification with proficiency, but differences across groups were minimal, and even learners in the highest proficiency group fell far short of the English native speakers, especially in external modification of requests. Rose (2000) observed minimal use of supportive moves (mostly grounders, e.g., "*I don't know that question.* Can you teach me?") by only the highest proficiency group. More detailed analyses of the development of mitigation strategies are needed, and we would expect that much of the interesting development would be most evident from stage three onward.

It is worth pointing out that examining major analytical categories (e.g., directness level or use of mitigation) for developmental patterns is not without flaws. As noted above, Hill (1997) found a move toward conventional indirectness with increased proficiency among his learners. However, he points out that the global trend toward native speaker use of conventionally indirect requests concealed a number of patterns in the use of specific substrategies that did not converge toward NS norms. For example, want strategies (*I want to / I would like to*), which were hardly ever used by the native speakers of Irish-English, were overused by learners from the beginning and continued to increase as proficiency improved. The increase of ability strategies (*can / could you*) seen from low to intermediate did not continue at the advanced level; permission strategies (*may I*), though slightly on the rise, remained greatly underused; but willingness strategies (*would you*), while stable from low to intermediate, sharply increased at advanced level. So although an analysis based simply on major categories would appear to indicate that Hill's learners were moving closer to NS norms in their use of conventionally indirect requests, analysis of substrategies actually indicated the opposite. That is, the spike in use of conventional indirectness was the result of learner overuse of want and willingness strategies, actually a movement away from native speaker norms as proficiency increased. The same was true for mitigation: despite what appeared to be another developmental trend, Hill again noted patterns at the substrategy level that indicated movement away from native speaker norms, such as an overuse of syntactic downgraders (e.g., interrogative, negation, continuous, conditional) at the expense of those of the lexical/phrasal variety (e.g., politeness markers, understaters, downtoners), which were used more frequently by the native speakers. This was particularly evident in the learners' use of conditionals (e.g., *If you don't mind*), which Hill argued was transferred from very common Japanese forms such as *moshi yokattara* (if it's okay), and is regressive rather than developmental. The same general developmental trend was found in external modification with the frequency of supportive moves per request increasing with proficiency, and advanced learners' use approaching native-speaker levels. Here again, despite the apparent developmental trend, Hill found regressive patterns in the use of specific substrategies, such as overuse of apology moves (e.g., *So I'm sorry very much*, *I'm feel bad but*, *Sorry to interrupt you but*) as external modifiers. One important lesson to be learned from Hill's study is that without examining more closely the use of specific substrategies within a given strategy category, analysts may arrive at incorrect conclusions, unless the pattern displayed at the macro level reproduces the patterns of the subsumed strategies.

Our discussion so far has addressed learner development in terms of pragmalinguistics, but what about sociopragmatics? Quite early on, Scarcella (1979) argued that "the acquisition of politeness forms appears to precede the acquisition of the socio-linguistic-interactional rules and mechanisms underlying the use and distribution of these forms" (p. 285). It would appear that this claim finds considerable support in the literature on L2 request development. Scarcella's own study—which formed the basis of her conclusion—found that while use of indirectness by NSs on a role play task that varied the status of the hearer formed a cline across status levels, ESL learner groups at two proficiency levels varied minimally in their use of indirectness according to status. Given that adult learners bring considerable universal pragmatic knowledge to the L2 learning task (cf. Chapter 5), Scarcella's learners likely had knowledge of social status as a factor affecting language use (as would be evident in their L1 use), but they were not yet able to match this knowledge with the appropriate linguistic forms in the L2. Ellis (1992) noted that J's and R's requests, for the most part, were not varied according to addressee, indicating no sociopragmatic development at all, despite having displayed acquisition of a range (albeit small) of requesting strategies. Hill's (1997) participants (even the most advanced learners), who demonstrated knowledge of a wide range of request forms, showed little variation in use of direct and conventionally indirect requests and internal modification according to hearer status, indicating their inability to map target language forms to appropriate social categories. However, they did use external modification more frequently with equal-status hearers than those of higher status, showing some evidence of sociopragmatic awareness. Trosborg (1995) and Rose (2000) both reported virtually no situational variation in request strategy across all learner groups, despite having found evidence of a fairly wide range of request forms. These findings underscore the fact that despite already possessing considerable universal pragmatic knowledge, adult L2 learners appear to require a great deal of time to develop the ability to appropriately map L2 forms to social categories. This appears to be especially true in foreign language contexts.

But not all the news is bad. Achiba (2002) noted that there were some rather interesting aspects in which Yao's requests took into account various sociopragmatic factors. For example, while Yao's use of direct requests persisted for goals such as initiation and cessation of action (e.g., "Oh just give me another story," "Here don't eat too much"), she preferred conventional indirectness in requesting goods and joint activity (e.g., "Could I please have one choc chip?" "Let's pretend this is Safeway"). There was also variation observed in requests depending on addressee, with, for example, all of the *want* statements used with adults rather than peers, the majority of requests with *let's* used with peers rather than adults, and *please* used almost exclusively to Yao's mother. Schmidt also reports some sociopragmatic awareness in Wes's responses to Scarcella's (1979) test of verbal routines, for example, on an item designed to elicit an apology for being late, Wes initially responded with "Hi! I'm sorry. Somebody call," but he then noted that "No, this is Japan need two story. Here I'm only just say 'Hi, sorry, you waiting long time?'" (p. 154), demonstrating the level of pragmatic sophistication with concomitant grammatical infelicities that have made him famous. Thus, Wes and Yao did appear to develop some sociopragmatic competence in the target language, no doubt largely due to the fact that their learning took place in an acquisition-rich environment, with ample opportunity for input and interaction.

Summing up the request studies, perhaps the most striking finding is the proposed five-stage development sequence drawn from the work of Ellis (1992) and Achiba (2002). Stage one is a pre-basic variety (see Chapter 5), in which requestive intent is conveyed through highly context-dependent, minimalist realizations. Stage two brings with it reliance on imperatives and unanalyzed routines, which are then unpacked for more productive use in the third stage. This stage also sees a shift away from imperatives toward the use of conventional indirectness. The fourth stage involves the addition of many new forms to the pragmalinguistic repertoire for requests, and the final stage is characterized by the increasing ability to fine-tune requests for various contexts. Another obvious trend worth noting is that learners begin to gradually modify their requests, both internally and externally, as proficiency increases (particularly from stage three onward). Hill's findings, however, make a strong case for not taking the results of major category analyses at face value. Despite the move toward what appeared to be more native-like requests in terms of directness, his analysis of substrategies showed that more advanced learners were actually moving away from native speaker norms in their choice of pragmalinguistic devices that realized conventional indirectness or modification. So while more advanced learners may have more closely resembled native speakers in using more conventional indirectness or in mitigating their requests, the ways in which they were doing so were decidedly not native-like. Concerning the sociopragmatics of request development, findings are mixed. It would be fair to say that learning context plays a key role here, with learners in second language settings (e.g., Wes, Yao) achieving some level of sociopragmatic development, and learners in foreign language contexts (e.g., learners of English in Denmark, Japan, and Hong Kong) reaching little or none. Given that the literature on requests has provided a good deal of evidence of pragmatic development, it is interesting to see whether the same will be true for studies of other speech acts, which we consider next.

Other Speech Acts

For research on speech acts other than requests, we start with Bardovi-Harlig and Hartford's (1993a) study of suggestions and refusals in an academic advising context, one of the first longitudinal studies of pragmatic development. Based on their earlier work on advising sessions (Bardovi-Harlig & Hartford, 1990), which indicated a number of differences in nonnative speaker and native speaker use, Bardovi-Harlig and Hartford (1993a, p. 281) proposed a "Maxim of Congruence: Make your contribution congruent with your status." They note that in advising sessions, congruent contributions from the advisor include advising, recommending, and requesting information from the student, and those congruent with student status are making requests for advice, information, and permission. Incongruent acts for students include correcting the advisor and rejecting his or her advice. When congruence is not possible, a status-preserving strategy (SPS) must be employed. Bardovi-Harlig and Hartford list six such strategy types but focus on the following four:

- Appear congruent. Use the form of a congruent speech act where possible.
- Mark your contribution linguistically. Use mitigators.
- Frequency. Avoid frequent noncongruent turns.
- Use appropriate content.

(Bardovi-Harlig & Hartford, 1993, p. 281)

The data for this study were drawn from academic advising sessions that took place at intervals of about two months to about four-and-a-half months. Even after such a short observational period, results showed some change over time in the use of suggestions by nonnative speakers. Bardovi-Harlig and Hartford identified three types of suggestions: initiated suggestions (offered by the speaker without a prompt or question), responses to prompts, and responses to questions. Of these, initiated suggestions are status-incongruent for students (and thus require SPSs), while the other two strategies are status-congruent. Both groups used suggestions with about the same frequency in the early and later sessions, but there were differences across groups in choice of suggestion type. In the early sessions, native speakers favored initiated requests and nonnative speakers relied more on responses to questions, but in the later sessions, both groups used initiated suggestions about equally. This suggests that the nonnative speakers moved from a passive to an active role in schedule building. Native speaker suggestions were a great deal more successful (i.e., accepted by the advisor) than those of nonnative speakers, with one key exception being that nonnative speakers' success rate for initiated suggestions on the later sessions rose to a level approaching that of native speakers. This greater success rate of native speaker suggestions is likely due to their more effective use of mitigators—native speakers used about twice as many mitigators as nonnative speakers, who also frequently employed aggravators, as in the following examples:

(4.12) Nonnative speakers' use of aggravators

In the summer I *will take* language testing for the first summer session, the first one, the second summer session I *will take* the socio [linguistics class].

Yeah, *I'm going to* take, ah . . . applied . . . transformational syntax.

So, I, *I just decided* on taking the language structure . . . field method in linguistics.

(Bardovi-Harlig & Hartford, 1990, p. 289)

Changes were also found over time in the use of rejections. In the early sessions, nonnative speakers rejected about half of their advisor's suggestions, resulting in a frequency of rejections that was almost 10 times that of native speakers. However, by the later sessions, the frequency of nonnative speaker rejections had decreased rather dramatically to about one-fourth the level of the early sessions, approaching native-speaker levels. The success rate of nonnative speaker rejections improved somewhat, but still lagged well behind the 100% success rate of native speaker rejections. Another key area of change in rejections is the more frequent use by nonnative speakers of what Bardovi-Harlig and Hartford call "credible content," i.e., rejecting a course for an acceptable reason such as a time conflict or having already taken it previously, rather than, say, a lack of interest (e.g., *I think I am not interested in Montague grammar*), which tended to provoke strong reactions from advisors. Bardovi-Harlig and Hartford conclude that nonnative speakers "do develop competence in their handling of the advising session. What they primarily learn is the institutional rules. That is, they learn what the advising session is for and how it is generally structured" (p. 298).

Another refusal study was T. Takahashi and Beebe's (1987) cross-sectional study involving a standard interlanguage data set: native speakers of Japanese and English, and Japanese-speaking learners of English. The learners were divided into two groups based on location: an EFL group in Japan, and an ESL group studying in the United States. The two sets of learners were grouped into low and high proficiency. The focus of the study was on transfer, which Takahashi and Beebe expected to find in both contexts and at both proficiency levels, with more transfer occurring in the EFL setting and among higher-proficiency learners. Regarding the relationship between transfer and development, Takahashi and Beebe (1987) rather famously posited that higher levels of proficiency result in more negative first language transfer because increased fluency gives learners "the rope to hang themselves with" (p. 153). We return to this issue later in our discussion of pragmatic transfer and development. As expected, evidence of transfer from Japanese was found in the English refusals of both the EFL and the ESL groups in, for example, a preference for making a statement of philosophy (e.g., *Things with shapes eventually break*) or principle (e.g., *I make a rule to be temperate in eating*), and use of dissuading strategies (e.g., threat or statement of negative consequences, guilt trip) in a wider range of contexts. Further, more transfer was found in the EFL setting. The effects of proficiency on transfer were not so clear. It was found that lower-proficiency EFL learners marginally transferred more than those in the high-proficiency group, with the opposite pattern obtaining for the ESL learners. Takahashi and Beebe note that ESL data "weakly confirms" their hypothesis, while the EFL data "even more weakly" refutes it (p. 148), and opt to argue that there were real proficiency differences only for the ESL group. However, given the lack of independent proficiency measures, this strikes us as rather unconvincing. They offer an account of the greater levels of transfer in the high-proficiency ESL group, for example, refusals of a higher formality (e.g., *I am very delighted and honored to be asked to attend the party, but . . .*, and *I deeply appreciate your work*), which did not occur with lower-proficiency ESL learners.

From refusals, we now move to another speech act—greetings, which is also represented by two studies. In her account of the acquisition of Indonesian greetings by her six study-abroad learners, DuFon (1999) reports that learners were exposed to a range of Indonesian greetings. Some of these were semantically similar to English.

Halo 'hello'

Selamat 'happy' + time of day

Apa kabar? 'What's new / How are you?'

Other greetings were not semantically similar to English.

Dari mana? 'Where are you [coming] from?'

Sudah makan 'Have you eaten yet?'

Sudah mandi? 'Have you had your bath yet?'

When it came to their own use, learners displayed a clear preference for greetings that were semantically closest to English, and one learner even reported resistance to using the less English-like greetings because to him they didn't "seem like a greeting, but more of just a question. Almost as if they were just skipping the greeting"(DuFon, 1999, p. 303). Several learners also reported that they initially understood such greetings as information-seeking questions. For the most part, however, DuFon's account of greetings dealt with how learners were greeted, and how they responded, and she says little about development other than an initial preference for greetings semantically similar to English, with a gradual expansion of the greeting repertoire to include formulas that were initially interpreted as information-seeking questions. She does note that some learners demonstrated a rather advanced level of understanding of the politeness values of various greetings in different contexts, indicating some development of sociopragmatic awareness. One learner—a native speaker of Japanese—systematically compared greetings in Indonesian, Chinese, and Japanese in a dialogue journal entry, showing a level of metapragmatic awareness that indicates the benefits of individual multilingualism. A further study on greetings is that of Omar (1991), who conducted a cross-sectional study on the greetings of American learners of Kiswahili studying at Indiana University. Of interest to Omar was whether learners would indicate awareness of the norms governing greetings in Kiswahili, which involve more elaborated interaction than found in the rather formulaic greeting typical of American English. Kiswahili greetings typically involve a large number of turns, repetition of the same forms, and questions concerning one's family members. Omar reports that learners of Kiswahili are put off by this. Learners were classified as beginners and nonbeginners. For the most part, learners' greetings were inappropriately unelaborated, and there were few differences across the two levels. Omar notes that, if anything, it was the beginning learners whose greetings were more elaborate.

The studies of the speech acts reviewed in this section are a bit of a mixed bag. Bardovi-Harlig and Hartford's study clearly charts the progress of very advanced learners of English in negotiating their academic schedules through more appropriate use of refusals and suggestions, even over a relatively short period (as little as two months). However, their findings also show that even the most advanced learners continue to have difficulty with the finer points of mitigating their speech acts. This is not surprising, given that request studies have also shown that mitigation develops later, and studies such as Kerekes (1992) have demonstrated that learners also take time to accurately comprehend qualifiers. The two studies of greetings offer differing results as well, with Omar finding no evidence of compliance with the elaborated Kiswahili greetings, but DuFon finding that her participants relied on Indonesian greeting formulas that more closely resembled those they were familiar with from English, only slowly making use of what (to them) were more exotic greeting routines. These conflicting findings are likely explained, at least in part, by differences in learning context. DuFon's learners had the distinct advantage of residing in Indonesia when studying Indonesian, which included living with host families. Omar's participants had very different circumstances, that is, studying an uncommonly-taught language in an environment that afforded little or no intensive exposure to the target language, or opportunities to use it. Another possible explanation for the conflicting findings is individual learner differences (see Chapter 8), particularly motivation. Traveling to Indonesia to participate in a four-month study-abroad program likely indicates considerably more personal investment on the part of DuFon's learners than taking language classes most likely intended to fulfill a university foreign language requirement. DuFon's participants were also experienced second language learners, having already learned another second language prior to learning Indonesian. Omar does not offer details on the prior second language learning of her participants, so we cannot comment on their motivation or language learning prowess. And, finally, Takahashi and Beebe's focus on transfer offers little information regarding development and does not convincingly support their hypothesis that (negative) transfer from the first language correlates positively with proficiency in the target language. It does, however, offer a nice segue into our next section, where we take up the issue of pragmatic development and transfer in more detail.

Pragmatic Transfer and Development

Pragmatic transfer has been attested in many of the single-moment studies comparing interlanguage performance with corresponding first language and second language data (see Maeshiba et al., 1996; S. Takahashi, 1996, for review). Here, we will consider research addressing the relationship of pragmatic transfer and development. As noted above, T. Takahashi and Beebe (1987) advanced the positive correlation hypothesis, predicting that second language proficiency is positively correlated with pragmatic transfer. Lower-proficiency learners, according to the hypothesis, are less likely to display pragmatic transfer in their L2 production than higher-proficiency learners because they do not have the necessary linguistic resources to do so. Higher-proficiency learners, on the other hand, do have such resources, so their L2 production will tend to reveal more pragmatic transfer. As noted above, while Beebe and T. Takahashi's (1987) study on the English refusals of Japanese learners of English at two different proficiency levels did not demonstrate the predicted proficiency effect, some studies have found that learners' limited second language knowledge prevented them from transferring complex first language conventions of means and form, and that increasing proficiency in the target language can apparently facilitate negative pragmatic transfer.

One such study is Cohen's (1997) account of his experience in a four-month intensive JFL course at the University of Hawai'i. His diary entries indicate that he intended to adhere to implementations of the Quantity and Manner maxims common in mainstream North American culture, which would have amounted to talking more and being more specific than was appropriate in Japanese, or, as he puts it, to "use more speech than Japanese do" (p. 150). For example, Cohen noted a specific desire to supply more than *sumimasen* in apologizing, but since his low degree of foreign language knowledge and control prevented that plan from being implemented, Japanese conversational norms were involuntarily observed. Cohen's experience lends support to the positive correlation hypothesis—despite his stated desire to violate target language norms and intentionally produce utterances in the L2 that observed pragmatic norms from his L1, he was unable to do so because he lacked sufficient Japanese resources.

Findings from Hill (1997) would also appear to support the positive correlation hypothesis. Recall that although Hill's highest-proficiency learners appeared to be moving toward native-like request production when main strategies (i.e., level of directness) and use of mitigators were considered, closer examination of substrategies for both categories turned up pragmalinguistic features that both deviated from native English speakers, and—more importantly where transfer is concerned—appeared to be the result of first language influence. For example, advanced learners' use of conditionals such as *If you don't mind* were likely a direct translation from Japanese (i.e., *moshi yokattara*, 'If it's okay'), as was their overuse of apology moves (e.g., *So I'm sorry very much*, *I'm feel bad but* and *Sorry to interrupt you but*) as external modifiers. It appears, then, that Hill's more advanced learners transferred these forms to English from Japanese as soon as they had the requisite linguistic skills in the target language.

But not all studies support Takahashi and Beebe's hypothesis. Maeshiba et al. (1996) carried out an apology study with intermediate and advanced Japanese-speaking ESL learners in Hawai'i. In addition to a production task, participants also completed a metapragmatic assessment questionnaire on seven contextual factors (i.e., severity of offense, offender's obligation to apologize, likelihood for the apology to be accepted, offender's face loss, offended party's face loss, social distance, and social dominance). Assessments of the various groups indicated the highest levels of agreement for status, obligation to apologize, and likelihood of acceptance, and the lowest for offender's face loss, offended party's face loss, and social distance. Maeshiba et al. predicted that transfer of apology strategies could be based on similarities and differences in assessment of contextual variables, with positive transfer occurring with similar assessments, and negative transfer where assessments differed. For the most part, these predictions were borne out. An important finding was that the advanced learners outpaced the intermediate group in both types of transfer, showing more positive transfer and less negative transfer. These results do not support the positive correlation hypothesis.

One could attempt to continue working with Takahashi and Beebe's hypothesis by looking for explanations for the conflicting findings offered by these studies. For example, one possible explanation for the different outcomes of Hill (1997) and Maeshiba et al. (1996) is that apology strategies in Japanese and English vary less in terms of syntactic complexity than request strategies do. How exactly the grammatical complexity of speech act strategies in first language and second language and pragmalinguistic transfer interrelate developmentally has not been studied thus far. Such a line of inquiry would move forward considerably the study of the relationship between pragmatic development and pragmatic transfer. In fact, it would enable researchers to explore more complex relationships than the rather facile hypothesis according to which advanced learners are prone to negative pragmatic transfer because their L2 grammar makes it possible. Although the phenomenon of pragmatic transfer is well documented, the conditions of transfer and especially its interaction with other factors are less clearly understood. Reminiscent of Kellerman's psychotypology (1983), studies by Olshtain (1983) and Robinson (1992) suggest that learners may be more prone to transfer their pragmatic first language knowledge when they hold a universalist view as opposed to a relativist perspective on pragmatic norms. To date, only one interlanguage pragmatic study (S. Takahashi, 1996) has been carried out with an explicit focus on transferability, that is, learners' perception of equivalence between conventions of means and form in first language and second language.

After reviewing the existing literature on second language pragmatic transfer, S. Takahashi (1996) argues that "in addition to product-oriented research on pragmatic transfer, we . . . need to undertake process-oriented studies of pragmatic transferability, exploring the conditions under which transfer occurs" (p. 190), and her study of the transferability of Japanese indirect request strategies to English makes a significant step in that direction. She was interested in how proficiency in the target language (i.e., English) as well as requestive imposition influenced learners' perceptions of the transferability of request strategies from their first language (i.e., Japanese). She outlined two criteria for pragmatic transferability, that is, learner assessment of the contextual appropriateness of a given strategy and their assessment of the equivalence of strategies in the first language and the target language in terms of contextual appropriateness. Based on this, Takahashi proposed a pragmatic transferability scale, which posits that strategies rated high for contextual appropriateness and viewed as contextual equivalents are more transferable, while those that are rated low for appropriateness and considered contextually different are less transferable. Participants in her study low- and high-proficiency Japanese male undergraduates. Preliminary work was carried out to establish what Takahashi refers to as conventional equivalent pairs (CEPs) and functional equivalent pairs (FEPs). The former were basically literal translation equivalents, while the latter were equivalent in terms of their communicative effect. For example, the Japanese request form *V-te itadaki-tai-n-desu-kedo* "I would like you to VP" would have the functional English equivalent "I was wondering if you could VP," which is quite different from its literal translation. A transferability judgment questionnaire was constructed to measure perception of the contextual appropriateness of five Japanese indirect request strategies and their contextual equivalence vis-à-vis their CEP counterpart. Scores from these two were then used to compute pragmatic transferability rate. It was found (among other things) that CEPs were rated higher in terms of equivalence than FEPs, with no differences across the two proficiency groups. Takahashi (1996, pp. 209–210) noted that her "Japanese learners of English could not identify the English requests that were the real functional equivalents of the Japanese request strategies" no matter what their level of proficiency, indicating that both groups "equally relied on their first language request conventions or strategies in second language request realization." By examining the cross-linguistic correspondences of a specific subset of first and target language pragmatic features, Takahashi's study represents a more sophisticated approach to pragmatic transfer and development.

Chapter Summary

This chapter has examined acquisitional patterns in various areas of interlanguage pragmatics. After discussing the rather meager evidence of progression in pragmatic comprehension, we considered how several features of discourse and pragmatic ability (other than speech acts) change over time. We noted a tendency for learners to rely on routine formulas and repetition at first gradually giving way to an expansion of their pragmatic repertoire. Also evident is overgeneralization of one form for a range of functions, occasionally resulting in pragmatic failure. As we will elaborate in the next chapter, aspects of pragmatics that are closely related to grammatical proficiency are problematic for learners without the requisite knowledge of L2 grammar. These studies also show, however, that even lower-proficiency learners are capable of controlling what might appear to be rather challenging aspects of target language pragmatics, and that learners' pragmatic knowledge may not be accurately represented in their production. Next we looked at speech acts. Investigations of requests in particular point to some rather stable findings, namely, the tendency to rely on direct strategies in the early stages of development, with a gradual move to conventional indirectness, followed by the introduction of internal and external modification of requests as proficiency increases. The longitudinal studies also suggest a possible five-stage developmental sequence for L2 request development. Concerning the sociopragmatics of request development, findings are mixed. Learning context would seem to play a key role here, with learners in second language settings generally achieving some sociopragmatic development, and learners in foreign language contexts making much less progress. Finally, we addressed the relationship between pragmatic transfer and development, a research issue that could benefit from a richer investigative perspective than the effects of general L2 proficiency on pragmatic transfer.

CHAPTER FIVE

The Development of Pragmatics and Grammar

Most developmental research on interlanguage pragmatics isolates pragmatics from other components of communicative competence. Separating out the focal object of study from related material is a common research strategy in second language acquisition and elsewhere in the social sciences, and as in studies of lexis, morphosyntax, and phonology, it has been utilized to good effect. But equal in importance to the development of pragmatics as an autonomous component of communicative competence is to relate it to other aspects of communicative ability. In this regard, Canale (1983) expressed caution about the epistemological status of the Canale-Swain construct of communicative competence (Canale, 1983; Canale & Swain, 1980), arguing that "this theoretical framework is not a *model* of communicative competence, where model implies some specification of the manner and order in which the components interact and in which the various competencies are normally acquired" (p. 12, italics added). Walters (1980) echoed the need to investigate the relationship among the components of communicative ability, asking

> Are they [the various components] by and large independent like the syntactic and phonological components of a grammar? Or, do they frequently interact in complex ways like syntax and semantics? Do these components suggest a hierarchical organization, or do they represent parallel levels of analysis? (p. 388)

Some early studies, conducted as explicit test cases of Canale and Swain's framework, set out to investigate the integrity and

159

interdependence of the framework's components, addressing such questions as "[t]o what extent are grammatical ability and socio-cultural ability independent as claimed in the Canale and Swain model? In what ways are they interdependent, i.e., in what ways does the sociocultural component depend on the grammatical component?" (Walters, 1980, p. 339). Walters's questions address the possible independence of the two competencies and the dependence of pragmatics on grammar. A further possibility to consider is that grammatical development may require already established pragmatic knowledge.

This chapter will review what the research literature has to say about the relationship of interlanguage pragmatic and grammatical development. We will start by referring to recent studies that specifically addressed the issue and a programmatic call to subject the relationship between pragmatics and grammar to renewed scrutiny. Next, we will provide evidence for the primacy of pragmatics in interlanguage development. This section will be followed by studies documenting the opposite developmental pattern, that is, grammatical knowledge precedes its pragmatic deployment. Specifically, this section will comment on available grammatical knowledge that (a) is not put to pragmatic use; (b) enables non-target-like pragmatic use; and (c) is used in a way that is pragmalinguistically target-like but sociopragmatically non-target-like. Finally, we will suggest how these seemingly contradictory findings may be reconciled. We will refer to formal linguistic knowledge, including lexis, morphosyntax, and phonology, summarily as "grammar" and distinguish among these components as necessary.

Reopening the Research Agenda

Despite researchers' initial interest in the connection between pragmatics and grammar, most interlanguage pragmatics studies have singled out pragmatics as their sole focal object, commenting on grammar as one factor that might influence pragmatic development. Renewed attention to the relationship between pragmatic and grammatical competence was marked by Bardovi-Harlig and Dörnyei's (1998) study of ESL and EFL learners' pragmatic and grammatical awareness, operationalized as learners' scores on an error recognition and severity rating task. The main groups in the study were ESL learners enrolled in an intensive language program at a U.S. university and EFL learners studying at secondary schools and university programs in Hungary, as well as ESL and EFL teachers. The student groups were separated into high and low proficiency for analysis. The instrument was a set of 20 video-taped scenarios, featuring a female and a male student engaged in typical university interactions. The target utterance (the second pair part in each dialogue) was marked on the screen and appeared on the answer sheet. Respondents first assessed whether the target utterance was appropriate/correct. If their judgment was negative, they were then asked to estimate the severity of the problem. It was found that error recognition and ratings differed significantly depending on the ESL/EFL context, the learners' proficiency, and student versus teacher status. The ESL learners identified more pragmatic errors and rated them as more severe than the grammatical errors, whereas the EFL learners recognized more grammatical errors and assessed them as more serious than the pragmatic errors. Proficiency interacted with learning environment: the low-proficiency Hungarian students gave lower ratings to both grammatical and pragmatic errors than the high-proficiency EFL group, whereas the high-proficiency EFL students rated the grammatical errors as far more severe than the pragmatically inappropriate utterances. Compared to the low-proficiency ESL group, the high-proficiency ESL learners assessed pragmatic inappropriacies as somewhat more serious, however, their severity ratings of grammatical errors *decreased* significantly. In a replication of Bardovi-Harlig and Dörnyei's (1998) study with Czech EFL students, Niezgoda and Röver (2001) found that their ESL students rated pragmatic errors as significantly more severe than grammatical errors, which confirmed Bardovi-Harlig and Dörnyei's finding. Unlike Bardovi-Harlig and Dörnyei's Hungarian EFL group, however, the Czech students noticed a much higher number of pragmatic *and* grammatical errors and judged both error types as more serious than the ESL sample. Low-proficiency learners in both the EFL and ESL groups recognized more pragmatic than grammatical errors and rated pragmatic errors as more severe, whereas high-proficiency learners showed the opposite tendency. The findings from both studies strongly suggest that pragmatic and grammatical awareness are largely independent. What they do not examine (and indeed did not intend to examine) is how awareness, measured by judgments of grammatical acceptability and pragmatic appropriateness, is related to learners' ability to express pragmatic meaning and use grammatical forms in spoken (and written) discourse.

A second, programmatic initiative to explore the relationship between interlanguage pragmatics and grammar was proposed by Bardovi-Harlig (1999). In this paper, she outlined a research agenda on the acquisition of pragmatics that recommends in-depth study of specific, related grammatical and pragmalinguistic subsystems. This proposal moves developmental interlanguage pragmatics a significant step beyond most of the broad comparisons of grammatical and pragmatic development that have been conducted thus far. It is grounded in a consistent finding in research on advanced learners' pragmatic ability, namely, "high levels of grammatical competence do not guarantee concomitant high levels of pragmatic competence" (Bardovi-Harlig, 1999, p. 686). How have researchers arrived at this very stable result? Typically—and irrespective of the research design—previous studies have compared learners' performance of a *particular* pragmatic feature (mostly a speech act) with the performance of that speech act by native speakers and a *general* measure of L2 proficiency such as standardized proficiency tests, grade level, or even indirect measures of proficiency, such as length of residence in the target community or length of formal study. Such studies have found repeatedly that high general proficiency is not matched by native-like performance in the pragmatic feature examined (Bardovi-Harlig, 2001). They confirm early work in language testing, reviewed by Canale and Swain (1980), which showed that "performance on measures of grammatical ability (e.g., Michigan Test of English Language Performance, TOEFL) would not significantly predict performance on communicative tasks (e.g., oral interviews, information-getting, narratives, description, referential communication)" (Walter, 1989, p. 338).

Most developmental studies of interlanguage pragmatics to date have adopted the research strategy of treating pragmatic ability as an autonomous component of communicative competence in order to examine how particular subcomponents of pragmalinguistic ability are acquired and what levels of attainment learners reach. While this approach does reveal patterns of pragmatic development (cf. Chapter 4), it does not offer insights on how a *particular* pragmalinguistic feature is related to the *particular* grammatical knowledge implicated in its use. It is precisely this question that Bardovi-Harlig (1999) recommends to SLA researchers' attention. Although at present, only a few studies have made the relationship between pragmatics and grammar their central issue, much previous research offers observations and comments about it. We will therefore discuss pertinent evidence regardless of a study's research focus. In this body of literature, two—apparently contradictory—sets of outcomes are reported. One group of results documents that learners use L2 pragmatic functions before they acquire the L2 grammatical forms that are acceptable realizations of those functions. The other set of findings indicates that learners acquire L2 grammatical forms before acquiring their pragmalinguistic functions. We will take a closer look at each of the two scenarios.

Pragmatics Precedes Grammar

The Universal Pragmatics Principle

The proposition that learners' L2 pragmatic ability can be ahead of their grammar is at odds with the commonsense view that in order to do things with words in a target language, the "words"—used synecdochically for the grammar—must already be in place. Like many stubborn myths about language learning and teaching, this belief persists in foreign language curricula and teaching materials around the world. Even if language instruction ultimately aims to enable students to "communicate" in the target language, pragmatic ability must be grounded in a solid foundation in L2 grammar, which is later put to pragmatic use. The myth of the primacy of grammar disregards the indisputable reality that unlike children, normal adult L2 learners are already fully pragmatically competent in at least one language—and most people in more than one, given the fact that the majority of the world's population grows up multilingually rather than monolingually. Adults and children thus face quite different learning tasks in pragmatics, as predicted by Bialystok's (1993) two-dimensional model of language use and proficiency (cf. Chapter 2). Children primarily have to develop analytic representations of pragmalinguistic and sociopragmatic knowledge, whereas adult L2 learners mainly have to acquire processing control over already existing representations. To some extent, adults have to acquire new representations as well, such as unfamiliar sociopragmatic distinctions and practices, new pragmalinguistic conventions, their social meanings, and their contextual distributions, but in developing L2 specific pragmatic ability, adult learners can build on a broad basis of prior knowledge.

Regardless of ethnolinguistic specificities, competent adult members of any community bring a rich fund of universal pragmatic knowledge and abilities to the task of learning the pragmatics of another language (Blum-Kulka, 1991). Such knowledge is conceptualized differently in various theories of pragmatics, discourse, and interaction, as noted in Chapter 1. But consistent with comprehensive perspectives on pragmatics (Levinson, 1983; Mey, 1993) and theories addressing specific aspects of pragmatic knowledge (Brown & Levinson, 1987; Grice, 1975; Gumperz, 1982; Leech, 1983; Psathas, 1990), universal pragmatic competence minimally comprises implicit knowledge and ability to use of the following:

- Goffman's "system constraints" of interaction and their extensions in conversation analysis, including principles and practices of turn taking, repair, the sequential accomplishment of actions, and preference organization (e.g., Hutchby & Wooffitt, 1998).
- Differences between ordinary conversation and at least some other, usually institutionalized, speech exchange systems (e.g., Drew & Heritage, 1992; Markee, 2000).
- Acts of speaking, writing, and using hybrid modalities, such as the main categories of illocutionary acts—verdictives, exercitives, commissives, behabitives, expositives (Austin, 1962), or representatives, directives, commissives, expressives, declarations (Searle, 1976).
- Specific communicative acts: greetings, leave takings, requests, suggestions, invitations, offers, refusals, acceptances, (dis)agreements, apologies, complaints, compliments, expressions of gratitude (Ochs, 1996, p. 425f.).
- Conversational implicature, inferencing heuristics, and indirectness (Gibbs, 1994; Grice, 1975; Searle, 1975).
- Indexicality as an implicit expression of epistemic, affective, and social stance (Ochs, 1996) and contextualization (Gumperz, 1996).
- Politeness as a mutually face-saving strategy (Brown & Levinson, 1987).
- Major realization strategies for communicative acts, such as levels of directness in requesting (Blum-Kulka, House, & Kasper, 1989; Fukushima, 2000).
- Routine formulae for managing recurrent communicative events (Coulmas, 1981; Nattinger & DeCarrico, 1992; Wray, 2002).
- Sociopragmatic (contextual) variability in actional and linguistic choices (Blum-Kulka, 1991; Brown & Levinson, 1987; Hymes, 1972).
- Discursive construction of social identities and relations (Bakhtin, 1986; Antaki & Widdicombe, 1998).

- Collaborative and autonomous accomplishment of activities (Levinson, 1979) and genres (Bakhtin, 1986).

From the perspective of linguistic anthropology, Ochs (1996) subsumes some of these competencies under a "universal culture principle," proposing that "There are commonalties across the world's language communities and communities of practice in the linguistic means used to constitute certain situational meanings. This principle suggests that human interlocutors use similar linguistic means to achieve similar social ends" (p. 425). But since the competencies summarily listed above constitute the *pragmatic* knowledge and skills that competent adult members draw on in their communicative practice, they specifically point to a universal pragmatic principle, not just a universal culture principle, which would also encompass cross-culturally shared nonlinguistic, non-discursive, and nontextual phenomena. For the most part, universal pragmatic competencies are implicit and proceduralized types of knowledge and ability whose availability for conscious inspection is quite limited. Prime occasions for noticing and meta-commentary are violations of expected lines of conduct (e.g., *Don't interrupt me*, *He was really rude*). It may well be that because universal pragmatic competencies are omnipresent, taken for granted, and acquired in social interaction rather than formally learned, their role in adult second and foreign language learning is not easily recognized. However, as noted in Chapter 2, such diverse theories of second language acquisition as the interaction hypothesis (Long, 1996), sociocultural theory (Lantolf, 2000b; Ohta, 2001b), conversation analysis (Markee, 2000), and language socialization (Pallotti, 2001; Poole, 1992) attribute (in different ways) foundational acquisitional roles to interaction and partici-pation. Although this is usually not made explicit, without L2 learners' preexisting ability to engage in interactions of various sorts—in other words, if learners were Garfinkelian interactional dopes—even the most persistent efforts at co-construction and collaboration would be doomed to failure. Whether or not *linguistic* universals are at work in adult second language acquisition, *pragmatic* universals enable learners to participate in L2-mediated interaction from early on and to acquire L2-specific pragmatic knowledge.

Functional-Linguistic Theories of Second Language Acquisition

Whereas the Canale and Swain framework of communicative competence conceptualizes its components in a modular fashion, functional-linguistic theories from Halliday to Givón reject the idea of separating pragmatics, semantics, and syntax into distinctly bounded units or levels. The European Science Foundation (ESF) project on *Second Language Acquisition by Adult Immigrants* (Perdue, 1993, 2000), for instance, adopted as its descriptive framework a version of functional grammar that conceptualizes language as "bidirectional form-function mappings" (Dittmar, 1992, p. 250, citing Cooreman & Kilborn, 1991, p. 197). Pertinent to our concerns is the notion of *grammaticalization*, or syntacticization, a process operative in the phylogenesis and ontogenesis of languages, albeit in different ways (see papers in Dittmar, 1992, for various definitions in historical linguistics, Creole studies, and first and second language acquisition). Giacalone Ramat (1992) usefully refers to grammaticalization processes in second language acquisition as "acquisitional grammaticalization," defined by Skiba and Dittmar (1992) as

> The transformation of pragmatic and semantic formats of expression (words, unanalyzed "chunks")
>
> 1. Into specific productive syntactic patterns of the individual learner variety, which are important for the organization of meaning and which tend to converge in the long run with the target variety; and
>
> 2. Toward morphosyntactic norms of the target language. (p. 324)

In functional perspective, empirical evidence of acquisitional grammaticalization in adult learner varieties converges on the view that "pragmatic categories precede syntactic ones" (Dittmar,

1992, p. 256). The primacy of pragmatics hypothesis is supported in functional-linguistic studies of temporality (Dietrich, Klein, & Noyeau, 1995) and modality (Giacalone Ramat & Crocco Galèas, 1995) in second language acquisition and in some interlanguage pragmatics research.

Evidence for the Primacy of Pragmatics

One SLA celebrity whose pragmatic skills advanced to great effectiveness while his grammar lagged behind is Wes, the participant in Schmidt's (1983) study. As we discussed in Chapters 2 and 4, over the three-year observation period, Wes made little progress in his grammatical knowledge, whereas his pragmatic and discourse competence improved considerably. Wes's case impressively illustrates the dissociation of grammatical from pragmatic and discourse ability. He demonstrates that a restricted interlanguage grammar does not necessarily prevent pragmatic and interactional competence from developing, and that high acculturation is not necessarily related to target-like grammar, whereas it appears to be strongly related to pragmatic and interactional competence.

In a study examining the comprehension and production of requests, apologies, and commands by beginning learners of Spanish as a foreign language, Koike (1989) explicitly focused on the structure and development of pragmatic ability and their relationship to grammatical competence. She sums up the results of her study as follows.

> The L2 pragmatic component of interlanguage in the context of speech acts suggests characteristics which are different from those of an L2 grammatical component. . . . Simply because learners do not employ L2 pragmatic forms corresponding to those of the L1, even when they have studied a number of possibilities to express the speech act, does not signify that those forms are not present in their competence. Rather . . . *since the grammatical competence cannot develop as quickly as the already present pragmatic concepts require, the pragmatic concepts are expressed in ways conforming to the level of grammatical complexity*

acquired. For this reason, the pragmatic information may be added peripherally to the early-acquired basic command form through lexical options (e.g., imperative + *por favor* ['please']). (p. 286, emphasis added)

One impressive illustration of Koike's conclusion can be found in a study of disagreements in authentic native-nonnative interactions, conducted by Salsbury and Bardovi-Harlig (2001). In one of these conversations, the nonnative interlocutor MR expressed the epistemic stance of hypotheticality through what the authors refer to as "pre-conditionals" (extract (5.1); Int 2 is a native English speaking interviewer).

(5.1) Pre-conditionals in MR's argumentative discourse

1	Int 2:	Yeah, I know, sometimes because of religion, they
2		say being gay is bad, but I don't understand that,
3		because in religion they say you should love
4		people.
5	MR:	No, no, excuse me, this is no my, I express,
6		express bad, my question is, is bad when people
7		is, <u>for example, do you have a boyfriend</u>, your
8		boyfriend you think is the man, but maybe he has
9		<u>other, other couple, but maybe he is gay, but this</u>
10		<u>is bad</u>, when the people say, ok, I am gay, ok, but
11		I like, only this people, I love you only you, but
12		when this man, maybe woman, maybe man, is bad
13	Int 2:	Ah!
		⋮
14	Int 2:	Well, sometimes a lot of, I have gay friends, and
15		sometimes their parents give them freedom . . .
16		the parents were very shocked, but then it was ok.
17	MR:	<u>What do you think maybe you had, you have a</u>
18		<u>baby, after your child is gay? No problem?</u>
		⋮
19	MR:	Yes, I think it is difficult for the people, is
20		gay, because other people don't understand . . . but
21		when you live this problem, it's . . . I understand
22		them, but it's, <u>maybe my child, is, I think I</u>
23		<u>need a psychologist, maybe I need, yeah.</u>

(Salsbury & Bardovi-Harlig, 2001, p. 144f.)

In all three of her turns, MR conveys hypotheticality without the conventionalized L2 grammatical forms, as is apparent from rendering the underlined utterances in a target version: *If you had a boyfriend who was gay and you did not know about it, that would be bad* (lines 7–10); *If you had a child that was gay, wouldn't that bother you?* (lines 17–18) (Salsbury & Bardovi-Harlig, p. 146); *If my child was gay, I might need a psychologist* (lines 22–23). As Salsbury and Bardovi-Harlig comment, MR's pre-conditionals are composed without the conjunction *if*, the conditional past tense, and modal verbs such as *will* and *may*. But MR conveys conditionality through the modal expressions *I think* and *maybe*. We will have more to say about the multifunctional (over-)use of these modal devices later in this chapter.

Further support for Koike's conclusion is provided by scholars working in a functional-linguistic framework. In the early stages of adult second language acquisition, learners perform actions in L2 in a "pragmatic mode" (Givón, 1979), in which heavy reliance on situational and discourse context enables them to accomplish tasks for which they lack grammatical knowledge. Several extensive European studies of predominantly untutored adult second language acquisition, such as the EFS project and the Project on *"Modalität in Lernervarietäten im Längsschnitt"* (a longitudinal study of learner varieties, or P-MoLL, e.g., Dittmar & Ahrenholz, 1995), document how learners of German as a second language perform instructions in pragmatic mode by using verbless directives or directives including formulaic, uninflected verb forms, as in extracts (5.2) and (5.3) from Ahrenholz (2000).

(5.2) Angelina giving instruction (12 months of residence in Germany)

mit de   journal   de aschenbäsch in de boors
with the newspaper the ashtray   in the bag

(Please put) the ashtray (with the help of) the newspaper in the bag.

und eh kom   de(r) stühl
and uh come (to) the chair

(adapted from Ahrenholtz, 2000, p. 349f)

(5.3) Franca giving instruction (6 months of residence in Germany)

du e:hm ah (.) (eh come si puo dire) (3) das tasche
you um ah   (uh how can you say)   the bag
ier   eh in eh: fussbo:den
here uh in uh floor

You (can put) the bag here on the floor.

(adapted from Ahrenholz, 2000, p. 354)

The modal conditions underlying these instructions (and instructional directives generically), nonfactuality (the action has not yet been done) and necessity (the action is necessary to achieve the goal of the instruction, Dietrich, 1992), are conveyed implicitly in these early learner utterances, whereas the object, goal, and location referents are expressed through explicit and specific nouns.

Turning to a very different learner population, Walters (1980) found that ESL-speaking children and adolescents between the ages of 7 and 15 addressed appropriately polite request strategies with ungrammatical forms to adult recipients. The most elementary request realizations only made reference to the requestive goal.

(5.4) Basic requests

Rice . . . Rice.

Ticket?

Card?

(Walters, 1980, p. 341)

These requests illustrate some properties of a developmental stage called the "pre-basic variety" in functional-linguistic theories of learner varieties (Klein, Dietrich, & Noyeau, 1995, p. 262):

(A) They are lexical; they mainly consist of bare nouns, adjectives, verbs, adverbials, and a few particles

(B) There is no functional inflection

⋮

(D) They are heavily context-dependent.

From a pragmatic perspective, Walters (1980) elaborates (D) by noting that the requests "rely heavily on context, both linguistic (previous utterances in the conversation) and sociocultural (the status and ability of the addressee to comply)" (p. 341). Although it is not clear from the cited request utterances how they were tailored to addressee status, they do demonstrate the children's sociopragmatic ability to enact the required directives and specify the requestive goal at the pre-basic stage of grammatical ability. Likewise, the earliest request utterances by Ellis's (1992) adolescent learners cited in Chapter 4 illustrate request performance at the pre-basic stage of grammatical development.

At the "post-basic" end of the learner varieties continuum, Walters (1980) shows that children successfully encode the action and appropriately mark their requests for politeness with more complex yet partially non-target-like grammar.

(5.5) Post-basic requests

(1) We borrow your basketball please?

(2) We can go in front of you?

(3) You give me the paper?

(4) Can you tell me where is the can openers, please?

(5) Do you know where is the can opener?

(6) Do you give me 35 cents for the lunch?

(7) May you give us the towels to clean-up our milk?

(8) Can you know where is the can opener?

(9) Are you have some rice?

(Walters, 1980, p. 341, numbering added)

Since these are cross-sectional data from several learners, analysis of the grammatical knowledge they display must be tentative. However, it is still insightful to describe them in terms of hypothetical grammatical development. Within the framework of processability theory (Pienemann, 1998), the request utterances display quite different developmental stages. Other things being equal, the canonical word order for question formation in (1), (2), and (3) places the learners at the stage of category procedure (Pienemann's stage 2). In (9), the fronted "are" appears to be a form of marking questions, one process of the stage of phrasal procedure (Pienemann's stage 3). Sentences (5) and (6) could be produced by learners who have acquired do-fronting but not yet the morphological forms of *do*, resulting in such utterances as *do she know*. In that case, (5) and (6) could be evidence for the phrasal procedure level, just as (9). If the same learners also produced *does she know*, however, this could be taken to demonstrate control of interphrasal information exchange marked by subject-verb agreement, which would place the learner at S-procedure level 5. In (4), (7), and (8), the learners produced yes/no inversion and different modal verbs, suggesting that they are able to apply a level 4 S-procedure. (S-procedures refer to interphrasal information exchange). The uninverted auxiliaries following the embedded wh-clauses in these utterances indicate that these learners have not yet reached the subordinate clause procedure (stage 6), which enables cancellation of inversion (Pienemann, 1998, p. 171). According to one theory of grammatical development, then, these utterances suggest different acquisitional stages, although they do not differ with regard to their illocutionary and politeness functions. However, the ungrammatical choices of modal verbs (7, 8) and the use of periphrastic "do" (6) and nonmodalized intonation questions (1, 3) instead of modal verbs show that the learners have not yet worked out the grammar and the pragmalinguistics of modal verbs in requests.

Turning to a yet another speech act category, Eisenstein and Bodman's (1986, 1993) study of expressions of gratitude showed how advanced ESL learners provided pragmalinguistically appropriate thanking strategies with ungrammatical forms.

(5.6) Thanking expressions use by advanced learners

Intensifiers:	I very appreciate
Tense:	I never forget you kindness
Word order:	I'll pay back you
Idiom:	This is the thing what I've wanted; thank you. Sound is good
Prepositions:	That's very nice from you; I hope to see you by us
Word choice:	I have never taken such a good dinner; it is so glad to me that I have such kind of good friend

(Eisenstein & Bodman, 1986, p. 175; 1993, p. 69)

The grammatical errors may make these thanking expressions less effective, but they are not *pragma*linguistic errors, and the ungrammatical features do not convey illocutionary force or politeness.

There is thus ample evidence from different learner populations—children and adults, second and foreign language learners, and learners acquiring different target languages—that when performing action in L2, beginning learners rely on a pragmatic mode when they have not yet developed the grammatical resources available to more expert speakers. More advanced learners may still produce ungrammatical utterances in L2 speech act performance, but if such ungrammatical features have no pragmalinguistic impact, they do not influence the illocutionary act or politeness value of such speech act realizations.

Grammar Precedes Pragmatics

The pragmatics literature cites rich evidence of L2 use, often produced by advanced learners, in which correct grammar is deployed in pragmalinguistically or sociopragmatically non-target-like fashion (Bardovi-Harlig, 2001). As we will discuss in this section, the grammar-precedes-pragmatics scenario comes in three different forms.

1. Learners demonstrate knowledge of a particular grammatical structure or element but do not use it to express or modify illocutionary force.

2. Learners demonstrate knowledge of a grammatical structure and use it to express pragmalinguistic functions that are not conventionalized in the target language.

3. Learners demonstrate knowledge of a grammatical structure *and* its pragmalinguistic functions yet put the pragmalinguistic form-function mapping to non-target-like sociopragmatic use.

We will examine each of these varieties in turn.

Grammatical Knowledge Does Not Enable Pragmalinguistic Use

The first form of the grammar-precedes-pragmatics scenario is well illustrated by studies designed to implement Bardovi-Harlig's (1999) research agenda. In a one-year longitudinal study, Salsbury and Bardovi-Harlig (2000, 2001) examined the emergence of modality in beginning ESL learners. The researchers compared the learners' acquisitional profiles in context-free modality inventories with the learners' use of modals in performing disagreements during oral interviews. Despite considerable variability in learners' modality profiles, modal expressions emerged in a consistent acquisitional pattern:

maybe > think > can > will > would > could

However, availability of modal verbs in learners' grammars did not necessarily translate to the use of these verbs in mitigating disagreement. Salsbury and Bardovi-Harlig (2000) observe that "even learners with grammaticalized expressions of modality rely heavily on lexical forms to unambiguously mark their pragmatic intent" (p. 73). A similar observation was made in earlier cross-sectional research on epistemic modality in interlanguage pragmatics. In her study of epistemic expressions in the English of

Finnish learners, Kärkkäinen (1992) found that lower-proficiency learners mainly modified their speech acts by parentheticals such as *I think* and *I know*. The higher-proficiency learners opted more frequently for modal adverbs and modal verbs, though not as frequently as the native speakers of English in her study, as indicated by the results summarized in Table 5.1. Kärkkäinen's findings suggest that implicit, syntactically integrated, nonroutinized expressions of epistemic modality are more difficult to acquire than explicit, extra-clausal (parenthetical), and routinized expressions.

A clear developmental pattern exemplifying how available forms do not enable concurrent pragmalinguistic use is seen in the acquisition of modal particles by adult naturalistic acquirers of German as a second language. In German, a number of lexical items that primarily function as adverbs and conjunctions have been grammaticalized as modal particles and are used both in their primary and modal meanings. Rost-Roth (1999) reports how her Italian participant Franca, whom we have already met in the work of Ahrenholz (2000), acquired the primary lexical meanings of these forms and their use as modal particles during four years of observation. The emergence of the particles in their two functions is summarized in Table 5.2.

Table 5.1

Relative Frequency of Epistemic Markers (Ratio Epistemic Markers / Total Words)

English NSs	Adverbs	Parentheticals	Modals	Adjectives
	0.71	0.45	0.45	0.13
NNS high	Adverbs	Parentheticals	Modals	Adjectives
	0.59	0.56	0.38	0.14
NNS low	Parentheticals	Adverbs	Modals	Adjectives
	0.74	0.36	0.24	0.22

Note. From "Modality as a Strategy in Interaction: Epistemic Modality in the Language of Native and Non-Native Speakers of English," by E. Kärkkäinen, 1992, in L. F. Bouton and Y. Kachru (Eds.), *Pragmatics and Language Learning,* p. 204. Urbana-Champaign, IL: Division of English as an International Language, University of Illinois, Urbana-Champaign.

Table 5.2

First Emergence of Particles in Franca's Production

Particle (Total Frequency in Corpus)	Realization in Primary Function	Realization Permitting Both Readings	Realization as Modal Particle
auch (424)	4th month	11th month	11th month
mal (46)	4th month	—	18th month
ja (2716)	4th month	24th month	31st month
aber (844)	4th month	—	—
nur (148)	4th month	—	—
vielleicht (376)	5th month	20th month	18th month
einfach (22)	14th month	—	28th month
schon (74)	18th month	34th month	32nd month
erst (7)	18th month	—	—
*denn** (3)	20th month	—	20th month
*halt** (1)	26th month	—	—
doch (9)	28th month	—	—
ruhig (5)	28th month	—	—

Note. Adapted from "Der Erwerb der Modalpartikeln. Eine Fallstudie zum Partikelerwerb einer italienschen Deutschlernerin im Vergleich mit anderen Lernervarietäten" [The Acquisition of Modal particles. A Case Study of the Particle Acquisition by an Italian Learner of German in Comparison With Other Learner Varieties], by M. Rost-Roth, 1999, in N. Dittmar and A. Giacalone Ramat (Eds.), *Grammatik und Diskurs / Grammatica e discorso. Studi sull'acquisizione dell'italiano e del tedescho / Studien zum Erwerb des Deutschen und des Italienischen* [Grammar and Discourse. Studies of the Acquisition of German and Italian], p. 174 (with frequencies added from p. 172). Tübingen, Germany: Stauffenberg.

As Table 5.2 shows, Franca was using the forms *auch, mal, ja, aber,* and *nur* in their nonmodal functions from her fourth month of residence in Germany, when the observation period started. Franca began using these forms as modal particles in months 11 (*auch*), 18 (*mal*), and 24/31 (*ja*). *Mal,* for instance, appeared early in its primary meaning as a temporal referent (for instance, to repeating events, as in *einmal, zweimal* "once," "twice"), whereas it only showed up as a modal particle (MP) in such unanalyzed routines as *guck mal* "look MP" and *sag mal* "say MP" (p. 182). The functional restriction of *mal* is also reported in other learner varieties of German (p. 183). In Franca's production across a variety of speech activities, unambiguous modal particle use of *aber* and *nur* were not registered at all during the four years of observation. Particularly remarkable is Franca's use of the particle *ja*, a form that she deployed in its primary functions as answer particle, listener response token, tag question, and connector from the earliest learning stage. In Franca's German interlanguage as well as in the productions of native-speaker controls, *ja* was, by a long shot, the most frequently used particle. However, of the 2716 *ja* tokens in the total of Franca's productions, only the three included in example (5.7) had a modal or partially modal reading.

> (5.7) Franca's use of *ja* as a modal particle
>
> (24th month)
> aber es war ja (.) ehm mit chaos
> but it was (M)P uh with chaos
> *But it was chaotic.*
>
> (31st month)
> danach kannst du ja die zwei eh pole
> then   can   you MP the two uh poles
> *Then you can (connect the wires to) the two poles.*
>
> (51st month)
> äh sie wollte   ja (so)
> uh she wanted MP (like that)
> *She wanted it (this way).*

The late emergence and sparse use of *ja* as a marker of epistemic modality in the discourse of Franca and other GSL learners contrasts sharply with its high frequency in native-speaker inter-action, where it indexes knowledge or assessments as shared between speaker and hearer.

(5.8) *ja* as modal particle by native speakers of German

is ja   wohl selbstverständlich
is MP MP   obvious
That's obvious isn't it.

ne halbe stelle bringt ja   nich soviel   geld
a half job   brings MP not so much money
*A half-time job doesn't bring in that much money
does it.*"

(adapted from Rost-Roth, 1999, p. 186f.)

Neither input frequency nor its consistent pragmalinguistic role as a marker of epistemic stance when positioned utterance-medially appears to facilitate the acquisition of *ja* as a modal particle by GSL learners. What may make *ja* in its epistemic function difficult to acquire is its syntactic placement and phonological composition. In informal spoken discourse, the particle's most common habitat, it appears syntactically and prosodically integrated, unstressed, and somewhat phonologically reduced. The low perceptual salience of the modal particle contrasts markedly with the exposed turn- or utterance-initial position of *ja* as an answer or response particle, or its utterance- or turn-final position as a question tag (*du kommst doch auch ja?*). In addition to these structural properties, which make modal *ja* less noticeable, its meaning is more opaque than those of the nonmodal usages. Of course, the fact that all modal particles are indexicals makes them a challenging learning task. As modal markers, they do not have a clearly circumscribed symbolic meaning, requiring learners to first notice, understand, and store in memory their situated meanings over a range of instances and then abstract from the instances generalizable indexical functions. Given the complexity of interactions that adult learners often have to cope with, it is perhaps not surprising that using modal particles productively is a very late item on natural acquirers' learning agenda.

Moving from particles to syntax, the relationship between syntactic structures and their illocutionary and politeness functions is an issue in S. Takahashi's studies on transferability (1996) and input enhancement (2001) of request strategies. In both studies, Takahashi found that advanced Japanese EFL students rejected the bi-clausal "I was wondering if you could VP" and "Would it be possible for you to VP," opting for mono-clausal structures such as "would/could you (please) VP" instead. Although no independent grammar test was conducted, the students had evidently been taught and understood the semantics of the bi-clausal structure. Takahashi (2001) concluded that "the Japanese EFL learners lack the L2 pragmalinguistic knowledge that an English request can be mitigated to a greater extent by making it syntactically more complex" (p. 173). In another study examining the request performance of Japanese college-level EFL students, Hill (1997) found that the progressive aspect as a syntactic mitigator was almost completely absent, whereas in a native English-speaking control group, the progressive was the single most frequent internal modifier: 46% of the native requests were modified by *I was wondering if* or the like. While these students clearly knew the primary semantics of the progressive as a grammaticalized aspectual category, they did not seem to understand that the progressive can be used with mitigating function.

Grammatical Knowledge Enables Non-Target-Like
Pragmalinguistic Use

A somewhat different form of the grammar-before-pragmatics scenario is observed when learners do put available grammatical knowledge to pragmalinguistic use, but such deployments diverge from target practice. Early emergence and/or high input frequency of particular form-function mappings are not necessarily related to target-like use. The lower-proficiency Finnish EFL learners in Kärkkäinen's (1992) study deployed parentheticals more than twice as often than adverbs, but especially the most common formula, *I think*, was often used "slightly unidiomatically" (p. 206), as in extract (5.9) (p. 209).

(5.9) NNS student has broken the TV set in a dormitory lounge

NS: Well, I'm kind of er in charge of it now and I found out that it's broken.

NNS: Yes, and I think I'm responsible for that.

In addition to Finnish-English discourse, the overuse and pragmatic overextension of *I think* as an epistemic expression has been noted in the interlanguage performance of learners with very different native language backgrounds, such as Spanish (Salsbury & Bardovi-Harlig, 2001, see above), Japanese (LoCastro & Netsu, 1997), and German (Kasper, 1981). Most of these authors refer to L1 transfer as one possible contributing factor that reinforces those semantic, syntactic, and processing properties of the routine that make it learners' all-time favorite epistemic marker, that is, its explicitness, extra-sentential position, and—because it does not require morphosyntactic exchange with other sentence elements—low processing costs.

At the more advanced stages of interlanguage development, learners can be found to accomplish action in L2 by using sophisticated grammatical knowledge that is, however, outside the scope of conventionalized L2 pragmalinguistic usage. Bodman and Eisenstein (1988) cite learners' transliterated thanking routines in their expressions of gratitude in English:

(5.10) Transliterated thanking expressions

May God increase your bounty.

May God grant you a long life.

You are a blessing to us from God.

As noted in Chapter 4, evidence of advanced grammatical knowledge put to pragmatically inappropriate use led Takahashi and Beebe (1987) to propose the positive correlation hypothesis, according to which advanced learners' superior grammatical knowledge enables negative pragmatic transfer.

Grammatical and Pragmalinguistic Knowledge Enable
Non-Target-Like Sociopragmatic Use

The third form of learners' grammar preceding their pragmatics is in evidence when learners know a grammatical structure
and its pragmalinguistic functions yet demonstrate lack of familiarity with the contextual and sociopragmatic conditions that
constrain target-like use. Several studies report on learners' use
of information questions as indirect strategies in requests for
action, warning, disagreeing, refusing, rejecting, or criticizing, in
contexts where more transparent strategies would be more
effective (e.g., Bardovi-Harlig & Hartford, 1991; Beebe & Takahashi, 1989a, 1989b). Extract (5.11) is from Bardovi-Harlig and
Hartford's advising session data (1991). The advisor wants the
student to take Linguistics 560. The student responds with a
series of questions.

> (5.11) Linguistics 560 (A = faculty advisor, S = graduate
> student)

	A:	Yeah. Are you going to be here next fall?
	S:	Mmmmm. Exactly, no. Actually, actually.
	A:	Then you'll have to do L560.
→	S:	Which one is that one? Oh.
	A:	It's American Culture.
→	S:	That one's required?
	A:	Yes it is. It's right . . . there.
→	S:	It's American Culture. What time is it? 4:20. [mumbles as looks at schedule] (softly) L560. This was . . . I was thinking if I could take your class Mondays and Wednes-days. 15 credits. It'd be crazy, too many credits.

[20 turns later]

	S:	So you know about 560, who teaches?
→	A:	Mr. Smith
→	S:	Mr. Smith, is the one who is next to Professor Brown?
	A:	No, no, Mr. Smith is not here. He's in Malaysia, so he'll be back next semester.

→   S: OK. Mr. Smith is twice a week. Do you have any idea what the syllabus is like? Do you have to write a paper, do you have to

      A: Ah yes. But I don't think it's going to be terribly difficult for you. I, I don't think it's going to be a real problem.

      S: Umm. I wish I could also take language testing.

(Bardovi-Harlig & Hartford, 1991, p. 47f.)

The use of the question strategy demonstrates that this student both has the grammar to form interrogatives and the pragmalinguistic knowledge to deploy questions in order to convey pragmatic intent indirectly. The non-target-like question use is indicative of the student's pragmalinguistic competence, not incompetence. However, it also suggests that the student does not have the sociopragmatic knowledge to assess when the use of a question strategy is appropriate and effective. Repeated questions as a strategy to convey rejection may be valued as less imposing than more direct rejections in some communities and therefore as a favored way of performing a dispreferred act, especially in institutional interaction with a status-higher interlocutor. But to many graduate advisors at North American universities, putting on them the onus of inferring the student's obliquely conveyed reluctance to take a proposed course is probably more imposing than an illocutionary transparent and mitigated rejection. Not surprisingly, Bardovi-Harlig and Hartford (1990) did not observe the question strategy in the rejections of native American English-speaking students.

A pragmatically famous, but no less hazardous, use of a question strategy was reported by Beebe and Takahashi (1989a), who observed how a customer in a sushi bar warned another guest about having her bag stolen by asking *Do you have a bag?* When communicative efficiency is at a premium—not only in a New York sushi bar but also in other North American contexts—abiding more closely by the Gricean maxims would be viewed as consistent rather than in conflict with polite conduct.

Pragmalinguistic knowledge and concomitant lack of sociopragmatic knowledge is also evident in Japanese ESL learners' verbal protocols, collected by M. A. Robinson (1992) in a study of refusals. Prompted to refuse to help a friend with her house moving, one learner responded as in extract (5.12a).

(5.12a) Refusing, DCT response

I hate to say that I can't help you, but on Sunday *I want to study* at libraly, because I should prepare for the term paper, the due date of it is Tuesday.

The concurrent verbal protocol (5.12b) revealed the learner's decision-making process that resulted in the choice of the volitional expression *I want*:

(5.12b) Refusing, concurrent verbal protocol

... on Sunday I will – I will – uh – I would I would like – I will – on Sunday – um – um yeah *friends would like is too polite* so uh – I want – okay I sa I want – I want to study – to study – um – I want to study - at library

(M. A. Robinson, 1992, p. 58, italics added)

The learner's self-repairs in the think-aloud protocol show not only that she knew the form *I would like* but also that she knew that *I would like* is more polite than *I want*. Her grammatical and pragmalinguistic knowledge were demonstrably intact. Where she went wrong was in her sociopragmatic hypothesis that *would like* is "too polite" when talking to American friends. As Scarcella (1979) noted, "adult L2 performers seem to use politeness features before they have acquired their co-occurrence and appropriate distribution" (p. 285).

Less dramatic but worth noting all the same is the observation that learners may overproduce a target pragmalinguistic strategy because their grammatical competence enables them to do so. Hill (1997) reports that with improved grammatical proficiency, the Japanese EFL students in his study increased their use of conditionals as a syntactic modifier of requests, as in extract (5.13).

(5.13) Conditional requests

If you don't in a hurry, please take me to the station (low EFL)

If you don't mind, I want to use your computer (intermediate EFL)

If possible, could you let me borrow it (advanced EFL)

Native English-speaking controls made very little use of conditionals in the same request contexts. Unlike the pragmalinguistic conventions discussed earlier in this section, the learners' requests were both pragmalinguistically and sociopragmatically target-like, yet using conditionals as a request strategy was not "done" (in Hymesian terms) that much by the native-speaker group. Hill notes that the overuse of hypothetical conditionals was very likely the result of transfer from Japanese since 51% of the Japanese requests in his pilot study contained this request strategy, such as *otsukai ja nakattara* "if you're not using it" or *moshi yokattara* "if it's ok."

Pragmatics and Grammar in Developmental Perspective

As the discussion in this chapter suggests, the relationship between pragmatics and grammar in learners' developing interlanguage is complex. The research evidence we have provided supports two seemingly incompatible hypotheses, namely, that communicative language ability moves from pragmatics to grammar and from grammar to pragmatics. In a double sense, this inconclusive state of affairs is an artifact of the levels at which the issue is often pitched—the level of learners' L2 development, and the level of specificity by which questions about the pragmatics-grammar nexus are asked.

In our discussion of the primacy of pragmatics, we referred to the functional-linguistic notion of a "pragmatic mode" that organizes L2 use in pre-basic varieties. The pragmatic knowledge that beginning learners draw on is composed of pragmatic universals and language and culture-specific practices, both of which become available to L2 learners through prior experience in one or more (necessarily diverse) speech communities and multiple communities of practice (Eckert, 2000). As shown without fail in longitudinal studies of uninstructed (or predominantly uninstructed) adult second language acquisition that started the observation period as closely as possible to the participants' arrival in the target language community, adult learners' initial participation in L2 interaction relies on the pragmatic mode for organizing whatever rudimentary L2 grammatical knowledge they have. As far as pragmatic categories are concerned, beginning adult learners, unlike children, have a head start (e.g., Bialystok, 1993; Koike, 1989). This is well illustrated by studies on the acquisition of deontic and epistemic modality in L2 German and Italian (Giacalone Ramat & Crocco Galèas, 1995). As Giacalone Ramat (1995) notes, "there is a contrast between what is found in first language acquisition where deontic modality clearly precedes epistemic modality, and second language acquisition, where both modal categories are present from the very beginning, although expressed by very different means" (p. 275). Giacalone Ramat's last clause points to one—perhaps the most important—reason for the seemingly contradictory research outcomes on patterns of pragmatic and grammatical development.

Adults learning L2 Italian and German obviously possess knowledge of epistemic and deontic modality, but more than that, they express both types of modality from early on and develop L2 resources to do so concurrently (Dittmar & Ahrenholz, 1995). However, beginning learners express deontic modality by means of modal verbs, whereas they express epistemic modality through cognitive verbs and epistemic adverbs, but not through modal verbs. Our friend Franca, for instance, produced the deontic modal verbs *wollen*, *können*, and *müssen* in the fourth month of her residence in Germany. She conveyed epistemic modality through such cognitive verbs as *wissen*, *kennen*, *glauben*, *denken*, *finden*, and the pervasive and very early use of the adverb *vielleicht* (maybe). Throughout the four-year observation period, epistemic modal verbs were not recorded in Franca's production. In order to understand the relationship of pragmatics and grammar in early learner varieties, pragmatic categories, no matter whether they are expressed in a non-target-like manner, have to be distinguished from the linguistic forms by which they are conveyed.

But what about the large body of research findings demonstrating that learners have the grammar but do not use it in pragmatically effective ways? In post-basic varieties, learners have established an increasing range of L2 grammatical forms and achieved some control over such forms, usually deploying them in their primary functions. For instance, verbs will be marked for tense and aspect to convey temporal relationship, although not always all at once, or necessarily in a target-like way (Bardovi-Harlig, 2000; Dietrich et al., 1995). But it will take far longer for learners to notice and achieve control over secondary meanings, such as using past tense and the progressive aspect as mitigation devices in L2 English. At this stage, then, the order of acquiring grammar and pragmatics appears to be reversed—form precedes function, as Klein et al. (1995) concluded with respect to the development of temporality in post-basic learner varieties, and Scarcella (1979) noted with respect to the politeness functions and contextual distribution of grammatical forms. But it has to be kept in mind that adult learners have the concept of mitigation and, when beyond the elementary stages, mitigate requests or other face-threatening acts through various grammatical devices. Their learning task is now to work out the pragmatic meanings to which grammatical forms can be put. In this process, L1 grammar and pragmatics can be a help or hindrance. As we saw earlier, Japanese learners of English used conditionals as request mitigators from a low-proficiency level onward, whereas even advanced learners did not deploy progressive aspect as a mitigating device. As Hill (1997) noted, conditionals are frequently used by Japanese speakers as polite requests, whereas the progressive cannot take on a mitigating function in Japanese.

To conclude, then, in their development of L2 pragmatics and grammar, adult learners face different learning tasks at different developmental stages: in the very early phases they build on their available pragmatic knowledge, making do with whatever L2 grammar they have and at the same time acquiring the grammar needed to accomplish actions in L2. As learners progress, their learning task increasingly changes to figuring out the various pragmatic, often secondary meanings that specific grammatical forms have beyond their primary meaning(s). This process will evolve differently for different grammatical forms and their pragmatic meanings, and will depend, among other things, on the activities learners engage in and on whether grammatical and pragmatic knowledge of other languages helps to acquire new L2 pragmatic meanings of grammatical forms.

Research exploring in depth the development of L2 pragmatics and grammar as its focal investigative question is still scarce. In her programmatic paper on this issue, Bardovi-Harlig (1999) recommends that such studies should be conducted longitudinally, starting the observation period at the beginning stages of L2 acquisition and collecting authentic data. Several European projects of adult second language acquisition that we referred to in this chapter have enriched our understanding of pragmatic and grammatical development substantially by adopting these design features. Furthermore, they demonstrated the advantages of very long observation periods such as two to four years.

After reviewing more of the literature than we were able to discuss in this chapter, we would like to add some further recommendations for future research on the pragmatics-grammar connection. First, the activity that participants engage in shapes their contributions functionally and formally. Therefore, resources permitting, it is preferable to record learners longitudinally on a variety of activities, as in the ESF project and P-MoLL. Data analysis should be activity-specific so that it allows for comparison of learners' performance across activities. When learners are observed only in one particular activity type, generalizations to performance in other activities or to "general" pragmatic and grammatical development will best be made in the form of hypotheses that can be put to the test in future studies that examine learner performance on different activities. Second, transcriptions of discourse gain much from including temporal, prosodic, sequential, and preferably nonverbal information because such phenomena of speech production and interactional conduct can be decisive for the analysis of pragmatic and grammatical development. A conversation-analytic transcription format (e.g., Hutchby & Wooffitt, 1998) is advisable for analyzing learner performance in interaction. Third, even though the focus remains on the learner, it is often impossible to analyze learner contributions correctly without placing them (leaving them, rather) in the interactional context in which they occur. Even if the research interest centers on, say, the learner's expression of epistemic modality or the performance of instructions, it is crucial to examine the interlocutor's preceding and response turns and to conduct a sequential analysis of the evolving interaction. Finally, the research report is more informative if it presents sufficiently contextualized data excerpts. Presenting multiturn segments of the interaction allows readers to act as co-analysts and thereby increases the reliability of the study (Peräkylä, 1997).

Chapter Summary

This chapter started out by underscoring the need for examining the relationship of pragmatic and grammatical development rather than focusing on each component of communicative competence separately. Specifically, we followed Bardovi-Harlig (1999) in recommending that research scrutinize how particular pragmalinguistic features emerge in relation to particular grammatical structures. We then discussed research evidence supporting two seemingly contradictory tendencies in adult learners' development of pragmatic and grammatical knowledge: evidence that pragmatics precedes grammar, and evidence that grammar precedes pragmatics. In order to capture the robust theoretical and empirical support for the developmental move from pragmatics to grammar, we proposed (adapting Ochs, 1996) a universal pragmatics principle, which specifies the discourse, pragmatic, and sociolinguistic competencies that adult learners bring to the task of acquiring the pragmatics of an additional language. Functional-grammatical approaches to adult second language acquisition in nontutored settings conceptualize L2 use in the earliest stages as determined by a pragmatic mode, in which learners accomplish actions in a pregrammaticalized fashion by relying on situational and discourse context in conjunction with whatever L2 knowledge they have available. While the acquisitional direction from pragmatics to grammar characterizes the early (especially untutored) stages of pragmatic development, the reverse appears to be the case with more advanced learners who "have the grammar." Here, we find three scenarios in which learners do not put to use their grammatical knowledge in ways that more expert language users would. First, learners demonstrate knowledge of a particular grammatical structure or element but do not use it to express or modify illocutionary force. Second, they demonstrate knowledge of a grammatical structure and use it to express pragmalinguistic functions that are not conventional in the target language. And third, learners demonstrate knowledge of a grammatical structure *and* its pragmalinguistic functions yet put the pragmalinguistic form-function mapping to non-target-like sociopragmatic use. Putting the evidence on early and later acquisitional stages together, it appears that learners at different stages of pragmalinguistic development face different learning tasks: early learners have acquired the L2 grammatical means to express already existing pragmatic categories, whereas later learners have to tease out the pragmatic meanings to which their now available L2 grammatical knowledge can be put. We closed the chapter by making a few recommendations for research on the pragmatics-grammar nexus in developmental perspective.

CHAPTER SIX

Learning Context and Learning Opportunities

In Chapters 4 and 5, we discussed, among other things, the knowledge and ability that adult learners bring to the task of acquiring L2 pragmatics and how they draw on L1 grammatical and pragmatic knowledge at different stages of L2 development. In this chapter, we shift our focus to the role of the environment in pragmatic development. Language acquisition requires that learners have access to the target language, and specifying this fundamental condition of language learning has engaged researchers of diverse theoretical persuasions for almost four decades. Despite the progress that has been made in both first and second language acquisition research, considerable controversy remains concerning the type of data that learners need to develop communicative competence, and how these data can be obtained most effectively. Second language acquisition researchers working in a cognitive-psychological and interactional framework recognize Corder's (1967) distinction between "input" and "intake" (though they do not necessarily use these terms). Input consists of the communicative data available to the learner in her environment, whereas intake comprises the subset of input that is "noticed" (Schmidt & Frota, 1986) or "apperceived" (Gass, 1997) and thereby made available for further processing. Some of the enduring research issues in this area focus on determining the properties of input with the greatest acquisitional benefits to learners, the role of the learner and her interlocutors in acquisitional terms, the role of feedback (positive and negative) in the learning process, and the acquisitional functions of the learners' own production. Some of these issues have been addressed in the interlanguage pragmatics literature, but for the most part, the research literature on the role of the environment in pragmatic development has addressed broader issues. This chapter will be structured along these broader lines, reviewing more specific findings when relevant. One putative environmental variable in second language acquisition is the learner's length of residence in the target community. We start by reviewing what is known about the impact of duration of stay on pragmatic development. Next, we examine the opportunities for obtaining L2 pragmatic input and engaging in interaction in different learning environments, including uninstructed settings and institutional discourse. We then turn to the opportunities to learn L2 pragmatics under instructed but noninterventional conditions. Lastly, we will scrutinize research that compares the pragmatic ability of L2 learners in second and foreign language learning contexts, including the effect of study abroad on pragmatic development.

Length of Residence as a Factor in Pragmatic Development: The Longer the Better?

The first study that addressed the question of the effect of length of residence in an L2 community of pragmatic development, and answered it in the affirmative, was conducted by Olshtain and Blum-Kulka (1985). Using a metapragmatic assessment task in a cross-sectional design, they investigated whether with longer duration of stay in Israel, nonnative speakers' assessments of contextualized request and apology strategies in Hebrew increasingly converged with native-speaker judgments. Based on Brown and Levinson's politeness theory, they hypothesized that nonnative speakers of Hebrew from diverse L1 backgrounds would gradually shift from a preference for negative politeness to a positive politeness orientation and a higher tolerance for directness. With regard to the subset of pragmatic strategies that differed significantly between native-speaker ratings and judgments by immigrants who had stayed in Israel for less than two years, their prediction was borne out. As Table 6.1 shows, over time, immigrants increased their high acceptance of "optimistic," that is, compliance-expecting strategies.

Consistent with native-speaker assessments, immigrants' increased preference for positive politeness was differentially pronounced in different contexts and varied with such factors as the requestive goal, as illustrated by the different ratings for the request utterances in Table 6.1. But approximation to a pragmatics of positive politeness as an index of low social distance was still evident in the ratings of these request utterances, as it was for the explicit but brief and nonintensified apology in response to a space offense, which showed the most dramatic increase in acceptance across the learner groups. In a similar vein, over time, immigrants developed a more positive view of direct request strategies and

Table 6.1

Developmental Increase in High Acceptance of Positively Polite Requests and Apologies

	Length of Residence in Israel			
Request or Apology Utterance	Less Than Two Years	Two–Ten Years	More Than Ten Years	Hebrew NS
Say, could you lend me 100IS until next week? (To a friend)	47%	56%	57%	61%
Is it possible perhaps to go to town with you? (Asking acquaintance for a ride)	51%	77%	86%	80%
I'm sorry (When bumping into other customer with shopping cart)	55%	64%	93%	95%

Note. Adapted from "Degree of Approximation: Nonnative Reactions to Native Speech Act Behavior," by E. Olshtain and S. Blum-Kulka, 1985, in S. Gass and C. Madden (Eds.), *Input in Second Language Acquisition*, pp. 319–320. Rowley, MA: Newbury House.

minimizing (in fact, rather nonapologetic) redressive action in the given contexts, as shown in Table 6.2.

But not all of the immigrants' metapragmatic assessments were subject to change. They did not necessarily develop in a linear fashion or converge most strongly with native speaker judgments in the group of immigrants with the longest time of residence in Israel. While all nonnative groups as well as the native speakers of Hebrew accorded conventionally indirect strategies acceptance ratings of 50% and higher, Table 6.3 shows that immigrants who had lived in Israel between two and ten years rated conventional indirectness as appropriate less often than all other groups. The groups with the longest residence increased their acceptance rating again but differed more strongly from native raters than one or both of the lower groups. This may suggest that despite a shared high acceptance of conventional indirectness, long-term immigrants and Israelis held different views of the contexts in which conventionally indirect requests were most appropriate.

Olshtain and Blum-Kulka's study shows two main tendencies: immigrants accommodated their assessments of contextualized speech act strategies to community pragmatic norms and

Table 6.2

Developmental Decrease in Rejection of Directness

	Length of Residence in Israel			
Request Utterance	Less Than Two Years	Two–Ten Years	More Than Ten Years	Hebrew NS
Lend me the money please	37%	36%	18%	22%
I hope you can take me back				
to town with you	53%	34%	39%	34%
This can happen, madam, it's				
not so terrible	62%	40%	31%	32%

Note. Adapted from "Degree of Approximation: Nonnative Reactions to Native Speech Act Behavior," by E. Olshtain and S. Blum-Kulka, 1985, in S. Gass and C. Madden (Eds.), *Input in Second Language Acquisition*, p. 320. Rowley, MA: Newbury House.

Table 6.3

Maintained High Acceptance of Conventional Indirectness

	Length of Residence in Israel			
Request or Apology Utterance	Less Than Two Years	Two–Ten Years	More Than Ten Years	Hebrew NS
Say, could you lend me 100IS until next week?	64%	50%	55%	72%
Is it possible perhaps to go to town with you?	68%	61%	78%	62%

Note. Adapted from "Degree of Approximation: Nonnative Reactions to Native Speech Act Behavior," by E. Olshtain and S. Blum-Kulka, 1985, in S. Gass and C. Madden (Eds.), *Input in Second Language Acquisition*, p. 320. Rowley, MA: Newbury House.

such convergence correlated positively with duration of stay, and they continued to accept pragmatic strategies that they viewed as appropriate initially and that were also strongly accepted in the community. It is no coincidence that the second finding applies to conventional indirectness, which Blum-Kulka (1987) had found to be the request strategy preferred by native speakers of Hebrew and American English alike. One problem that compromises the 1985 study is the arbitrary division of duration of stay. Standard deviations were not reported, but the within-group variation in years of residence may well have exceeded the between-group differences, making it impossible to determine the actual relationship between residence and pragmatic accommodation.

Turning from metapragmatic assessment to pragmatic comprehension, in a series of studies, Bouton (e.g., 1992, 1994b, 1999) investigated how length of residence influences nonnative speakers' understanding of implicature in American English. As we reported in Chapter 4, upon arrival in the United States, the international students participating in Bouton's studies successfully understood relevance and minimal requirement implicatures, whereas they diverged from native-speaker controls in their comprehension of formulaic implicatures such as the Pope question, sequence and scalar implicatures, indirect criticism, and irony. With increasing length of residence on a U.S. university campus, they very gradually improved their ability to understand the difficult implicature types, but progress was slow and not complete: after 17 months, they still had problems with the same implicature types as upon arrival. After 33 months, the nonnative group understood sequence implicatures and two out of four indirect criticism items on the multiple-choice questionnaire, whereas they continued to understand the Pope question, irony, and scalar implicatures differently from the native group. After between four and seven years of residence, students effectively understood all implicatures types. Bouton argued that the slow progress in understanding implicature through exposure alone indicates a need for instruction. In Chapter 7, we report how students' implicature comprehension profited from targeted pedagogic intervention. Although Bouton's work does show how the comprehension of implicatures is related to students' length of residence in the target community, one may wonder to what extent pragmatic comprehension and pragmatic ability generally may be influenced by the *quality* of nonnative speakers' exposure and social contacts conducted in English, rather than the quantitative measure of length of residence. As Klein, Dietrich, and Noyau (1995) conclude from their longitudinal study of second language learners' acquisition of temporality,

> Duration of stay is an uninteresting variable. What matters is intensity, not length of interaction. Therefore, ordering learners according to their duration of stay is normally pointless because too crude a measure for what really matters: intensity of interaction. (p. 277)

Although not coterminous with intensity of interaction, L2 input is closely related to the interactions in which learners' participate. While Olshtain and Blum-Kulka (1985) and Bouton (e.g., 1999) do not provide information about the input opportunities afforded to the participants in their studies, other investigations have examined the relationship of input and pragmatic learning in different social settings outside of language classrooms.

Input and Interaction in Noninstructional Settings

Ordinary Discourse

Kim (2000) scrutinized the effect of input in noninstructional settings and two learner variables (i.e., age of arrival in the United States and cultural identity) on Korean ESL speakers' oral and written production of requests and apologies. Variables operationalizing the amount of input outside ESL classrooms were the number of hours per week spent with English-speaking roommates, at an English-speaking workplace, with English-speaking friends (separated into native and nonnative speakers), reading English books, newspapers, magazines, dictionaries, watching television, and listening to the radio. Two of the input variables (i.e., "Time speaking English with native speakers" and "Work experience in English environment") correlated significantly with performance ratings. The last factor showed by far the strongest statistically significant correlation with total amount of informal input. Age of arrival and informal input also correlated significantly. However, regression analysis revealed that there was an interaction among three independent variables—age of arrival, total input, and cultural identity (about which we will have more to say in Chapter 8) and this interaction predicted performance ratings, whereas none of these variables alone was significantly related to performance scores individually.

Examining how age at arrival and input influenced strategy choices in participants' request and apology productions, Kim found that for both speech acts, early arrivals and high-input generators approximated native speakers' strategy distribution more closely than late arrivals and low-input generators. A comparison of the written dialogue completion and oral discourse confirmed a rather stable finding from research on native and nonnative speakers' speech act performance, namely, that the types of speech act strategy tend to be stable across different modalities of data elicitation, whereas their propositional and linguistic implementation is more elaborate in spoken (especially interactive) discourse (but cf. Edmondson & House, 1991). Kim found this pattern repeated in the native-speaker productions and those of high-input generators but not in the performance of low-input generators, irrespective of age of arrival. So, whereas in the dialogue completion task, a high-input generating participant wrote extract (6.1a), she produced extract (6.1b) in the oral task.

(6.1a) High-input generator, written version

I'm so sorry I'm late, something came up last minute.

(6.1b) High-input generator, spoken version

I'm so sorry I'm late. I just got caught up in a conversation and I got kind of heated and I didn't realized how much time it passed.

Low-input generating participants, on the other hand, showed the opposite pattern. Their oral productions were simplified versions of their written responses.

(6.2a) Low-input generator, written version

I didn't write my paper because I have a cold and allergy. I was sleeping all day because I have a headache and my body was very hot. Nose was very terrible.

(6.2b) Low-input generator, spoken version

I didn't write my paper. My condition is no good. I have a cold. My body is no good.

The written and oral responses by the same learner contrast strikingly in control of discourse cohesion, propositional specificity, and syntactic complexity, suggesting that written conditions enabled this learner to perform her competence at a much higher level than oral production, for which she had not yet developed the necessary degree of processing control. If this data sample is representative of the low-input generating group, it points to an important issue for future investigation: how environmental factors such as quality and quantity of input may influence learners' acquisition of pragmatic ability differently according to modalities, activity types, and genres (cf. Perdue, 1993).

Kim's study raises additional questions about the impact of environmental factors relative to other variables as well. One of her dependent variables was age of arrival, reflecting her interest in determining whether a maturational factor may be involved in acquiring pragmatic ability. Age of onset was one factor interacting with input and cultural identity but had no independent effect on speech act production. However, age of arrival was related to amount of input. As the social settings and activities that children and adolescents interact in differ from those in which adults participate, the quality of input will also be quite different (cf. Beebe, 1985; Rampton, 1995). Kim's study, using quantitative measures of input that were not designed to capture qualitative differences in input and interaction, invites subsequent research that explores qualitatively the relationship between target language input to learners at different age levels and the effect of these factors on L2 pragmatic development. Another issue that awaits exploration is the possible interaction of age and length of residence. Since in Kim's study, length of residence was neither a control nor a predictor variable, it is impossible to determine whether effects that appeared to be related to age of arrival may not be effects of duration of stay, or both. Do ESL speakers who arrived in the target community at age 12 and are now 21 produce more native-like requests and apologies than speakers who arrived at age 18 and are now 27? And if indeed they did, would such a difference be due to biological maturation processes, or rather an effect of the socialization that teenagers and young adults experience in different communities of practice, inside and outside of educational institutions? Whereas Kim investigated the role of informal input in long-term residents' L2 pragmatics, most of the studies that remark on the influence of learning context and input in shaping opportunities for learning pragmatics have focused on sojourners who were staying in the host community between a couple of months and several years. Also in contrast to the quantitative studies discussed thus far, the remaining research that we will review in this section has adopted ethnographic and discourse-analytical methodologies. Rather than relating samples of learners' L2 pragmatics to the time spent in the L2 community or domains and activities within the target setting, they investigate learners and their co-participants in concrete interactional engagements. These studies, therefore, document the actual input that learners obtain and permit researchers to assess how qualitative aspects of the input are related to other factors in the host environment.

Two ethnographic studies provide rich insights into the input and interaction opportunities encountered by Anglo European learners of Japanese during sojourns in different cities in Japan. In an investigation of dinner table conversations between Japanese host families and their North American guest students during a home-stay program, Iino (1996) examined how the observed interaction practices were shaped by participants' ethnolinguistic ideologies. Based on a critical macro-sociolinguistic analysis of "auto-exotizing" views of Japanese culture and language (Coulmas, 1992, p. 300), Iino described how the guest students were discursively constructed as *gaijin* (white foreigners) by the host families, a process he referred to as "gaijinization." In his study, gaijinization included such discourse practices as code-switching from the regional dialect (*Kyoto ben*) to the standard Tokyo dialect and various other forms of foreigner talk adjustments that have been reported in the literature on the topic. But Iino also reported actions that were not noted in previous studies and that bore directly on gaijinization, such as particular topic selections. One such topic—in fact, the most common topic in the observed conversations—was to compare Japan with the United States. As Iino acerbically comments, "not only the professional Japanologists but also lay Japanese people seem to have a kind of obsession with comparing and anthropologizing everything from politics to the size of cucumbers between the two nations" (Iino, 1996, p. 235f.; cf. Siegal, 1994, p. 267). In Iino's analysis, the emphasis on and confirmation of presupposed cross-cultural differences was deployed strategically as a "preventive apology from both sides for potential misconduct such as preparation of food, eating manners, and ways of speaking" (p. 237). Not unrelated to the contrastive approach were topics emphasizing the uniqueness of Japanese culture, which might be conveyed pragmatically as compliments that treated trivial skills such as *gaijin* eating with chopsticks as remarkable accomplishments or as criticism for overstepping hard ethnolinguistic boundaries such as *gaijin* enjoying *natto* (fermented bean paste). Iino argues that the Japanese language was treated here as "the same symbolic ethno-emblem as *natto*" (p. 244). Foreigners were not expected to speak Japanese properly, and if they did, they were perceived as *henna gaijin* (strange foreigner). By treating indigenous food, nonstandard dialects, and in fact, the Japanese language as belonging to a restricted culture, some Japanese hosts conveyed the belief that these cultural objects should not be acquired by outsiders, or not in the same way as by cultural members. This exclusivity extended to routine expressions used by the guest students that are pragmatically appropriate in native-speaker interaction and yet elicited laughter and surprise when heard from a nonnative speaker, such as the formula *tsumaranai mono desu kedo douzo* (this is a useless thing, but please accept) said by an American student when she presented a gift to her hosts (p. 220). The input and feedback on the pragmatics of Japanese that students received were thus quite closely related to their hosts' ethnolinguistic attitudes.

In a more comprehensive ethnographic study, Siegal (1994, 1995, 1996) examined how four women of Anglo European ethnicity acquired communicative competence in Japanese during a one-year sojourn in Hiroshima. The participants interacted in a variety of social domains, speech events, and social relationships, took courses in Japanese language and culture, and, to varying extent, studied the written language. The different forms of engagement with Japanese people and language, and especially the positions taken by the learners themselves in different contact environments, significantly shaped their language learning. The ways in which the students were situated by Japanese co-participants and their own stances in various interactional contexts constituted their identities in the host communities in acquisitionally consequential terms. Like Iino, Siegal observed that obtaining input that reflects acceptable and appropriate language use within the Japanese community was not always an easy matter and depended fundamentally on how the nonnative speakers were viewed by Japanese co-participants. In encounters where the social category of foreigner was salient, input opportunities tended to be reduced in quantity and quality. The learners repeatedly experienced service encounters during which clerks would disappear in order not to have to talk to the foreigner. When interactions in various contexts did take place, language addressed to the students was often marked by various features of foreigner talk, such as mixing English words (in Japanese pronunciation) in the Japanese discourse or choosing less polite language than what could be contextually expected, as in this interaction at a travel agency.

> (6.3) At a travel agency
>
> Clerk: *hai*
>   Yes.
> Sally: *konshuu wa kankoku ni ikitai kara (xxxx) kippu o kaemasu ka.*
>   I would like to go to Korea this week, can I buy a ticket?
> Clerk: *hai. dekimasu yo.*
>   Yes. You can *yo.*

(Siegal, 1994, p. 226)

Siegal observed that the opening *hai* conveyed the clerk's availability but not the polite welcome of *irasshaimase* by which another student was greeted at a different travel agency. Also, the sentence-final *yo* rather than *yo ne* lent to the clerk's response a rather aggressive note. In a later encounter, the same clerk addressed Sally by the second person pronoun *anata* ('you'): *anata hitori de yoroshi desu ne* ('You are going by yourself, right'). In native speaker interaction, pronominal reference (instead of position, name, or no explicit address) would not be appropriate in this context. On Siegal's analysis, the foreigner talk adjustment was the marked use of the second person pronoun *anata* (you) as addressed to Sally by the same clerk in a later encounter: *anata hitori de yoroshi desu ne* (you are going by yourself, right). The pronominal reference (instead of position, name, or no explicit address) is inappropriate in native-speaker interaction. The foreigner talk modifications in the native interlocutors' speech provided pragmatically and sociolinguistically distorted input that, rather than facilitating the students' development of communicative competence in Japanese, contributed to non-target-like style-mixing. Similarly, the students' attempts to engage linguistically naïve native speakers as language informants was often unsuccessful because they provided contextually inappropriate lexical items and literal translations of English expressions that were not functionally equivalent in Japanese. From such data, Siegal concluded that "merely being surrounded by a rich context does not necessarily aid in the acquisition of native-like language use and, indeed, can even act as an impediment to native-like language use" (p. 274).

However, the students in Siegal's study experienced *gaijinization* to different degrees—their category membership as Anglo European female foreigners was not always salient, and, consequently, their opportunities for receiving acquisitionally useful input also varied. Foreigner status interacted with, and could effectively be overridden by, social factors that structure interpersonal relationships in Japan, notably age and status. As a woman in her mid-40s, Mary was usually the recipient of polite style in service encounters, whereas the younger participants were spoken to with less formal politeness, as befitting their status and age bracket as students. How consequential social status within the host community can be for learning opportunities was clearly seen in Karen, the only participant in the study who was married, financially well off, and a university teacher. She participated actively in many domains of Japanese society, adopted numerous

aspects of a Japanese lifestyle, and her pragmatic and sociolinguistic ability in Japanese progressed rapidly. However, despite
the fact that the learners' social position within Japanese society
provided differential access to learning opportunities, the richest
context for developing conversational ability in Japanese was
informal conversations with close personal friends. Siegal comments that

> The informal conversations . . . indicate both native
> speaker and non-native speaker use of informal conversa-
> tional forms such as pragmatic particles, modal auxiliaries,
> and *aizuchi* [i.e., listener behavior]; stylistically, nonnative
> speakers were exposed to a conversational style that was
> in many ways typically Japanese, for example, having their
> sentences finished by native speakers and co-constructing
> conversations. It is also the place where learners can
> become attuned to different aspects of conversation, such
> as voice quality and *aizuchi*. (Siegal, 1994, p. 326)

The positive acquisitional role played by informal conversations
with peers was also noted by Shea (1994), who concluded that a
congruent perspective and symmetric production are the most
productive learning environments (cf. Chapter 2). Interactions
with peers are all the more important in vertically structured
societies, where interlocutors' speech in asymmetrical encounters
is nonreciprocal and therefore does not appropriately model
target-like language use for the nonnative participant (LoCastro,
1998). Asymmetrical participation structures are also typical of
many kinds of institutional discourse in less hierarchically structured societies. Adult L2 learners have to figure out how to
participate in a variety of institutional settings. When institutional activities are unequal power encounters, nonnative participants often (though by no means always) find themselves in the
role of clients whose institutional knowledge and decision-making
power are limited. In the next section, we examine the input
opportunities for learning the pragmatics of institutional discourse.

Institutional Discourse

An extensive research literature reports on nonnative speakers' interactions in various institutional settings, such as workplaces (Day, 1994; Roberts, Davies, & Jupp, 1992), business contexts (Firth, 1996; Wagner & Firth, 1997), and various types of counseling and advising (Bardovi-Harlig & Hartford, 1990; Erickson & Shultz, 1982; Fiksdal, 1990; Gumperz, 1992; Tyler, 1995; Tyler & Davies, 1990). These studies have examined how participants accomplish the activities they are engaged in with varying degrees of success and failure, and what contributes to either outcome. Rarely have researchers scrutinized institutional discourse from the perspective of L2 learning. One notable exception is Bardovi-Harlig and Hartford's series of studies of academic advising sessions. As we noted in Chapter 4, their longitudinal study found that the sociopragmatic performance of nonnative students' suggestions and rejections became increasingly more target-like, whereas the students showed little pragmalinguistic development in the forms they chose to implement the two speech acts (Bardovi-Harlig & Hartford, 1993a). In a later paper, Bardovi-Harlig and Hartford (1996) provided an account for the differential developmental patterns by examining the input made available to students in the advising session interaction. They identified two sources of evidence for expected and appropriate student participation provided in the advising sessions themselves: explicit teaching and the advisors' own contributions. Advisors made clear to the students that they should take responsibility for their course of study and take an active role by suggesting the courses they were interested in. These expectations were conveyed to the students in various phases of the session. Early in the session, advisors solicited course suggestions from the students, such as:

(6.4) Advisors' solicitations

Now, what courses do you want to take in the fall?

Do you have some idea of what you want to take?

(Bardovi-Harlig & Hartford, 1996, p. 175)

Advisors expressed disapproval when students came unprepared or were indecisive about their course selections and displayed satisfaction when students provided suggestions. Students were thus directly informed that they were expected to make course suggestions. Advisors also provided explicit information about appropriate content of course suggestions and rejections of advisors' course recommendations. Appropriate content for course suggestions required institutional knowledge about what courses were or were not admissible in the program or appropriate to the student's specific course needs. Advisors helped students understand institutional requirements by teaching them, for instance, what courses could be taken as electives in linguistics and that photography was not one of them. Students were also able to access information about legitimate course selections through sources outside the advising session, such as discussions among students and the graduate catalog. In order to learn *what* course suggestions they could make, students could thus rely on multiple explicit sources. Advisors also provided negative evidence about admissible content for rejecting a course. Students learned that illegitimate reasons included the assumed ease or difficulty of a course, or lack of interest in a course that was central to their specialization. They received positive and negative evidence of admissible content and directives about making course suggestions. Their successful sociopragmatic development demonstrated that they noticed the input and effectively learned these aspects of advising session interaction.

For appropriate pragmalinguistic choices of suggestions and requests, on the other hand, negative and positive evidence was rarely forthcoming. Incorrect utterance forms usually went uncorrected because the advisor responded to the inferred intent rather than the forms (p. 179). As advising sessions are dyadic and private encounters, students had no opportunity to observe how native English-speaking peers interacted with their advisors.

Because of the complementary institutional roles of advisor and advisee, the advisor's suggestions seemed to be disqualified as relevant input. Advisors deployed a large range of forms for their course suggestions, some of which were indexes of institutional status and therefore inappropriate for students to emulate, such as:

(6.5a) Advisors' course suggestions

I'm going to have you take . . .

What we could do is let you take the L511 course now.

Others were more status-neutral and input-relevant, such as:

(6.5b) Advisors' course suggestions

You could take *Testing*.

You need to take L100.

The other thing that's a possibility is *Language and Society*.

(Bardovi-Harlig & Hartford, 1996, p. 181)

Perhaps because they perceived all advisor talk as status-bound, students did not appear to "intake" these forms or notice that advisors' suggestions were often quite mitigated. A particularly striking example of a student intensifying his own suggestion rather than adopting the mitigator from the advisor's preceding turn is extract (6.6).

(6.6) A student's course suggestion

A: What were the other courses *you were thinking of*?
S: Yeah, *I'm going to* take, ah . . . applied . . . transformational syntax.

(Bardovi-Harlig & Hartford, 1996, p. 182)

As Bardovi-Harlig and Hartford (1996) comment, "examples such as this one, and the fact that NNSs showed no change in the use of mitigators in the longitudinal study, suggest that the advisor's suggestions serve as neither a model for local accommodation within a single advising session nor as intake leading to a change across sessions" (p. 182). From this study, then, it appears that relevant input is status-bound—a hypothesis that warrants further examination. Whether or not other institutional environments show similar input and intake characteristics is a question that awaits future study. As the authors caution, no generalizations from one activity type to another should be made until comparative research has shown whether and where such generalizations are empirically sustainable. Compared to ordinary discourse, institutional interaction has the advantage for researchers investigating pragmatic input opportunities that it is relatively prestructured, predictable, and repetitive. Yet institutional activities as contexts for learning L2 pragmatics remain sorely underexplored, with one major exception: the second or foreign language classroom.

Input in Instructional Settings

As environments for developing pragmatic ability in a target language, L2 classrooms have a bad reputation. A number of studies show that compared to interaction outside the classroom, L2 pragmatic input in instructional discourse is functionally and formally limited. For example, in classroom interaction, openings and closings are shorter and less complex, the range of discourse markers is smaller (Kasper, 1989; Lörscher, 1986), and contributions would often not be considered polite outside the classroom (Lörscher & Schulze, 1988). But does this apparent uselessness of classroom discourse for L2 pragmatic learning hold up against empirical scrutiny? The studies cited above examined teacher-fronted interaction in foreign language classrooms in Denmark and Germany, conducted almost exclusively in the target language, English or German. Uniformly, the turn organization in these classrooms was IRF structured, that is, the teacher performed an initiation, a student offered a response, to which the teacher provided feedback or follow-up (Chaudron, 1988, p. 37). In the IRF-structured speech exchange system, the teacher controls topic nomination, maintenance and change, turn allocation, and third-turn assessment, initiates and terminates different activities within the unit of the lesson, and frames the beginning and end of the lesson itself through boundary routines (Ellis, 1990; Lörscher, 1986). The students' opportunities for performing any of these activities are severely limited. But how about the input opportunities afforded by the IRF routine? In a study examining German EFL students' discourse-pragmatic ability in English after nine years of instruction, these students displayed no difficulties with identifying transition-relevant places and taking turns at talk (Kasper, 1981). Based on a far more detailed microanalysis than the older study, Carroll (2000) came to a similar result. The Japanese college students he observed had no trouble producing precision-timed entries into talk. Neither student group had much contact with English-speaking interlocutors outside class. Whereas the German students received virtually monolingual English input from highly proficient nonnative English-speaking teachers, very likely, the Japanese students' precollege English education was conducted predominantly in Japanese, whereas their college English class was taught in the L2 by a native speaker of English. There is therefore good reason to hypothesize that students' universal interactional competence (Chapter 5) and teacher input jointly enabled them to identify transition-relevant places and fine-tune turn starts.

The German students were less successful in using discourse markers. Response tokens such as *okay* and *right*, although pervasive in teacher talk, were absent from the students' response turns. So were response tokens conveying emotively intensified change-of-state (*Oh goodness/wow/grief*), although the learners did use, often not entirely effectively, the solo *Oh* receipt token. *You know* was both under-used and incorrectly replaced by *I see*, and *I mean* was entirely absent from these high intermediate students' interactions in English. Not only were *You know* and *I mean* found rarely in teacher talk but some students also reported that, according to their teacher, *I mean* was incorrect in English (a case of transfer avoidance from German). Similarly, the students performed face-threatening speech acts without appropriate politeness marking. Lörscher and Schulze's (1988) observations appear to apply to these students; their teachers did not adequately model for them how to mitigate or intensify speech acts in English. In the absence of such input, students did not have an opportunity to extend their considerable grammatical knowledge of English to speech act modification. Finally, conversational openings and closings were troublesome in the students' discourse, in part because they did not choose appropriate routine formulas and did not perform cohesive second pair parts. There was thus a match between most aspects of the (lack of) input students received in their nine years of teacher-fronted EFL instruction and the students' own interlanguage discourse.

Of course, in light of the possible status-boundedness of intake (Bardovi-Harlig & Hartford, 1996), it cannot be claimed with any certainty that students' discourse-pragmatic ability would be more target-like if their teachers had modeled for them discourse management, politeness marking, and openings and closings as they would be appropriate in noninstructional ordinary interaction. But other studies suggest that this may be the case. In a longitudinal study of teacher talk in first-year Japanese as a foreign language (JFL), Ohta (1994) observed how affective particles were used by three teachers, all female native speakers of Japanese. Compared to conversational settings outside the classroom, these teachers used a narrower range and lower frequency of affective particles, a finding similar to the use of discourse and politeness markers in the EFL classrooms that we discussed above. Intriguingly, the teachers' use of particles varied according to their instructional philosophy. The teacher who held a structurally oriented view of teaching diverged most strongly from particle use in noninstructional conversation, whereas the two communicatively oriented teachers frequently provided assessments marked by the particle *ne*, which brought the input they supplied to students more closely to the practices of active listening in conversational Japanese. Because in the IRF-structured classroom, listener responses typically occur in the follow-up turn, students were massively exposed to the teacher's third-turn acknowledgments or assessments. In a more recent comprehensive study, Ohta described how teachers modeled *ne*-marked assessments for the students, as in extract (6.7).

(6.7) *ne*-marked assessments

1	T:	Anoo Jamie-san wa (.) donna kuruma o motte imasu ka?
		Um, Jamie (.) what kind of car do you have?
2	S:	Ah kuruma wa motte imasen.
		Ah I don't have a car.
3	T:	Ah soo desu ka? <u>Zannen desu ne:.</u>
		Is that right? <u>*That's too bad ne:.*</u>
4		Kim-san wa donna kuruma o motte imasu ka?
		Kim, what kind of car do you have?
5	K:	Ie kuruma ((laughs))
		A nice car
6	T:	Ah ii kuruma o motte imasu ka? ((All laugh)) <u>Ii desu ne:.</u>
		Ah you have a nice car? ((All laugh)) <u>*That's nice ne:.*</u>

(Ohta, 2001b, p. 193)

As can be seen in lines 3 and 6, the follow-up turn in the IRF routine provides a discourse slot for third-turn assessments, by which the teacher displays attention and positive affect to Jamie's and Kim's preceding contributions. Because the IRF provides a recurrent and predictable slot for teachers' assessments, students have ample opportunity to become attuned to the importance of active listening in Japanese and notice the practices by which it is accomplished. But beyond modeling, teachers guided students explicitly in their use of listener responses, even through choral repetition, and aligned themselves with assessments provided by students. Within the period of one academic year, all of the four first-year focal students used assessments in response to interlocutor contributions, and two of them used one type of alignment response (Ohta, 2001b; cf. also Chapter 4).

The acquisitionally productive role of interactional routines specific to the classroom was shown in Kanagy's studies of English-speaking children's acquisition of pragmatic routines in a JFL immersion kindergarten (Kanagy 1999a; Kanagy & Igarashi, 1997). A large part of the teacher's utterances and the activities she engaged the students in were managed by formulaic routines, such as greetings, taking attendance, classroom organization, pre-lunch and end-of-lesson routines, cleaning up, and others. The routines examined in Kanagy and Igarashi's (1997) study were part of the children's linguistic environment from day one, yet the children incorporated them differentially into their own production. In her more recent study of the same classroom setting, Kanagy (1999a) examined children's increasing participation in the daily interactional routines *aisatsu* (greeting), *shusseki* (attendance), and *jiko-shookai* (personal introduction). Through the teacher's verbal and nonverbal modeling, repetition, praise, corrective feedback, and scaffolding provided by both teacher and peers, the children gradually learned to engage competently in these routines, which required control not only of the linguistic components but also of the appropriate nonverbal conduct.

While it may be true that the IRF format proved effective in socializing children to the Japanese immersion classroom as a community of practice, it does not support many aspects of L2 pragmatic ability that are needed for communication outside the classroom. The discontent with IRF-structured classroom interaction as an environment for learning L2 pragmatics prompted some early research comparing teacher-fronted with student-centered classroom organization formats, such as pair work (Long, Adams, McLean, & Castaños, 1976) and role play (House, 1986). These studies found that the student-centered activities substantially increased the range of speech acts and discourse functions performed by the students, but they did not examine the participants' productions from the perspective of pragmatic input. This issue was addressed in a study by Porter (1986), who examined (among other things) whether in problem-solving tasks, ESL learners with a Spanish L1 background provided native-like pragmatic input to each other. Comparing how the learners and native English-speaking controls expressed opinions, agreement, and disagreement in the task-structured interaction, Porter found that the learners performed all three speech acts more directly, used less mitigation, and the range of pragmalinguistic expressions was narrower than in the native speaker discourse. In expressing opinions, mitigators that the native group used frequently but that did not, or very rarely, show up in the learners' productions included hypothetical *would* (e.g., *I would argue / choose, I would do X*) and the modal past of cognitive verbs (e.g., *it seemed to me, I figured / thought*), a common interlanguage phenomenon, as we noted in Chapter 5.

Participants from both groups displayed attention to the other's ideas, but whereas the native speakers implemented their assessments with a range of routines (e.g., *That's a very good point; Good question; You have a point there*), the learners' response tokens were partly idiomatic (e.g., *Yeah, I know what you mean; As you said*) and partly not (e.g., *Yeah, you have reason; Yeah, that's true; That's a good arguing*). Systematic differences were also observable in the learners' and native speakers' politeness styles in agreements and disagreements, as shown in Tables 6.4 and 6.5.

The negative politeness style in the native speakers' agreements and disagreements contrasted strongly with the learners' positive politeness style, which was not only direct but also almost completely unmitigated, and even featured intensified disagreements. Porter (1986) therefore concluded on a rather pessimistic note that

> Learners' lack of appropriate language use patterns suggests that only native speakers (or perhaps very advanced nonnative speakers) can provide truly "appropriate" input that will build sociolinguistic competence. . . . Communicative activities in the classroom will provide valuable production practice for learners, but they will not generate the type of sociocultural input that learners need. (p. 218)

Fortunately, later research presents a more encouraging picture of the pragmatic input that learners provide to each other. Ohta (1995, 1997) compared how second-year students of Japanese as a foreign language (JFL) learned to use polite request strategies in Japanese in teacher-fronted exchanges and role plays involving

Table 6.4

Expressing Agreement

Native Speakers	Learners
Focus on agreement	
That's the same as mine	Well, in the first, third we have the same
Well, that's close	It's agree, no? We're agree.
We're kind of agreed on some of them	We are agree.
Well, I thought she was pretty bad too, but . . .	
Hedging	
I could go along with switching a little bit	
Well, I'm somewhat convinced by what you say	
That is a somewhat good idea, I guess, in the extreme case	
I think basically you have a somewhat legitimate argument	
No hedging	
	All right.
	I change my mind.
	I am agree. I can change it.
	It's OK. I think is OK.
	Yeah, I change to seven.

Note. Adapted from "How Learners Talk to Each Other: Input and Interaction in Task-Centered Discussions," by P. A. Porter, 1986, in R. R. Day (Ed.), *Talking to Learn: Conversation in Second Language Acquisition,* p. 217. Rowley, MA: Newbury House.

two students of differing JFL abilities. The collaborative interaction between the students created a range of opportunities for using Japanese that was not available in teacher-fronted exchanges. Both the stronger and the weaker learner capitalized on their available interactional skills and shifted expert-novice roles during interaction. It was not the case that only the weaker learner profited from the activity at the cost of the stronger partner. Also, there was no evidence of participants' picking up

Table 6.5

Expressing Disagreement

Native Speakers	Learners
Indirect	*Indirect*
Acknowledge other's view and state your own.	No!
	Well, I disagree with you.
A: I ranked them- those two the worst.	I'm no agree with that.
B: Really. I ranked Abigail and Slug the worst.	But that is no important.
	Is wrong.
	No, no, forget it!
Focus on own ignorance or task difficulty	
At this point, I was very arbitrary	I'm not sure about
But I don't know how it works	Is very difficult
I thought . . . but who would know for sure	I didn't really pay attention of that part
Oh! It didn't even enter my head	
Hedging	
I wouldn't necessarily agree with that even though	
So I had him kind of toward the end of my list	

Note. Adapted from "How Learners Talk to Each Other: Input and Interaction in Task-Centered Discussions," by P. A. Porter, 1986, in R. R. Day (Ed.), *Talking to Learn: Conversation in Second Language Acquisition,* p. 217. Rowley, MA: Newbury House.

each other's errors; rather they assisted each other in reaching more advanced levels of communicative ability. As Ohta comments, "from a developmental perspective, pair work clearly provides an environment which allows learners to participate freely in using Japanese for their own purposes as they take part in meaning-making activity which increases the salience of the language used" (Ohta, 1995, p. 115).

How can the opposite conclusions that Porter and Ohta arrived at be explained? It appears that the theoretical perspectives adopted in each study enabled a very different treatment of the data. Porter's (1986) focal construct was that of *task*, as understood in the then-current version of the interaction hypothesis. Ohta (1995, 1997) adopted a sociocultural perspective, in which the *activity* is the central locus of language learning (cf. Chapter 2). As Coughlan and Duff (1994) demonstrate, the same task can generate quite different activities. How learners define a task and transform it into an activity depends on a number of factors. One that appears particularly consequential for assessing the learning potential of peer group interaction for pragmatics is its situational context. The peer activities observed by Ohta were embedded in form-focused JFL instruction. Although the students used the target language for a variety of purposes, they seemed to attend to learning Japanese at the same time. Learning and using Japanese appeared to be working synergistically, as suggested by the recurrent shifts to the metalinguistic level in the peer inter-action and the fact that the teacher was around to monitor and assist students in the peer activity. The task in Porter's study, by contrast, was not situated in an ongoing language classroom. The instruction to participants is not included in the report, but task-based interaction would typically orient them to complete the task, with no particular consideration given to language learning. There is no evidence from Porter's report that the learners trans-formed the task, conducted in a laboratory setting outside of the classroom, into a learning activity. Furthermore, the learners and native speakers clearly defined the activity differently: the native speakers, by simultaneously attending to its transactional and interpersonal dimension, the learners by attending to referential and illocutionary clarity. These differences in task definition indi-cate that learners might benefit from instruction in the pragma-linguistics of peer collaboration. Components of an instructional sequence could include relevant models prior to the peer work and various forms of debriefing, such as peer and teacher feedback, or comparison of students' own speech act performance with that of the native speakers as in Tables 6.4 and 6.5. These recommenda-tions have implications for research methodology. Rather than evaluating the benefits and limitations of peer input on the basis of a one-shot task administration outside the classroom setting, longitudinal observation of task implementation in classroom activities will offer a more valid basis for such an assessment. As we discussed in Chapter 2, understanding how acquisitionally useful a task is requires that the activities generated by it be examined longitudinally (cf. Brooks, Donato, & McGlone, 1997). This applies to the capacity of the task to elicit learners' production of L2 discourse as well as generating pragmatic input: two aspects that are inseparable in collaborative peer interaction.

As the discussion in this section has suggested, the apparent usefulness of language teaching as an environment for providing L2 pragmatic input depends on a variety of factors, and not least on the adopted theoretical perspective and research methodology by which such an assessment is made. The research reviewed in the previous section suggests that contact with the target community *per se* does not supply learners with high-quality pragmatic input. This section indicates that it is not the instructional setting as such that determines the quality of pragmatic input. Different classroom arrangements and their implementation in activities, both teacher-fronted and student-centered, have the potential to provide acquisitionally relevant pragmatic input. Evaluating whether and how this potential is brought to fruition requires that pragmatic input be examined in situated classroom activities. Thus far, we have discussed the evidence for input opportunities in noninstructional and instructional settings separately. We will now turn to studies that have compared the benefits of foreign and second language learning contexts for L2 pragmatic development.

Comparing L2 Pragmatic Learning in Foreign and Second Language Settings

Several cross-sectional studies have examined whether foreign and second language learning contexts have a differential impact on learners' L2 pragmatic ability. Takahashi and Beebe (1987) compared Japanese EFL and ESL learners' production of refusals and found that the ESL learners' refusals were more target-like. In a study of politeness assessments of requests, also by Japanese EFL and ESL learners, Kitao (1990) reported that the ESL learners' judgments converged more with those of native speakers of English. In a correlational study, Röver (1996) found that German EFL students' use of pragmatic routines was highly and significantly related to their having stayed in the United Kingdom or the United States. The experience abroad was particularly helpful in the case of situational routines, such as *Do you need help out today?* as a North American grocery store check-out routine. Even students who had spent only six weeks or less abroad demonstrated a much superior knowledge of situational routines. In a more recent study, Röver (2001) replicated this finding. Interestingly, neither learners' comprehension of implicatures nor production of speech acts benefited from stay abroad in this study. The decisive variable was learners' general proficiency in English. The most proficient learners who had not stayed abroad scored almost as highly as native American English-speaking controls, suggesting that these learners' EFL instruction provided an effective environment for learning to understand implicature and producing speech acts in American English. On the other hand, in a study on the effectiveness of instruction on advanced EFL students' pragmatic fluency, House (1996) observed that students who had enjoyed a longer stay in an English-speaking environment outperformed their peers who had not benefited from such exposure both before and after instruction, irrespective of the adopted teaching approach (cf. Chapter 7).

Two studies that compared second and foreign learners' pragmalinguistic and grammatical awareness came to partially different conclusions about the effects of the learning environments for acquiring L2 pragmatics. Bardovi-Harlig and Dörnyei (1998) compared EFL students in Hungary with ESL learners at a U.S. university. In a replication study, Niezgoda and Röver (2001) contrasted EFL students in the Czech Republic with ESL learners at another U.S. university. In these studies, the learners' ethnolinguistic background was not matched across settings. The ESL learners in the original study identified more pragmatic errors and rated them as more severe than the grammatical errors, whereas the EFL learners recognized more grammatical errors and assessed them as more serious than the pragmatic errors. Proficiency interacted with learning environment: The low-proficiency Hungarian students gave lower ratings to both grammatical and pragmatic errors than the high-proficiency EFL group, whereas the high-proficiency EFL students rated the grammatical errors as far more severe than the pragmatically inappropriate utterances. Compared to the low-proficiency ESL group, the high-proficiency ESL learners assessed pragmatic inappropriacies as somewhat more serious. However, their severity ratings of grammatical errors decreased significantly. Niezgoda and Röver (2001) found that the ESL students in their study rated pragmatic errors as significantly more severe than grammatical errors, which replicated Bardovi-Harlig and Dörnyei's finding. Unlike Bardovi-Harlig and Dörnyei's Hungarian EFL group, however, the Czech students noticed a much higher number of pragmatic and grammatical errors and judged both error types as more serious than the ESL sample. Low-proficiency learners in both the EFL and ESL groups recognized more pragmatic than grammatical errors and rated pragmatic errors as more severe, whereas high-proficiency learners showed the opposite tendency. The two studies indicate that levels and development of pragmatic and grammatical awareness may be associated with different learning environments in a rather complex fashion. As Niezgoda and Röver (2001) report, their Czech participants were students in a university EFL teacher education program that included 15 hours of monolingual EFL classes per week, taught by highly qualified EFL instructors following a "communicative" approach. Bardovi-Harlig and Dörnyei's (1998) EFL students were enrolled in regular EFL classes where, due to exam requirements, more attention was paid to grammar than to pragmatics. The different sensitivity to pragmatic inappropriateness displayed by the two EFL groups indicates rather strongly that learning opportunities for pragmatics within foreign language contexts may vary considerably. Not all foreign language environments are equal.

So far we have considered studies in which the learner groups with or without exposure to the target language environment were composed of different individuals. The longitudinal studies to which we now turn examine how participation in a study-abroad program affects the pragmatic ability of foreign language learners.

Pragmatic Development at Home and Abroad

In his foreword to Barbara Freed's edited volume *Second Language Acquisition in a Study Abroad Context* (1995), Charles Ferguson notes that "in the USA, where the level of foreign language competence is admittedly low for an industrialized country, teachers and students alike are familiar with and often cite such views as: the only way to achieve real fluency in a foreign language is to go to a place where it is spoken" (p. xii). Without even trying to unpack "real fluency," we can safely assume that this commonsense notion is understood to include the ability to act and interact effectively in a range of target contexts, using the target language. According to this widespread ideology of foreign language learning, foreign language classrooms provide environments in which grammar and literacy can successfully be learned, but they are inadequate contexts for developing pragmatic, discourse, and sociolinguistic ability, especially in informal spoken interaction. As we have discussed in this chapter and several other places in this book, research evidence does not support the summary dismissal of foreign language teaching as an effective environment for L2 pragmatic learning. Rather, it suggests that it is not the instructed learning context as such but the ways in which it is organized that enables or hinders the acquisition of L2 pragmatics. We have also seen earlier that residence in the host country alone holds no guarantee for successful pragmatic learning but that such learning depends on a range of societal and local conditions as well as the learners' agency within the host contexts. The study-abroad research that we will consider now is designed to allow us to identify more precisely what gains students make while on a study sojourn in an L2 community. As participants in these studies are tested minimally before and after the study-abroad period, the research format resembles a pretest-posttest design, with the study abroad experience as a treatment variable.

Some studies also test participants during their stay in the host country and are thereby able to inform on early and later changes in the learners' pragmatic ability. Some studies include a control group of students who did not go abroad but continued to participate in foreign language classes at home, and can thus shed light on whether the gains that the study-abroad students made were in fact attributable to the study-abroad experience. Finally, some studies include native speakers of the target and/or the students' first language to assess approximations to target practices and changes in L1 transfer. Participants in study-abroad research with a focus on pragmatic and sociolinguistic development were college or high school students who had participated in foreign language instruction anywhere from several months up to seven or eight years, with the period spent abroad lasting between eight and twelve months. The focal learning objects included specific speech acts, politeness, pragmatic routines, discourse markers, speech levels and honorifics (in Japanese), and a sociostylistically sensitive particle (in French). In addition, some studies also examined whether the students' sociopragmatic sensitivity to context factors changed during their stay abroad.

Whereas the majority of studies reports some gains in the students' acquisition of the focal pragmatic objects during their sojourn in the host community, the overall impact of the study-abroad experience appears as rather mixed. Marriott (1996) investigated the acquisition of Japanese politeness by eight Australian English-speaking secondary school students during a year in Japan. The students had received varying amounts of instruction prior to their departure, but Mariott assessed their overall proficiency as low. Changes in the students' Japanese ability were measured by oral proficiency interviews, conducted before and after their stay in Japan. The examined politeness features included the use of honorific style and forms, politeness routines, and performing requests. The learners made the greatest gains in their use of politeness formulas, as demonstrated in their native-like production of opening and closing routines in the post-exchange interview. They also quite effectively performed a request in a role play, but because no comparative pre-exchange data were available, we can only speculate as to what extent their experience abroad was instrumental to their successful request performance. A striking change from pre- to post-exchange was evident in students' use of plain style. Prior to their year abroad, they had employed plain forms only sparingly and incorrectly. After returning, their use of plain forms strongly increased, and even though some uses were target-like, most were not (cf. Hashimoto, 1993). In another paper, Marriott (1993) points out an important context-related difference in the order of learning informal and formal speech styles.

> In contrast to native speakers who acquire the honorific styles in the order of plain style, polite *desu/masu*-style and *gozaimasu*-style, foreign learners in instructed settings generally learn the polite style first, then rather later the plain style and perhaps later the *gozaimasu*-style . . . interaction within the domains in which [the students] participated in Japan—home, school, and friendship—had the strongest influence upon their language development and consequently they acquired the plain style, which is the most prominent style in these domains and represents the basic style which is acquired by Japanese children. (p. 175)

By the same token, upon return, students deployed fewer addressee honorifics to outgroup members, another move away from L2 usage. However, Marriott qualifies this assessment by noting that for teenage speakers, informal style may be accepted in contexts where it is not in line with adult norms. Although Marriott (1996, p. 220) contends that "the principal factor in their acquisition of Japanese is the amount and type of input and interaction available to learners," that factor alone cannot account for the differential success with which the students acquired politeness. For the acquisition of routine formulas, massive exposure alone seems to be sufficient, as was also found by Röver (1996) for the acquisition of pragmatic routines by EFL learners. Learning to choose speech levels and addressee honorifics, on the other hand, appears to require negative feedback from interlocutors.

According to the students' self-reports, such feedback was almost entirely absent during their stay in Japan.

A predominantly sociolinguistic focus was adopted by Regan (1995, 1996), who examined the effect of a nine-month study abroad in France and Brussels on six Irish university students' development of *ne* deletion in French negation (*ça ne fait rien →* *ça fait rien*). The participants in the study had had six years of French instruction prior to their sojourn abroad. Development of the students' *ne* deletion was measured through their use of the particle in two sociolinguistic interviews, conducted prior to their departure to France and Belgium, and upon return to Dublin. Using VARBRUL analysis, Regan determined the contribution of stylistic, structural, and individual variables to *ne* deletion in the students' discourse. These advanced students were already familiar with the *ne* deletion rule prior to their stay abroad, but upon their return, their deletion probability had increased from 0.19 to an astounding 0.80. While at their stage of grammatical development, the learners appeared to be ready to tune in to subtle sociolinguistic variation, they still had not quite worked out the stylistic constraints on *ne* deletion and retention. In fact, they deleted more in formal contexts than before their sojourn abroad, and both before and after, they deleted more when *ne* occurred as an element in formulaic expressions. In both instances, the learners overgeneralized the deletion of the particle, compared to native-speaker use (even though that use appears to be in flux, as Regan notes), indicating that they might have come to understand *ne* deletion as a typical feature of spoken French, irrespective of other context factors.

That some aspects of students' interlanguage pragmatics may develop away from target use during residence in an L2 community was also observed by Kondo (1997b), who examined Japanese EFL learners' apology performance before and after one year of home stay in the United States in comparison with L1 speakers of Japanese and American English. In some respects, the students' apologies became more target-like, whereas in others

they did not. While the learners approximated or even outperformed native speakers of American English in their use of the
apology strategies of lack of intent, explanation, and repair offer,
they also increased their use of admission of fact and concern for
the hearer, following, and in fact overshooting, the native Japanese
norm. Kondo cites the positive correlation hypothesis as an explanation of the increased negative transfer (cf. Chapter 4). A striking
example of the students' much improved apology performance
after the year abroad is seen in extracts (6.8a) and (6.8b).

(6.8a) Damaged car—before study abroad

I am very sorry

Illocutionary Force Indicating Device (IFID) + Intensifier

(6.8b) Damaged car—after study abroad

I am very sorry	*IFID + Intensifier*
that I scratched your	*Admission of fact*
parked car with my bike.	
I didn't mean it	*Lack of intent*
but I did it anyway.	*Admission of fact*
I'm sorry.	*IFID*
Can I do anything for you?	*Repair offer*

(Kondo, 1997b, p. 277, slightly modified)

Although the later apology seems to be doing too much of a good
thing, it illustrates well that learners can acquire formulaic apology strategies through extended interaction in the target community. Learners' apology strategies also became more explicit after
their stay abroad, moving away from Japanese and closer toward
target practices. In a companion study, Kondo (1997a) examined
whether the same learners changed their sociopragmatic assessments of context factors in the same apology situations. In contrast
to a previous study (Maeshiba, Yoshinaga, Kasper, & Ross, 1996),
all groups of Japanese respondents provided similar ratings,
which differed from those given by native speakers of American
English. After the study-abroad experience, the learners' ratings
of severity of offense and likelihood of apology acceptance became

more similar to those of the English native speakers. The students converged less in their assessments of obligation to apologize, and their ratings of distance and dominance remained close to those given before their departure. It appears from these results that context-internal apology factors may be more prone to change through exposure and interaction than participant factors, an issue worth investigating in future research.

The studies discussed so far showed some movement of the focal pragmatic and sociolinguistic features in the direction of target usage, but since they did not include control groups of students who continued to participate in foreign language instruction at home, it is impossible to say with any certainty whether the effects were due to the stay in the target community. The importance of a control group is particularly striking in a study by Rodriguez (2001), who investigated the effect of a semester in Spain on the pragmatic ability of a group of North American students of Spanish as a foreign language, compared to students who continued their Spanish classes in the United States. The study focused on students' appropriateness assessments of request strategies and their relation to context factors. Although both groups improved during the semester in that they approximated native-speaker judgments more closely on the posttest than on the pretest, no difference was found between the groups in Spain and the United States. Over time, both groups increased their assessments of question strategies such as *¿puedes?* (can you) or *¿podría (yo)?* (could (I)) as appropriate and of *necesito* (I need) as inappropriate, and they judged the same context variables as contributing either to the appropriateness or inappropriateness of situated request strategies. This study, then, shows no advantage at all for the study-abroad students, thus far a unique result. Rodriguez surmises that this rather surprising outcome may have to do with the choice of requests as the focal research object. Since the students were exposed to plenty of requests in the classroom context, requests may be an insensitive indicator of environmental effects. To this it may be added that judgment tasks are perhaps not as discriminating as production tasks. Having to produce their own contextualized selections of request strategies and forms, as free-recall tasks require, may well make differences between students with and without the experience of staying in the target community more apparent.

Particularly insightful are studies that also probe students' pragmatic development during their stay abroad, rather than only before and after. These studies enable observation of the learning process over time, not only its end product. Similar in focus to Kondo (1997a) and Rodriguez (2001), Matsumura (2001) examined whether Japanese EFL learners' sociopragmatic assessments changed as a result of exposure. Perceptions of social status were operationalized as respondents' choices of advice-giving strategies addressed to interlocutors of different social status. A group of 101 Japanese EFL students spending eight months in Vancouver was compared with a control group, who continued taking English classes in Kyoto, and with native speakers of English. The multiple-choice instrument designed for this purpose was administered before, after, and twice during the students' stays in Canada. Contrary to expectations, the Vancouver and Kyoto students' strategy choices to high-status interlocutors' converged with those of the North American respondents throughout the period of the study. All groups selected indirect and hedged forms of advice in this status constellation. However, the exchange students' strategy choices to equal- and lower-status interlocutors, which differed from those of the North American students prior to departure, became target-like during the early phase of their stay in Canada. Rather than making their strategy choices dependent on interlocutor status alone, they now took into consideration other contextual aspects as well, such as the setting and what the advice was about. The control group did not shift their strategy preferences in these contexts during the period of the study. Confirming earlier findings, Matsumura (2001) concludes that "the effects of study abroad on the acquisition of pragmatic competence were not necessarily associated with length of stay. The commonly shared belief among many Japanese learners that the longer they stay in a target speech community, the more their proficiency improves, did not hold true for the learners in the present study" (p. 667). He adds that this outcome should not be taken as a justification for shortening educational exchange programs. Rather, it strongly indicates that much research is needed to obtain a better understanding of the amount and quality of exposure that benefits different aspects of L2 pragmatic ability.

The most complex studies of pragmatic development during study abroad that we are aware of examine how native speakers of different varieties of English learn several aspects of the pragmatics of French and German. Hoffman-Hicks (1999) charted American students' development of greetings, leave-takings, and compliments in French during an eight-month study abroad in Strasbourg. Although the study-abroad groups' improvements were not spectacular, they clearly made gains that their colleagues at home did not make. Some aspects of the Strasbourg groups' leave-takings became more target-like. From early on, they began to include in their leave-takings appropriate routine formulae, where students in the United States continued to produce nonformulaic, overlong expressions. The study-abroad experience was also beneficial for students' acquisition of discourse markers, whose frequency, range, and distribution expanded. Compliments, on the other hand, proved more resistant to change through exposure in the target speech community. Here, in most respects, the two student groups remained quite similar. This was true for students' preferred compliment structures *J'aime [bien/beaucoup] NP* and *NP est [très] ADJ* (both transfers from the English compliment formats 'I [really] like/love NP' and 'NP is/looks [really] ADJ') and that, as Hoffman-Hicks notes, are "particularly nonnative-like in French" (p. 262). But whereas the Strasbourg group also increasingly used the preferred French compliment format *PRO est [très] ADJ*, no such development took place in the U.S. group's compliment productions. Shortly after arrival, the study-abroad students also started adjusting to some of the sociopragmatics of French interaction by complimenting and greeting less and adopting a more reserved demeanor, while the U.S. group persisted in transferring a positively polite interactional style to their French discourse.

Despite the gains made by the study-abroad students, both groups' French pragmatics remained non-native-like in many respects. Particularly noteworthy was the Strasbourg group's tendency toward verbosity. Compared to native-speaker controls, they overused terms of address and produced longer, creatively constructed expressions where native speakers would use briefer routine formulas. They also included additional expressions of gratitude, advice, and requests in their leave-takings where native speakers abstained from such expanding actions. The waffling effect, noted by Edmondson and House (1991) as a feature of more advanced learners' interlanguage pragmatics, was much in evidence in these students' use of French. Likewise, the students' compliments remained quite non-target-like, both in sociopragmatic and pragmalinguistic terms. One reason why the students did not profit more from their sojourn in the target speech community seems to have been the difficulty of establishing contacts with native speakers, as Hoffman-Hicks engagingly discusses in the concluding section of her report. While some of the study-abroad participants expressed disappointment about the unwelcoming reception they had experienced from French people, they did, understandably enough, not consider what their own contributions to such lack of engagement might have been—and that one such contribution may have been their own pragmatics when interacting in French. The importance of raising students' awareness about target pragmatic practices *before* they depart on a study-abroad program is one of the many useful lessons to be learned from research on the benefits of sojourns in the L2 community.

A recent study by Barron (2002) examined how Irish students who had learned German as a foreign language at secondary school and university for seven to eight years developed their production of offer-refusal exchanges, pragmatic routines, and mitigation during study abroad in Germany. Participants completed discourse completion and metapragmatic assessment questionnaires three times during the study, prior to their departure, after two months in Germany, and at the end of their stay. Following the last session, they also conducted a set of role plays with subsequent retrospective interviews. Already after two months in Germany, the students' production of the offer-refusal exchange became more target-like. Before exposure to target practices, they regularly produced a ritual re-offer (of food, drink, services) after a ritual refusal, a sociopragmatic transfer from Irish English. As is apparent from the students' retrospective comments, they soon became very aware of the different pragmatic norms, not least as the result of critical incidents that some of them had experienced. Missing out on a badly wanted drink because no re-offer is made after an initial polite refusal can be a powerful motivator for pragmatic convergence. Even so, the nonnative speakers still re-offered more than the German control group at the end of the study-abroad period. The learners also improved their use of pragmatic routines, producing more target-like and fewer non-target-like formulaic expressions such as *ich wundere mich*, a transfer from 'I wonder . . .' (but meaning 'I am surprised') as a request formula. In expressions of appreciation, they also shifted from the transfer-based *Du bist / Sie sind sehr nett* ('You're very kind') to the target-like *Das ist abernett von Dir / Ihnen* (literally 'That is [modal particle] kind of you'), which expresses an evaluation of the action done by the recipient rather than a character assessment. But the learners also increased their use of overgeneralized routines and nonroutinized expressions where routine formulas would be more target-like, leading Barron to conclude that the development of pragmatic routines was a nonlinear process. The routines were learned more slowly than the offer-refusal exchange, as shifts to more native-like use were first evident at the end of the study-abroad period. Learners' development of mitigation also presented a rather complex picture. They already produced native-like syntactic mitigators before departure and continued to do so throughout the study-abroad period, although in some request contexts, they deployed less syntactic mitigation than either the German or Irish-English controls. One conspicuous finding was that the learners' use of such lexical mitigators as modal particles and adverbs actually decreased over time. The gains that the learners made during their stay in the target language community suggest that the input and interaction opportunities were beneficial for their pragmatic development. But the many aspects of their pragmatic performance that remained non-target-like or even diverged further from target practices also indicate that they had little benefit from negative feedback, an observation made in many studies reported in this chapter.

One observation made by Ferguson in his foreword to Freed (1995) was that "despite the increased sociolinguistic competence of the overseas learners, their stylistic variability still deviates from that of native speakers" (p. xiii). For the most part, the research reviewed in this section supports this generalization. A recurrent finding was that during study abroad, students acquired a more informal style than at home in the classroom, which they extended to encounters in settings and with interlocutors that required more distance politeness. Very likely, this effect is age-graded, considering the typical age bracket for exchange students studying at high school or university. Since most of the input that these students receive is from peers and the informal host family setting, it is understandable that the informal varieties of their interlanguage develop the most, whereas learning to associate pragmalinguistic and sociolinguistic choices with different contextual parameters during a year or less abroad may be too ambitious a goal for students in this age group.

Appraising the Influence of the Learning Environment

The studies we have reviewed in this chapter dispel three myths about the effect of the environment on learning L2 pragmatics. For developing pragmatic ability, spending time in the target community is no panacea, length of residence is not a reliable predictor, and L2 classrooms can be a productive social context. Eleven themes that specify these general findings have emerged from the studies.

1. How helpful time spent in the target community is in acquisitional terms depends on the quality and quantity of input available to learners (Hoffman-Hicks, 1999; Kim, 2000).

2. To no small extent, the source of opportunities for pragmatic development is located at the microsociological and macrosociolinguistic level. Ideologies held in the target community on its own ethnolinguistic uniqueness can make relevant pragmatic input more difficult to access (Iino, 1996; Siegal, 1994). Target community members' political views of the foreign students' home country may influence the extent to which they seek or make themselves available for contact with sojourning students (Hoffman-Hicks, 1999).

3. Situationally salient social categorization shapes input. When learners are primarily categorized as foreigners, the input they receive may be radically different from speech addressed to target community members. Foreigner talk features may include code switches to English and impolite use of the learners' L1 (DuFon, 1999) or the target language (Siegal, 1994). However, when learners' membership in other social categories such as age or social status in the target community is salient, or when situational role overrides more stable social categories, native-speaker input appears to be consistent with target pragmatic practices.

4. Cultural and pragmatic stereotypes can function as a bi-directional barrier to providing and receiving pragmatically relevant input. For instance, the stereotype that "Americans are direct/not polite/egalitarian" can induce target community members to discourage learners from using native practices such as ritually self-humbling formulaic expressions (Iino, 1996). Conversely, pragmatic stereotypes may also prevent learners from noticing polite language use that is readily available in the input (Bardovi-Harlig & Hartford, 1996). In this case, pragmatic ideologies act as a constraint on the process of converting input to intake.

5. Whether learners perceive interlocutor input as relevant for their own target language use can depend on interlocutor status. Current evidence suggests that co-participants in the same social and situational roles provide relevant models (Shea, 1994; Siegal, 1994); whereas interlocutors in different status roles do not (Bardovi-Harlig & Hartford, 1996). However, whether learners accept status-unequal co-participants as pragmatic models may be mediated by the setting, as learners do learn pragmatic features from teacher talk (Ohta, 2001b).

6. In noninstructional discourse, corrections and other kinds of negative evidence on learners' interlanguage pragmatics may be virtually absent (Barron, 2002; Iino, 1996; Marriott, 1995; McMeekin, in progress), or feedback opportunities may vary for different learning targets. DuFon (1999) noted that learners of Indonesian were regularly given feedback on incorrect uses of *belum* and *tidak* in experience questions, presumably because Indonesian native speakers categorized such errors as grammatical and believed that grammatical errors can be corrected without loss to the student's face. On the other hand, students' use of inappropriate address terms, even though (or because) it may be more damaging to the social relationship, was not usually corrected.

7. Pragmatic salience, combined with input frequency, facilitates acquisition (DuFon, 1999). This goes some way to explain why even after short stays abroad, learners expand their repertoire of discourse markers (Hoffman-Hicks, 1999) and pragmatic routines (Barron, 2002; Hoffman-Hicks, 1999; Kondo, 1997b; Marriott, 1995; Roever, 2001; Röver, 1996). But for many speech activities, pragmatic routines are not learned fast or are learned incompletely or incorrectly (Barron, 2002; Bouton, 1999; Hoffman-Hicks, 1999). The conditions for learning pragmatic routines in an L2 environment are still far from being understood.

8. The pragmatics of different social domains and activity types may be learned in different ways, as dramatically evident in interactions between learners and native speakers in informal conversations with close friends (Shea, 1994; Siegal, 1994), at the host family's dinner table (Iino, 1996), and in academic advising sessions (Bardovi-Harlig & Hartford, 1996). It is therefore crucial to investigate opportunities for sociopragmatic and pragmalinguistic input in the target community with specific attention to the interactional organization of different activity types.

9. The same attention to activity type has to be paid to input and interaction in instructional settings. Although L2 classrooms often supply little L2 pragmatic input, different interactional arrangements can provide learners with rich and relevant L2 pragmatic data. As environments for learning L2 pragmatics, language classrooms have some distinct advantages compared to interaction in noninstructional settings. Teachers can explicitly model and guide students in their use of target practices, engage students in awareness-raising activities of L2 pragmatics, and provide feedback on students' productions. Peer activities enable students to collaboratively work on tasks and support each other's development of pragmatic ability through using the target language and metapragmatic discussion (Ohta, 2001b). Interventional research on the effect on instruction in pragmatics, discussed in Chapter 7, suggests that students' L2 pragmatic ability benefits from such arrangements.

10. Language teaching can help maximize students' pragmatic gains during study abroad in several ways. Prior to students' departure, foreign language teaching has the important task to prepare students for the pragmatic practices in the target speech community (Barron, 2002; Hoffman-Hicks, 1999). While in the host setting, students will profit from language courses or courses related to L2 culture and society that encourage them to discuss and reflect on their experiences with L2

interactional practices. Without such preparation and support, progress in L2 pragmatic development can be slow and partially unsuccessful (Barron, 2002; Bouton, 1994, 1999; Hoffman-Hicks, 1999).

11. Different aspects of L2 pragmatics vary in the learning difficulty they pose for learners with different backgrounds, are differentially available in the input, may be more or less usable in the learners' own production, and, consequently, take different time to acquire. Some features of L2 pragmatics appear to develop in nonlinear ways (Barron, 2002; Hill, 1997; Hoffman-Hicks, 1999; Kondo, 1997b; Matsumura, 2001). Research on these properties of pragmatic learning requires repeated data collection during the period of investigation, observation of different activity types, and sequential analysis of the learners' and their interlocutors' discourse contributions.

Chapter Summary

This chapter focused on the opportunities for pragmatic development afforded by different learning environments. We started out by reviewing some early studies that related pragmatic learning to length of stay in the target community and concluded that duration of residence was too coarse a factor to meaningfully explain pragmatic development. Rather, the activities in which learners participate, and the occasions for engagements as listeners and speakers they offer, seem to be relevantly related to pragmatic learning. Ethnographic studies of learners' interactions in noninstructional target contexts demonstrate vividly that the societal and local positioning of learners in the host community can both enable and constrain their learning of L2 pragmatics (Iino, 1996; Siegal, 1994). Focusing on a particular institutional activity, the academic advising session (Bardovi-Harlig & Hartford, 1996), we saw that nonnative students effectively acquired the speech act categories called for in this type of encounter, whereas they were not successful at learning how to mitigate their speech acts in a status-congruent way. The critical variable here was not the input itself, which was available for speech act choice and mitigation alike, but appeared to be whether students assessed the input as relevant for their own contributions. Moving on to instructional settings, we questioned whether the poor reputation that language classrooms have as environments for learning L2 pragmatics is justified by the empirical evidence. The literature both supports and contradicts the commonsense view. Since some studies clearly demonstrate that pragmatics can be learned under conditions of instruction, the right question to ask is not "Can pragmatics be learned in the classroom?" but "How can classrooms be arranged so that activities and materials most effectively support students' pragmatic development?" Finally, we turned to studies comparing pragmatic learning in foreign and second language settings. The main part of this section was devoted to study-abroad research that focuses on students' learning of L2 pragmatics in the host community. The upshot of this literature is that the gains students make during study abroad is rather mixed, resulting in many cases in an overgeneralized informal speech style. This finding, together with others showing that students may actually develop parts of their interlanguage pragmatic ability away from target usage during residence abroad, strongly indicates that students would benefit from instruction in pragmatics prior to and during their stay in the host community. We concluded the chapter by drawing a number of conclusions from the reviewed research and offering some recommendations for future study.

CHAPTER SEVEN

The Role of Instruction in Learning Second Language Pragmatics

Classrooms essentially offer two kinds of opportunity for learning the pragmatics of a second or foreign language—students may learn as a result of planned pedagogical action directed toward the acquisition of pragmatics, or they may learn from exposure to input and production of output through classroom use of the target language even when pragmatics is not an intended learning target. This chapter addresses the first type of classroom learning. Specifically, we will examine what research on pedagogical intervention has to say about the effects of different instructional strategies for L2 pragmatic learning. How pragmatics is learned in instructed environments in which pragmatics has not been the object of pedagogical intervention was discussed in Chapter 6 (see also Rose & Kasper, 2001). The rationale for examining the effects of instruction in pragmatics is underscored by Schmidt's (1993) contention that simple exposure to the target language is insufficient—pragmatic functions and relevant contextual factors are often not salient to learners and so not likely to be noticed despite prolonged exposure. Schmidt also notes that even the learning of first language pragmatics is facilitated by a range of strategies caregivers employ to teach children communicative competence, that is, that children learning first language pragmatics do so with more than mere exposure to the target language. Furthermore, it is also true that outside of instructional settings, adult learners tend to receive little feedback and sometimes lack relevant input for the learning of pragmatics (for discussion, see Chapter 6). Bardovi-Harlig (2001) makes a strong case for the necessity of instruction, documenting that second language learners who do not receive instruction in pragmatics differ significantly from native speakers in their pragmatic production and comprehension in the target language. Because instructed learning of second language pragmatics is a subset of instructed second language acquisition, we will begin by situating our review of research on the classroom teaching of pragmatics within the larger research domain. We will then discuss the learning targets, learner characteristics, and learning contexts represented in the small, but growing, body of published research on the effects of instruction in second language pragmatics. Next, we turn to three central questions relating to the effect of instruction on pragmatics: whether pragmatics is teachable, whether instruction in pragmatics produces results that outpace exposure alone, and whether different instructional approaches yield different outcomes. We conclude by discussing research design issues in studies on instruction in second language pragmatics.

Research on Instructed Second Language Acquisition

In a recent meta-analysis of instructed second language acquisition research, Norris and Ortega (2000) identified some 250 published research reports on instructed SLA, and from these they selected 49 experimental studies that met their criteria for inclusion in a quantitative meta-analysis. Their study was designed to answer six basic questions central to instructed SLA research:

1. How effective is L2 instruction overall and relative to simple exposure or meaning-driven communication?

2. What is the relative effectiveness of different types and categories of L2 instruction?

3. Does type of outcome measure influence observed instructional effectiveness?

4. Does length of instruction influence observed instructional effectiveness?

5. Does instructional effect last beyond immediate post-experimental observations?

6. To what extent has primary research provided answers to these questions? (Norris & Ortega, 2000, pp. 428–429)

The outcome of their meta-analysis led Norris and Ortega to conclude that "the current state of findings within this research domain suggests that treatments involving an explicit focus on the rule-governed nature of L2 structures are more effective than treatments that do not include such a focus" (pp. 482–483). They also noted that results from explicit instruction were less heterogeneous than those resulting from implicit instruction. Despite these findings, however, Norris and Ortega urged caution because primary research to date "has not focused on the systematic accumulation of findings in direct response to [research questions 1–5], as evinced in study designs, data analysis and study reporting" (p. 489). They also provided a list of nine recommendations for improving research practice (pp. 497–498). Norris and Ortega's work makes a significant contribution to the field of instructed second language acquisition, but although it serves as an excellent model for assessing the cumulative evidence of quantitative research on the effects of instruction in pragmatics, a quantitative meta-analysis of this sort would be out of the question at this time—there are simply not enough studies to consider. Such an analysis will have to wait for the publication of a significantly larger number of well-designed studies, something we hope to see in the years ahead. At the same time, the quantitative approach taken by Norris and Ortega in no way obviates the need for classroom research that examines the impact of different instructional arrangements on the learning of pragmatics from various qualitative research perspectives.

Learning Targets

Research on the effectiveness of classroom instruction has targeted a variety of discoursal, pragmatic, and sociolinguistic targets of instruction, such as discourse markers and strategies, pragmatic routines, speech acts, overall discourse characteristics, and pragmatic comprehension.

Among the studies that have examined the effects of instruction on discourse markers and strategies are Wildner-Bassett's (1984, 1986) work on gambits in English and Yoshimi's (2001) study of Japanese interactional discourse markers. Wildner-Bassett selected as the object of instruction formulas and conversational routines for speech acts such as expressions of agreement and disagreement, or requests. Because her participants were adults in a corporate context, the type of activities she utilized invoked real-life tasks for her learners, including language used for checking into a hotel and rebooking a flight. Yoshimi's (2001) study focused on the Japanese discourse markers *n desu*, *n desu ne*, and *n desu kedo*, all of which "play important roles in organizing the presentation of an extended telling, and in expressing the speaker's interpersonal orientation in such a telling" (p. 224). For example, *n desu* signals to the hearer that the speaker has not yet finished her telling, while *n desu kedo* marks a piece of information as critical background knowledge necessary to the understanding of the narrative in question. The various functions of these three interactional markers represent a range of important, and often subtle, aspects of the pragmatics of Japanese oral narratives, and were of immediate use to her highly motivated, advanced learners of Japanese.

Pragmatic routines represented in the literature include the various functions of Japanese *sumimasen* in Tateyama, Kasper, Mui, Tay, and Thananart (1997) and Tateyama (2001), as well as hedging in academic writing and computer-mediated discourse in Wishnoff (2000). In Tateyama's studies, beginning learners of Japanese were taught the range of discourse-pragmatic functions realized by the routine formula *sumimasen*, such as getting attention, apologizing, and expressing gratitude. Learners were also made aware of additional forms that perform one or more of these functions, but not all three. Because participants in Wishnoff's study were far more advanced than Tateyama's learners of Japanese, Wishnoff's instructional goals involved the rather complex area of hedging expressions in academic writing. These included conditional statements (e.g., *could*), modifiers (e.g., *usually, some*), framing statements (e.g., *even though, I would argue*), verb choice (e.g., *it seems to me, it depends*), and quantifiers (e.g., *some, many*). Participants in this study were graduate students enrolled in an academic ESL writing course who viewed instruction in hedging as directly relevant and useful to their academic writing requirements outside the writing classroom.

Several studies have focused on specific speech acts and their realization strategies. Such studies include Olshtain and Cohen's (1990) work on apologies. Their study was expressly aimed at moving past the more basic apology forms—explicit indicators of illocutionary force such as *I'm sorry* and *I apologize*—to a wider range of semantic formulas used in apologies, such as explanation (e.g., *I didn't see you coming*), offer of repair (e.g., *Let me buy you a new one*) and promise of forbearance (e.g., *It won't happen again*), as well as the use of intensifiers (e.g., *I'm* very *sorry*). Billmyer (1990a, 1990b) and Rose and Ng (2001) have taken up compliments and compliment responses as the object of instruction. Manes and Wolfson's (1981) research on compliments has served as the main source of instructional content for these studies by providing the nine so-called syntactic formulas for compliments, the top three of which (e.g., *That dress is really nice, I really love that dress, That's really a nice dress*) accounted for some 85% of compliments in their corpus. For compliment responses, learners in both studies were taught a range of compliment response types (i.e., accept, deflect, and reject), and also made aware of the interactional utility of deflection as a preferred strategy. For Billmyer's participants, the learning targets were immediately applicable in real-life interaction, a rarity in the research literature, and quite a contrast to the learners in the study by Rose and

Ng (2001), for whom the instructional aims did not serve as direct a purpose. Requests have also served as the learning target in several studies. In the case of Fukuya and Clark (2001), the focus was on six mitigators (i.e., *perhaps, possibly, I'd be grateful if, I'd appreciate if, I was wondering if,* and *I know ... but*) used to soften the impositional force of requests. For Takahashi (2001), the target was instead two bi-clausal English request forms (i.e., *Would / could you VP* and *Would it be possible to VP*). Takahashi's previous work had demonstrated that Japanese learners of English were unable to determine the proper functional equivalents for these request forms in Japanese, which indicates lack of pragmalinguistic knowledge on their part concerning one manner in which request imposition can be mitigated in English. These request studies also contrast in terms of the learning targets' overt relevance to learners—while both studies involved the learning of requests, the second language context of Fukuya and Clark (2001) likely made the material covered of more apparent relevance to learners than the foreign language setting in Takahashi's study.

A smaller body of research has examined instruction in overall discourse characteristics. Among these are Lyster's (1994) study on the effects of instruction on sociostylistic variation in French, House's (1996) work on pragmatic fluency in English, and Liddicoat and Crozet's (2001) study on the "good weekend" question in French. Lyster focused on the contextually appropriate use of the French pronouns *tu* and *vous*, the latter of which is preferred in more formal contexts—an apparently difficult point for his Grade 8 French immersion students in Canada. House (1996) set rather more ambitious learning targets, which included gambits (e.g., uptakers, clarifiers, appealers, and starters), discourse strategies (e.g., grounders, disarmers, topic introducers), and speech acts (e.g., greeting, leave-taking). House (1996) notes that hers were "very advanced German university students of English" (p. 229), which no doubt accounts for such challenging material. For Liddicoat and Crozet's (2001) second-year French students, the learning target was interactionally appropriate responses to the French *T'as passé un bon week-end?* (Did you have a good weekend?), which should be elaborated and not formulaic, and should invoke indicators of attentive listener behavior. Thus, the instruction covered areas such as expression of opinions and feelings, as well as use of repetition and overlap.

Whereas most studies have concentrated on the production of the target features or their use in interaction, instruction specifically aiming at improving learners' pragmatic comprehension has received far less attention. Exceptions are studies on ESL learners' comprehension of implicatures in indirect responses by Bouton (1994a) and Kubota (1995). In both studies, learners were exposed to a range of implicature types, including the Pope-Q implicature (i.e., *Is the Pope Catholic?* in response to a question for which the hearer believes the answer is obvious), and implicatures based on Grice's maxim of relevance (e.g., A: *How about going for a walk?* to which B responds *Is it raining?*).

In sum, the interventional pragmatics studies have examined a fairly wide range of learning targets, including discourse markers and strategies, pragmatic routines, speech acts, and overall discourse characteristics. Studies of pragmatic comprehension, however, are less well represented. Rationale for selection of learning targets varies from one study to another. For example, in the case of the *sumimasen* studies (Tateyama et al., 1997; Tateyama, 2001), Takahashi's (2001) work on bi-clausal request forms, and Bouton's (1994a) implicature research, learning targets were identified as a result of observed learner difficulties in a particular area. In other cases—particularly the speech act studies—selection of learning targets appears to have been driven more by the availability of information derived from the speech act literature. This is particularly true in the compliment and compliment response studies, which rely heavily on work carried out by Manes and Wolfson (1981).

Learner Characteristics and Learning Contexts

Compared to the range of learning targets, the scope of learner characteristics represented in studies of the effectiveness of instruction in L2 pragmatics is rather smaller. Here we consider learners' first language, the target language, age, proficiency, educational context, and the status of the target language in the wider community. Lastly, we will discuss how research outcomes may be affected by the degree to which learners make a good faith effort to learn what they are being taught.

In terms of learners' first languages, English (Liddicoat & Crozet, 2001; Lyster, 1994; Tateyama, 2001; Tateyama et al., 1997; Yoshimi, 2001) and Japanese (Billmyer, 1990a, 1990b; Fukuya & Clark, 2001; Kubota, 1995; LoCastro, 1997; Takahashi, 2001) are equally represented. There are also studies involving NSs of German (House, 1996; Wildner-Bassett, 1984, 1986), Cantonese (Rose & Ng, 2001), and Hebrew (Olshtain & Cohen, 1990), with other studies drawing on mixed-language groups (Bouton, 1994a; Wishnoff, 2000). Reflecting the dominance of English as a target language in second language classroom-based research generally, by a wide margin, English has been the most frequently chosen target language in studies on instruction in pragmatics. The only other target languages represented at the time of writing are Japanese (Tateyama, 2001; Tateyama et al., 1997; Yoshimi, 2001) and French (Liddicoat & Crozet, 2001; Lyster, 1994). In terms of L1-L2 pairs, given the predominance of English L1 and Japanese L2, this pairing counts for about half of the studies. Future research needs to expand the range of first and target languages, not the least in order to enable investigators and language educators to better assess whether and to what extent findings from studies of a particular first or target language may be generalizable to other language pairings.

Another learner characteristic for which there is little variation across studies is age—with the exception of Lyster (1994), whose participants were adolescents, all of the interventional studies to date have involved adult language learners. Because younger learners may require different instructional measures to support their learning of L2 pragmatics, and it is not clear whether child learners in a second language context even require formal instructional intervention (Schmidt, 1993), interventional classroom research for this age group is urgently needed (for observational studies on child classroom learning of L2 pragmatics, see Chapter 6).

More information is available on the role of overall second language proficiency in instructed learning of pragmatics. Whether pragmatics is teachable to beginning learners is one area of concern. Tateyama's studies (Tateyama, 2001; Tateyama et al., 1997) demonstrate that short pragmatic routines are teachable to absolute beginners, indicating that pragmatics can be learned before students begin to develop analyzed second language knowledge. This finding is consistent with research on the role of unanalyzed chunks in first and second language acquisition, showing that routines allow learners to participate in conversation from early on and thus enable further opportunities for input, output, and interaction (cf. Chapter 4). A second issue is whether instruction is at all necessary—or at least facilitative—for learners of more advanced levels of proficiency. As we noted in the introduction to this chapter, a great deal of research documents that advanced learners often do not successfully acquire particular pragmatic practices in a second language without support through targeted instruction (Bardovi-Harlig, 2001; Schmidt, 1993). It appears that pragmatic practices that are difficult for advanced learners to acquire without instruction are in fact learnable through interventional measures (Bouton, 1994a; House, 1996; Olshtain & Cohen, 1990). The majority of studies have included learners of intermediate proficiency, and these studies have also produced the most mixed results. In some studies, students clearly profited from the instruction provided (Billmyer, 1990a, 1990b; Wildner-Bassett, 1984), while in others, only one of several treatments made a difference (Takahashi, 2001), pre-and posttest differences were found on only a few of several measures (Rose & Ng, 2001), initial gains had disappeared by the time of a delayed posttest (Kubota, 1995), or no differences were found between treatment and control groups (Fukuya & Clark, 2001). However, it is doubtful that the small or absent treatment effects derived solely from participants' proficiency—

students' educational background and issues of research design and procedures appear to have contributed to these outcomes.

The rather narrow range of learner characteristics is paralleled by the educational contexts in which the interventional studies have been conducted. With two exceptions—Lyster's (1994) study in a secondary school, and Wildner-Bassett's (1984, 1986) work in a business context—all studies that we are aware of were carried out in universities. More research set in other educational contexts is clearly needed. Concerning the status of the target language in the surrounding community, it is noteworthy that the majority of studies were conducted in a foreign language rather than a second language environment, that is, in contexts where students had little benefit of L2 input and interaction outside the classroom.

An issue that has received very little discussion in the literature so far is that of the degree to which participants actually make a good faith effort to learn what they are being taught, and the impact that this might have on results. Studies on the effects of instruction are generally reported with an implicit assumption that the learners participating in those studies did so in a good faith effort to learn what was being taught. To the degree that this is not the case, a given study is a less valid assessment of the effects of instruction. There is reason to believe that the high level of learner participation desired by researchers cannot always be taken for granted, or at the very least that there is considerable variation in learner effort across contexts and studies, as well as individual differences between learners in the same setting. As noted above, the learning targets chosen for various studies range from those that are directly relevant and applicable to real-life communicative events, to those that are entirely unrelated to learners' immediate concerns and have little application to learners' lives outside the classroom. The former are likely to promote a greater degree of learner effort, while the latter are likely to inspire considerably less. On the high end of the learner-effort scale, we would place studies such as Billmyer (1990a, 1990b) and Wishnoff (2000), both conducted in second language settings in which learners had felt a need for the instructional content, and perhaps more importantly, a context in which to apply their new knowledge to real communication. On the other end of the scale, we would put studies such as Kubota (1995) or Rose and Ng (2001), both of which were carried out in foreign language contexts and whose instructional targets were not the focus of the course in which the students were enrolled and did not have any application to language use outside the classroom. It is unlikely, then, that all students in these studies had a perceived need to acquire the learning targets. This is not to say that even students in a typical foreign language setting taking a mandatory language course cannot be genuinely interested in the target language and its use and make serious efforts to achieve the learning targets, but such engagement cannot be taken for granted, as studies on the effect of instruction in pragmatics usually do. Several studies did elicit feedback from learners on the instruction they received (Olshtain & Cohen, 1990; Tateyama, 2001; Tateyama et al., 1997), but these were intended to measure learner preferences, not the amount of effort expended by learners. What is needed is a measure of learner effort, or at least some informal assessment of the degree to which learners appear to take the learning process seriously.

So far, we have considered the learning targets, learner characteristics, and learning contexts represented in the literature on interventional research in second language pragmatics. Concerning learning targets, we noted that a fairly wide range of features have been targeted for intervention, including discourse markers and strategies, pragmatic routines, speech acts, overall discourse characteristics, and pragmatic comprehension. However, not all learning targets have received equal time—pragmatic comprehension studies are still few and far between. The learner characteristics represented to date offer less variety, with most research participants being adults studying at university, and the languages involved—both L1 and L2—either English or Japanese. We also noted that all proficiency levels are represented in the literature and that foreign language contexts weigh in more heavily than second language settings. Next, we will consider the types of question about the effect of instruction in pragmatics that the research literature has addressed and how these questions have been answered by research outcomes.

Research Issues and Findings

As a backdrop to discussing the overarching research issues and pertinent findings in interventional pragmatics research, a few words concerning the theoretical underpinnings of these studies are in order. Research on the effects of instruction in second language pragmatics has undergone a noticeable shift in theoretical orientation since its inception. Early studies (e.g., Wildner-Bassett, 1984, 1986) were mainly informed by pedagogical theory and practice—both of which continue to inform current investigations—but there has been a move more recently toward engaging SLA theory and research, which in turn is underwritten by psycholinguistics and cognitive psychology in general. The SLA-oriented interventional studies are based on three interrelated hypotheses: Schmidt's noticing hypothesis (e.g., Schmidt, 1993, 1995), Swain's output hypothesis (Swain, 1996), and Long's interaction hypothesis (Long, 1996). The first two hypotheses relate to different stages in the language learning process. The noticing hypothesis holds that in order for input to become intake and thus made available for further processing, it needs to be registered under awareness. The output hypothesis suggests a number of important acquisitional roles for target language production. Among these are the contention that during utterance production, learners may notice gaps in their interlanguage knowledge, making output one way of creating and testing hypotheses about L2. The output hypothesis also maintains that productive language use beyond formulaic speech requires analyzed knowledge that is not called upon in comprehension, and that automatization of language representations requires repeated productive use, as with any skilled behavior. Long's revised formulation of the interaction hypothesis integrates the noticing and output hypotheses and proposes that "negotiation of meaning, and especially the negotiation work that triggers interactional adjustments by the NS or more competent interlocutor, facilitates acquisition because it connects input, internal learner capacities, particularly selective attention, and output in productive ways" (Long, 1996, p. 451). In addition, many SLA theorists argue that meaning-oriented activities in the target language may not enable learners to detect relevant input features, thus prompting the need to employ some form of input enhancement to make input salient and encourage noticing (Sharwood Smith, 1993). When and how input may be most beneficially enhanced and, additionally, when and how feedback is best provided, are controversial issues (cf. Doughty & Williams, 1998; Doughty, 2001). As we shall see below, interventional second language pragmatics studies differ in the degree to which they draw on these various theoretical positions.

Studies on the effect of instruction in pragmatics seek to answer three types of questions:

1. Is the targeted pragmatic feature teachable at all?

2. Is instruction in the targeted feature more effective than no instruction?

3. Are different teaching approaches differentially effective?

The first question, whether pragmatics is amenable to instruction at all, is the most basic of the three questions, representing at best a starting point analogous to Long's (1983) early survey of instructed SLA research, which attempted to answer the question *Does second language instruction make a difference?* Question two—the comparison of the relative merits of instruction versus simple exposure—echoes Norris and Ortega's (2000) first research question, suggesting that this is the point where things begin to get more interesting. Knowing whether a given feature is teachable is one thing, but knowing whether instruction is more effective than exposure is another. One could argue, of course, that in foreign language contexts this question is rather moot given the generally limited opportunities for any level of exposure that is likely to result in acquisition. Still, the question is meaningful in a foreign language setting as well, because "exposure" here refers to the target language input in a classroom that is not organized so as to promote the learning of pragmatics in any planned fashion. The third question, which is number two on Norris and Ortega's list, further specifies the issue by addressing the differential effects of more than one type of instructional intervention. Studies that fall into the third category are likely to yield information that is most relevant for pedagogical purposes. It follows from this hierarchy of complexity that studies that attempt to answer these questions each entail their own requirements as far as research design is concerned. For example, teachability studies do not require a control group; instruction versus exposure studies need to include an experimental group receiving instruction in the target pragmatic feature and a control group that does not; and studies that address the differential effects of various instructional approaches comprise two or more experimental groups, each representing one instructional approach, and a control group if the research goals include the question whether any of the types of instruction is more effective than no instruction. Furthermore, all three research categories improve their validity if they include records of the classroom interaction to ensure that the instruction was delivered as planned in the research design. We will discuss research design issues in more detail later in this chapter.

Teachability

The most basic question that studies of the effect of instruction in pragmatics may consider is whether a particular area of pragmatics is at all teachable. Such studies typically adopt a one-group pretest-posttest design. Olshtain and Cohen (1990) chose as their learning target the more subtle aspects of apologizing, such as the differences between *excuse me* and *I'm sorry*, and the effects of context on the choice of intensifiers. LoCastro's (1997) pedagogical intervention dealt with politeness strategies in group discussion, such as requesting answers, directing the talk, and seeking (dis)agreement, whereas Liddicoat and Crozet (2001) set out to teach appropriately elaborated responses to the French question *T'as passé un bon week-end?* (Did you have a good weekend?). In these studies, treatment lengths varied from three 20-minute sessions (Olshtain & Cohen, 1990) to instruction spread out over a nine-week period (LoCastro, 1997). Assessment measures also varied considerably, from written DCTs (Olshtain & Cohen, 1990) to role plays (Liddicoat & Crozet, 2001) and observations of small group interaction (LoCastro, 1997). The type of instruction adopted in these studies could be characterized as explicit. One useful way of distinguishing explicit and implicit approaches to instruction is DeKeyser's (1995) criteria, according to which

> An L2 instructional treatment [is] considered to be explicit if rule explanation [comprises] part of the instruction . . . or if learners [are] directly asked to attend to particular forms and to try to arrive at metalinguistic generalizations of their own. . . . Conversely, when neither rule presentation nor directions to attend to particular forms [are] part of a treatment, that treatment [is] considered implicit. (p. 437)

We return to the issue of characterizing various approaches to instruction in more detail below in our discussion of studies in category three.

Thus far, results provided by teachability studies have been mixed. LoCastro (1997) found no change after nine weeks of instruction—participants continued to rely on bare head acts at the time of the posttest. Olshtain and Cohen's (1990) participants did not benefit from instruction in terms of overall frequency of semantic formulas used, but posttest responses did contain a wider variety of apology strategies and an increased use of intensifiers compared to the pretest, indicating some benefit from the pragmalinguistic aspects of the instruction. Learners did not, however, change their acceptability ratings of various apology realizations, with their posttest ratings continuing to differ from those of native speakers. Results of the first posttest conducted by Liddicoat and Crozet (2001) showed that the instruction had a greater impact on the overall content of the responses than on use of appropriate interactional devices such as feedback and repetition, that is, all of the content features that were included in the treatment (e.g., on-topic talk, sufficient detail, opinions/feelings) were present in the role play production of most learners, but the instruction had little impact on the interactive devices. There was some evidence of feedback in learner production, but repetition was much less frequent and overlaps were almost entirely absent. Results from a delayed posttest one year after the instructional period showed that learners retained most of the content features, but the only interactional practice they performed was feedback.

What accounts for these findings? One issue to consider—as Norris and Ortega (2000) do in their list of research questions—is whether outcome measures influence observed instructional effectiveness (or lack thereof). In the case of LoCastro's study, there is reason to believe that her pretest-posttest measures may have contributed to the lack of instructional effects, despite a relatively lengthy (compared to other studies) instructional period. She relied on transcripts of a single group discussion conducted in a reading class to determine whether individual learners had benefited from instruction on politeness strategies provided in a speaking class. If it was her goal to assess learners' ability to *use* these strategies in interaction, then more than a single observation—which varied the parameters of the discussion (e.g., gender, topic)—would have been advisable. If the aim was to assess learners' *knowledge* of the strategies, then some sort of individual measure (e.g., a written questionnaire) would have done the trick. It is entirely possible, then, that learners benefited from the instruction—in terms of both knowledge of politeness strategies and the ability to use them—but this did not register on a single occasion of small group interaction in a classroom context. A second issue has to do with quantity, and the related difficulty of the subject matter—was enough instruction provided to reasonably expect results for the particular learning target? For instance, Olshtain and Cohen (1990) provided a mere one hour of instruction, which can hardly be considered sufficient for learners to master the more advanced aspects of apologizing in English. On the other hand, the partial success of two of the studies by Olshtain and Cohen (1990) and Liddicoat and Crozet (2001) also poses interesting theoretical problems. For Olshtain and Cohen, the problem appears to have been that instruction—although effective in promoting more frequent (but not varied) use of apology formulas—was not effective in equipping learners to deal with tasks for which some knowledge of sociopragmatics was required. That is, learners were presented with contexts, together with a range of possible apology strategies, and asked to indicate whether they considered the various apologies "acceptable," "more or less acceptable," or "not acceptable," as seen below in extract (7.1).

(7.1) A student forgets to return a book to the professor

a._____ I'm terribly sorry. I forgot it.

b._____ Oh, damn! I forgot it.

c._____ Sorry, I forgot.

d._____ Oh, I'm very sorry. I completely forgot.

e._____ I'm really sorry but I forgot to bring it.

(Olshtain & Cohen, 1990, p. 63).

The fact that learners' ratings did not change as a result of instruction, and remained different from those of native speakers, indicates a lack of sociopragmatic knowledge on their part, that is, they knew the forms and their function, but they did not know their appropriate use in context. Olshtain and Cohen maintain that this is a simple exposure issue, and that an extended length of residence is the solution. But as we discuss in more detail in Chapter 6, exposure alone does not account for gains in pragmatic ability. Of course, Bouton (1994b) has demonstrated that some aspects of pragmatics (in his case, ability to interpret implicatures) do become (more or less) native-like over time, but Bardovi-Harlig (2001) points out that even after lengthy periods of residence in the target language context, pragmatic infelicities can remain. In terms of Bialystok's (1993) two-dimensional model, it might be argued that Olshtain and Cohen's findings are evidence of insufficient control of processing (especially of the mapping of forms to contexts), the type of learning problem that Bialystok considers the primary one for adult second language learners.

Liddicoat and Crozet's (2001) study also produced differential learning effects: participants were successful in acquiring the need for elaborated responses to the "good weekend" question in French, but were less successful in their use of the conversational devices (such as feedback and repetition) that ought to be deployed in responding, as Table 7.1 indicates.

Table 7.1 *Features of Performance in Postinstruction Roleplays*

	Dyads									
	A		*B*		*C*		*D*		*E*	
	S1	*S2*	*S3*	*S4*	*S5*	*S6*	*S7*	*S8*	*S9*	*S10*
Content										
question leads directly to talk on topic	✓	✓	✓	✓	✓	✓	✓	✓	✓	✓
detail	✓	✓	✓	✓	✓	✓	✓	✓	✓	✓
opinions/ feelings	✓	✓	?	X	✓	✓	✓	✓	X	✓
lively/dramatic	✓	✓	✓	✓	?	✓	✓	✓	✓	?
knowing	?	X	✓	✓	✓	✓	?	✓	✓	✓
Form										
feedback	✓	✓	✓	✓	✓	✓	✓	✓	✓	✓
repetition	X	✓	✓	✓	X	X	?	✓	✓	✓
overlap	X	X	✓	✓	X	X	X	X	X	?

Note. ✓ = feature present, X = feature absent, ? = ambiguous result. From "Acquiring French Interactional Norms Through Instruction," by A. Liddicoat and C. Crozet, 2001, in K. R. Rose and G. Kasper (Eds.), *Pragmatics in Language Teaching*, p. 138. New York: Cambridge University Press.

Liddicoat and Crozet argue that cultural aspects of language use may be more easily acquired, and that their particular learners were constrained by proficiency limitations and thus could not achieve the kind of automaticity needed for use of interactive pragmatic features. While we would prefer to withhold judgment on their first point because the available literature—both observational and interventional—generally shows that learners tend to struggle more with the larger cultural (or sociopragmatic) than with pragmalinguistic learning tasks, their second point meshes neatly with Bialystok's contention that low control of processing is the likely culprit for pragmatic infelicities in adults. Liddicoat and Crozet's intermediate-level learners of French were likely unable to simultaneously attend to the propositional content of their contributions and the interactive pragmatic features they were taught.

We now move to the second type of research question, which pits instruction against exposure.

Instruction Versus Exposure

Instruction versus exposure studies address the issue of whether pedagogical intervention in pragmatics leads to more effective learning than no instruction, or put another way, whether instruction is better than simple exposure. These studies provide a direct means of testing Schmidt's noticing hypothesis: the extent to which instruction that serves to draw learners' attention to the targeted features proves to be more beneficial than simple exposure to the target language is the degree to which the noticing hypothesis is supported. Methodologically, studies in this second group are quasi-experimental in nature, essentially two-group pretest-posttest designs without random assignment (Bernard, 2000). As in virtually all classroom-based research, the imperative to work with intact groups renders random assignment impossible. As with the previous group of studies, instruction in each of the studies in this group could be characterized as explicit.

A wide range of learning targets is represented in this group. Billmyer's (1990a, 1990b) study on the effects of instruction on compliments and compliment responses was among the earliest interventional studies, and remains the only study that we are aware of to collect data on learner performance outside the classroom. Bouton (1994a) selected the understanding of implicature as his learning target, while Lyster (1994) examined the use of French *tu / vous* in informal and formal contexts. Wishnoff (2000) investigated the effects of instruction in the use of hedging devices (e.g., verb choice, quantifiers, modifiers, and conditional statements) in both formal and informal texts, and Yoshimi's (2001) study focused on the Japanese interactional markers (*n desu*, *n desu kedo*, *n desu ne*) that feature prominently in the production of oral narratives. The range of instructional periods is also rather wide, with Wishnoff's two class sessions (a total of one-and-a-half hours) on one end, and Yoshimi's 24 hours of instruction spread over an entire semester at the other, a rather hefty amount of instruction compared to most studies. Billmyer and Bouton both provided six hours of instruction, while Lyster's learners were exposed to 12 hours. Assessment procedures included multiple-choice tests (Bouton, 1994a; Lyster, 1994), and production tasks that were oral (Lyster, 1994) and written (Lyster, 1994; Wishnoff, 2000; Yoshimi, 2001). As noted above, only Billmyer (1990a, 1990b) used as a measure of instructional effects learner production in actual face-to-face interaction (i.e., transcripts of meetings with native-speaking conversation partners). It is also worth noting that only Lyster (1994) employed more that one outcome measure.

Without exception, learners receiving instruction in pragmatics outperformed those who did not. Billmyer's (1990a, 1990b) instructed group outperformed the controls for frequency of compliments, norm-appropriate use, spontaneity, and adjectival repertoire, and favored the response strategy of deflection as they were taught, while the control group favored acceptance. In Bouton's (1994a) study, the experimental group achieved results as high as those observed with previous immersion students who had spent four years living in the United States, but there was no such improvement for the control group. Lyster's (1994) experimental participants outperformed uninstructed learners on all tasks except informal oral production, for which all learners used *tu* appropriately, differences that remained at the time of the delayed posttest. In the case of Wishnoff (2000), while use of hedges increased for both groups, the treatment group's hedging devices increased more than five-fold—a statistically significant difference across groups. And Yoshimi's (2001) instructed learners showed a dramatic increase in frequency of interactional markers, but no similar increase in their use by the control group was observed.

While in the cited studies, instruction proved superior to exposure, it is not the case that uninstructed learners showed no improvement at all. In both Billmyer's (1990a, 1990b) and Wishnoff's (2000) studies, learners in the control groups registered noticeable improvement in the features targeted in the treatment provided to the experimental groups. The fact that both studies dealt with subject matter that was of direct and immediate relevance to learners, and more importantly, concerned pragmatic features that learners in both groups were called upon to deploy in actual communicative use of the target language (spoken or written) outside the classroom, is a likely explanation for why learners in the control group improved despite a lack of targeted pedagogical intervention. The second language context no doubt played a significant role here. This is underscored by Yoshimi's (2001) findings: her uninstructed participants were exposed to the same texts as learners in the experimental group, but given the foreign language context did not have the opportunity to encounter and use the target discourse markers outside the classroom and so did not show any signs of improvement. An interesting question, however, is how to explain that Bouton's control group did not improve in the comprehension of implicatures, despite their residence in a second language context. A partial answer may reside in Bouton's (1988, 1994b) studies on the uninstructed acquisition of implicature: he found that after 17 months of residing in the United States, learners continued to have difficulty with four implicature types (i.e., indirect criticism, sequence implicatures, the Pope Q, and irony), but after four years of residence, they were able to interpret implicatures as well as native speakers, having difficulty only with items that required culture-specific knowledge that they did not have. Conceivably, implicature is less salient to learners than compliments, compliment responses and hedging in academic writing, and some implicature types, such as the Pope Q, may also be very infrequent in the input.

Although it was shown that learners who did not receive instruction made gains on some measures of the target pragmatic feature when they had ample opportunity for output (Swain, 1996), it was also true that some areas targeted for instruction proved resistant to improvement. For example, Wishnoff (2000) found that despite the greater frequency of hedging devices used by learners in her experimental group, there were no significant changes in the variety of hedges they used on the pretest and the posttest. The greater frequency of the targeted pragmatic category with concomitant stability in the variety of strategies used is analogous to Olshtain and Cohen's (1990) findings for apologies, discussed above. Both studies also provided a rather limited amount of instruction. Yoshimi (2001) noted that not all the targeted features were learned equally well, and even her experimental learners used the target forms only sparingly during communicative practice sessions, especially where more subtle aspects of the internal structure of tellings were concerned, such as marking shifts in scene or perspective to highlight the point of a story, a result not unlike that of Liddicoat and Crozet (2001) discussed above. In both cases, learners receiving instruction had difficulty in mastering the more subtle aspects of the target features. Here again we can appeal to Bialystok's contention that due to limitations in the control of processing, adult learners may be unable to attend to the more subtle aspects of talk-in-interaction.

In sum, studies that have pitted instruction against no instruction have provided ample support for the benefit of instruction in pragmatics. While it may be true that learners in acquisition-rich contexts who did not receive instruction in the target item(s) improved, and that participants in experimental groups did not uniformly master all of the targeted features, in each and every case, learners receiving instruction significantly outperformed those who did not. This also means that these findings offer considerable support for Schmidt's noticing hypothesis, showing that directing learners' attentional resources to specific target language features promotes learning. Indicative of this support is a related finding from Lyster (1994), who noted that features that learners in the experimental groups were exposed to but for which they received no explicit instruction (e.g., conditionals) were not learned as well, and appear to have been lost by the time of the delayed posttest, another indicator of the superiority of instruction over exposure. Having established with the first group of studies that pragmatics is teachable and with the second group that instruction outpaces exposure alone, the next logical question is whether different types of instruction yield different outcomes, the subject of the third group of studies we consider.

Different Teaching Approaches

A range of theoretical approaches to learning are by now well represented in the SLA literature on the acquisition of morphosyntax, but in pragmatics, such research is still in rather short supply. However, the move toward more direct appeals to theories of L2 learning is best represented in studies that set out to compare the relative effects of more than one type of pedagogical intervention. One reason that direct appeals to current SLA theory have been rare in interventional pragmatics research may be that it is not always obvious how principles proposed for instruction in grammar might translate to pragmatics—because pragmatics is never only form, the notion of focus on form (FonF) may appear inapplicable to pragmatics. Pragmalinguistic knowledge requires mappings of form, meaning, force, and context, which are sometimes obligatory (as in the case of prepackaged routines) and sometimes not (as in the case of nonconventional indirectness). And when we consider sociopragmatics, which refers to the link between action-relevant context factors and communicative action and does not necessarily require any links to specific linguistic forms at all, aligning sociopragmatics with FonF appears to be an even great stretch. Another reason why the interventional pragmatics literature has only recently begun to incorporate current SLA theory may be the terminological and conceptual inexplicitness in the SLA literature regarding just what FonF means from a cognitive perspective.

As an antidote to the prevailing conceptual confusion, Doughty (2001) provides the most detailed and coherent attempt we are aware of to map pedagogical concepts frequently invoked in the FonF literature to "plausible, psychologically real, cognitive correlates" (p. 206). For example, she lists "focus on form" with "simultaneous processing of forms, meaning, and use in working memory" and "noticing the gap" with "detection" and "cognitive comparison." The key categories in her model are cognitive microprocesses (e.g., working memory and noticing), cognitive macroprocesses (e.g., input processing and output production), and cognitive resources (e.g., long-term memory and mental representations of the target language). As Doughty notes, for FonF, the key question is whether pedagogical intervention addressing cognitive microprocesses can have a significant positive effect on cognitive macroprocesses. She also identifies what she considers the three central issues relevant to FonF in language teaching:

1. *The noticing issue*: Do learners have the cognitive resources to notice the gap between their IL utterances and the TL utterances around them?

2. *The interruption issue*: Is a pedagogical intervention that does not interrupt the learner's own processing for language even possible?

3. *The timing issue*: If so, then precisely "when," in cognitive terms, should the pedagogical intervention occur? (p. 209)

While it is beyond the scope of this chapter to summarize Doughty's entire argument, the literature she reviews leads her to conclude that the answer to the first two questions is "yes" and that "one of the most promising kinds of intervention is an immediate contingent recast, which can easily fit into [working memory] along with the original utterance to which it is to be compared" (p. 257). An interesting issue for us, then, will be to examine how FonF has been conceptualized in the interventional pragmatics literature, to what extent studies have incorporated recasts as part of the treatment, and what the effect of either or both interventions has been.

In attempts to extend FonF to pragmatics, recalling three sets of oppositions may be useful. The contrast between "focus on meaning" and "focus on form(S)" is paralleled by the opposition between language-in-use and metalinguistic information and allows for an analogous distinction between pragmatic and metapragmatic information. Just as the shift from focus on meaning to a focus on form can be triggered by a grammatical error in the learner's utterance and result in a recast, the shift from pragmatic action to metapragmatic comment can be triggered by a contextually inappropriate pragmatic feature. As long as such problems are clearly pragmalinguistic and involve short linguistic items that can be promptly located and unambiguously identified, they may lend themselves well to recast in an instructional setting. But if the problem is sociopragmatic, it may be more difficult to locate in the ongoing interaction. For example, a learner may employ a politeness style that strikes an interlocutor (or teacher) as too reliant on negative (or positive) politeness. Styles come as packages of features distributed over the entire discourse (Cook, 2001), so isolating and repairing a particular feature would be insufficient. Furthermore, in talk-in-interaction, the production and sequencing of communicative acts is jointly accomplished. If the learner starts out a complaint about rather loud violin playing from a neighbor's daughter by commenting to the neighbor that her daughter seems to be making excellent musical progress, and the neighbor instantly launches into apology, explanation, and a promise of forbearance, the learner will never have to perform anything close to a complaint, yet she has reached her communicative goal successfully. In a teaching sequence about complaining, there is thus no occasion for intervention during the ongoing interaction, even though the learner never did complain. But perhaps the most serious reservation against instant identification and repair of sociopragmatic problems is that such intervention presupposes firm sociopragmatic norms against which communicative action can be assessed, norms that privilege a particular course of communicative action and negatively sanction others. While such norms strongly constrain ritual communication and (to greater or lesser extent) institutional discourse, less prestructured encounters such as casual conversation present a wide range of allowable, and largely unpredictable, contributions, regulated by a "conversational contract" (Fraser, 1990) that is always subject to renegotiation. What counts as sociopragmatically appropriate is thus both guided by social, cultural, and personal preferences and the dynamics of the ongoing interaction. Because such preferences and the options and constraints emerging from the interaction itself elude instant repair, they can most adequately be addressed in metapragmatic discussion.

As an illustration of the difficulties posed by adapting strategies developed for instruction in linguistic form to teaching sociopragmatic information, a study by Fukuya, Reeve, Gisi, and Christianson (1998) is particularly revealing. One stumbling block in their study on teaching the sociopragmatics of requesting was to operationalize the distinction between focus on form and focus on formS. Another problem was to determine how a focus on form could be implemented through recasts during ongoing interaction, reflecting the difficulties discussed above. While recasting of sociopragmatic information is restricted to highly prestructured interactions, it appears more promising to extend the distinction between a focus on form and formS to pragmalinguistics. According to Long and Robinson (1998), form and formS focused instruction differ not so much in substance—what kinds of metalinguistic information is given—but in the role and contextualization of metalinguistic information in the syllabus and class activities. As long as the metalinguistic information is embedded in meaningful activities, triggered by an actual learner problem, and teachable at the learners' current stage of interlanguage development, the intervention would be considered FonF. Where pragmatics is concerned, then, it is not the quality of the metapragmatic information provided that determines whether a particular intervention provides focus on form or formS, but the role of metapragmatic information in the syllabus and its relation to practice activities. Metapragmatic comment generated by students' pragmatic action or observations would seem to be compatible with FonF. And indeed, without referring to FonF, several of the interventional studies in our third category illustrate what might better be termed FonFF in pragmatics—a focus on form and function.

Most studies comparing the effectiveness of different teaching approaches select two types of pedagogical intervention, and in all cases the intervention could be construed as explicit versus implicit. The operationalization of these constructs, however, varies across studies, particularly concerning the degree to which the studies could be considered exemplars of research on FonFF. A number of studies (e.g., Fukuya et al., 1998; House, 1996; Wildner-Bassett, 1984, 1986) report having incorporated corrective feedback into the treatment, although only Fukuya et al. (1998) specifically mention recasts. These studies also satisfy the key criteria of FonF: that any attention paid to form be done in the context of meaningful interaction, and that the forms themselves are not the organizing principle for the syllabus. By contrast, most studies comparing interventional approaches (e.g., Kubota, 1995; Rose & Ng, 2001; Takahashi, 2001; Tateyama, 2001; Tateyama et al., 1997) have a less direct relationship with FonF—in fact, given that in most of these studies the syllabus was organized around particular pragmatic features, they would more accurately be considered an extension of focus on formS to pragmatics. Although most of this research involved treatment that incorporated meaningful interaction, the pragmatic issues they addressed were planned as the core of the instructional treatment and did not arise from student problems encountered during meaningful language use. Instead, meaningful language use was an arena for the application of particular, predetermined forms. One could argue as well that these studies have much in common with those examining the effect of instruction versus no instruction discussed in the previous section, with a crucial difference being that while studies in the second group compared instruction to exposure, which was not manipulated to ensure that it contained the target features, studies in the third group involved two (or more) treatments that guaranteed that learners were exposed to and used the target features. The main feature distinguishing one group from another was the provision of metapragmatic information designed to make the target features more salient. These studies, then, are a more direct test of Schmidt's noticing hypothesis.

As with the instruction versus exposure studies, interventional research on different teaching approaches also provides support for noticing: in most cases, learners who received explicit instruction in the form of metapragmatic information regarding the target features outperformed those who did not. Wildner-Bassett's (1984, 1986) work on gambits to express (dis)agreement in a business context found that the explicit group outperformed those who received instruction based on the principles of suggestopedia in terms of the quality of gambits, and, perhaps more importantly, in their fluent (as indicated by a decrease in the use of filler and hesitation) deployment of gambits in role play interaction. Likewise, House's (1996) explicit group outperformed the implicit group in use of a range of pragmatic routines and discourse strategies such as the use of turn-internal gambits with interpersonal focus, managing discourse transitions, and topic initiation and change. Overall, explicit learners once again evidenced integrated these elements into discourse more successfully than was observed for the implicit group. And after only 50 minutes of instruction, Tateyama et al. (1997) found that beginning learners of Japanese as a foreign language engaged in role play benefited more when they were provided with metapragmatic information on the various functions of *sumimasen* than when they were not.

Rose and Ng's (2001) study on the effects of instruction in English compliments and compliment responses was one of the few that employed a control group in addition to two treatment groups. Although (following DeCoo, 1996) they use the terms *inductive* and *deductive* to characterize their instructional treatments, the distinguishing characteristics of the treatments is essentially the same as in other studies discussed so far—the provision (or lack) of explicit metapragmatic information. Three measures were used—a self-assessment questionnaire, a metapragmatic assessment questionnaire, and a discourse completion test (DCT). Across-group differences were not obtained for the first two measures, but DCT responses for compliments and compliment responses showed that learners in both treatment groups outperformed those in the control group. The increase in use of syntactic formulas for compliments was similar for learners in the two treatment groups, but explicit learners fared better where compliment responses were concerned, producing responses that were closer to those of an NS comparison group. Possible explanations for these findings are that Rose and Ng's learners were rather advanced, as evidenced by high scores on measures other than the DCT, thus enabling them to benefit from either type of instruction, at least where syntactic formulas for compliments was concerned. It could also be the case that the syntactic form of compliments is a rather easy pragmalinguistic feature of English to acquire. It would be of interest to see whether instruction in other pragmatic features produced similar findings. Also, the fact that learners in the explicit group outperformed their implicit counterparts in responding to compliments underscores the utility of metapragmatic discussion where sociopragmatics is concerned, as we noted above.

With four treatment groups, Takahashi's (2001) study on bi-clausal request forms boasts the most complex design represented so far. An explicit group was fronted by a teacher who provided metapragmatic information, a form comparison group had learners comparing request forms in transcripts to their own request forms, a form search group was required to search for request forms in transcripts, and a meaning-focused group listened to and read input containing the target forms. A pretest-posttest DCT revealed that learners in the explicit group outperformed all other groups in the use of target forms. Learners in the form comparison group used the target forms only minimally, while participants receiving form search and meaning-focused instruction did not use the forms at all. An immediate written retrospective and a follow-up questionnaire were used to determine whether groups that had not received explicit instruction had in fact noticed the target forms in the input. Results for these seem to indicate that this was not the case: while learners in the explicit group tended to mention both discourse features (e.g., order of elements) as well as linguistic form, learners in other groups tended to mention only discourse features. This study, then, provides rather unambiguous support for Schmidt's noticing hypothesis. Not only was it the case that learners in the explicit group outperformed learners in all other groups in the use of the target features, but the fact that the learners in the form comparison group—whose attention was drawn more to the forms than those in the form search and meaning groups—were next in line indicates the value of drawing learners' attention to specific target language features. Takahashi's use of the written retrospections and questionnaires to determine that learners in the form search and meaning groups apparently did not even notice the target forms is further evidence of a link between noticing and learning (or, in this case, a lack of both).

Despite the general trend noted so far in support of explicit instruction, it was not the case that every study comparing two (or more) approaches to instruction found that provision of metapragmatic information produced better results. Kubota's (1995) replication of Bouton's study on implicature comprehension actually found that learners in an implicit group outperformed those in an explicit group, although by the time of a delayed posttest, these differences had disappeared. Given the design and execution of Kubota's study (one 20-minute treatment in a two-hour class, which was also used for administering the pre- and posttests, and the use of items on the pretest and posttest as part of the treatment), there are a number of validity issues that militate against looking too hard for a theoretical (or other) explanation of these findings. Studies by Fukuya et al. (1998) and Fukuya and Clark (2001) were inconclusive, that is, posttests revealed no significant differences across treatment groups in the use of the target features. In both cases, the authors appealed to length of treatment as an explanation for the failure to find instructional effects, and Fukuya et al. (1998) even noted trends (although statistically insignificant) across groups that might indicate that the instruction was beginning to have an effect. Although some studies have produced impressive results even with short periods of instruction (e.g., Tateyama et al., 1997), there is no doubt a complex relationship between (at least) length of instruction, learner proficiency level, and difficulty of learning targets that must be considered in assessing the effects of length of instruction on pragmatic learning. Two studies that set out to do just that, and produced rather unexpected findings, are Tateyama et al. (1997) and Tateyama (2001). As noted above, the initial study found positive effects even after instruction limited to one class period. However, when Tateyama (2001) increased the instructional period to four sessions spread over eight weeks, posttest role plays revealed no differences across groups. Tateyama explained that data from a background questionnaire suggested that the students in the implicit group had more out-of-class contact with native speakers of Japanese, an obvious threat to internal validity, and a clear reminder of the importance of collecting as detailed information as possible on learners' exposure to the target language outside of the classroom.

In addition to studies that produced inconclusive results, just as in the instruction versus exposure studies, there were also cases in which certain aspects of the target language proved resistant to instruction. House (1996) found that even though learners in her explicit group had made considerable progress in incorporating pragmatic routines and discourse strategies into role play interaction, they continued to display negative transfer from German, for example, in reliance on content-oriented and self-referenced gambits instead of interpersonal gambits, overuse of *yes* in various interactional slots surrounding turn-taking, and especially problems in producing well-aligned responding turns. These lingering problems are reminiscent of those noted by Liddicoat and Crozet (2001) and Yoshimi (2001), both of whom also found that learners had difficulty incorporating some target features into online interaction. As we noted above, the explanation for these problems is likely to be limitations in control of processing (Bialystok, 1993). Takahashi also found that participants' use of *I wonder if you could VP* predominated across all situations, regardless of degree of imposition, providing no evidence of development in terms of sociopragmatic proficiency. The fact that even her explicit learners—who clearly benefited from the instruction in terms of frequency of use—still did not differentiate request forms appropriately across contexts is likely another indicator of the difficulty of learning sociopragmatics, especially in a foreign language context. Perhaps metapragmatic discussion on the use of the target request forms in context would be more effective for learning sociopragmatic distinctions than the teacher-fronted approach used for the explicit group, but that is an empirical question.

It is fair to say, then, that studies comparing different instructional approaches—despite some seemingly contradictory findings—provide considerable support for the value of explicit instruction (and thus the noticing hypothesis), even though they have yet to fully incorporate the theoretical concepts represented in FonF. In most cases where there was not some apparent methodological (or other) flaw, learners who had been provided with metapragmatic information regarding the target feature(s) outperformed those who did not. Of course, certain areas remained difficult for all learners, particularly where online use of the target features in interaction was concerned. Sociopragmatics was also frequently an area of difficulty, although there is evidence that better results are produced with metapragmatic discussion than without (Rose & Ng, 2001). Taken together with studies discussed in the previous two sections, we are able to come to some tentative conclusions. First, there is considerable evidence indicating that a range of features of second language pragmatics are teachable. These include a variety of discoursal, pragmatic, and sociolinguistic targets of instruction, such as discourse markers and strategies, pragmatic routines, speech acts, overall discourse characteristics, and pragmatic comprehension. Second, it appears that learners who receive instruction fare better than those who do not. Of course, given an environment that affords ample opportunity for exposure to and meaningful use of the target language, learners can acquire some, perhaps many, features of pragmatics without instruction. That is, instruction is not *necessary* for each and every pragmatic learning object in the sense that it *cannot* be learned without instruction. However, the fact that instructed learners outpaced their uninstructed counterparts indicates that pedagogical intervention has at least an important facilitative role, which is especially good news for learners in foreign language contexts. This overall outcome of studies on the effect of instruction is in complete agreement with research showing that without instruction in pragmatics, learners do not achieve sufficient ability in a range of pragmatic areas (Bardovi-Harlig, 2001). Nevertheless, because of the small body of studies and documented limits to instructional effects on some learning targets, these conclusions have to remain tentative at this point. More conclusive research outcomes depend in no small measure on research-methodological decisions, as Norris and Ortega (2000) emphasized for the literature on instructed SLA. Therefore, we will consider a number of design issues in our final section.

Design Issues in Research on Instruction in Pragmatics

The studies we have considered in this chapter are exponents of some type of (quasi-)experimental research, and although a detailed account of experimental methodology is beyond the scope of this book, some discussion is in order. Experiments measure the effect of a treatment by identifying causal relationships among variables. Several different types of experiment are commonly distinguished, depending on whether they have an experimental group and a control group, whether participants are randomly assigned to either group, and whether the effect of the treatment is measured by a pre- and posttest (see Bernard, 2000, for an overview). Interventional classroom research is usually quasi-experimental because the necessity of working with intact groups makes random assignment impossible. It is also true that with few exceptions (Fukuya et al., 1998; Rose & Ng, 2001), the interventional pragmatics studies do not make use of control groups, generally due to ethical or practical constraints. Conducting research without a control group produces less conclusive findings because there is always the possibility that any observed effects might not have resulted from the treatment(s). In a few cases (Fukuya & Clark, 2001; Tateyama et al. 1997), rather than examining the effect of a treatment and making claims about causality, post hoc designs were used to investigate the type and strength of relationships between variables. Hatch and Lazaraton (1991, pp. 99ff.) usefully refer to post hoc designs as a method of answering "what is going on" questions as opposed to the "what caused this" question of the experiment.

No matter what the research design is, participant selection affects research outcomes. In quasi-experimental designs, nonrandom participant assignment to groups poses a threat to internal validity. As noted above, this is generally the case in the interventional pragmatics research. Confounding participant variables are also a concern. In order not to compromise the internal validity of her transferability study, Takahashi (2001) controlled for gender (all participants were men) and age. External validity, the generalizability of research outcomes beyond the research setting, is the goal of most quantitative research, and it presupposes internal validity, as most research methods texts note (e.g., Hatch & Lazaraton, 1991; Bernard, 2000), but external validity also crucially depends on the similarity of the research participants and the wider population to which the researcher wishes to generalize. Issues of participant selection, assignment to groups, and the use of pre- and posttests represent several of the more basic considerations of experimental methodology in general. In addition, several issues arising from our discussion of the interventional pragmatics literature merit attention.

One critical task of experimental research on the effects of instruction in pragmatics—particularly studies that explore the differential effects of one or more pedagogical approaches—is to employ measures to determine that instructional treatments were applied as intended. This requires regular classroom observation, preferably including periods before, during, and after the intervention. Without such observation, it cannot be taken for granted that treatments were provided as intended. Few of the interventional pragmatics studies we have discussed indicated that measures were taken to verify that treatments were delivered as intended. Those studies that did note having done so made use of a various techniques, including participant-observation (Wildner-Bassett, 1984, 1986) and audiotaping of lessons (Rose & Ng, 2001). Audio, or preferably videorecordings, carefully transcribed and analyzed according to a specified discourse-pragmatic approach, provide essential documentation of how students and teachers implement the interventional agenda in classroom interaction and afford insights into the acquisitional potential of different classroom activities for learning the designated pragmatic practices. The findings of such observations should also figure prominently in detailed descriptions of research and be included in written research reports.

Another issue that merits attention is the assessment of outcomes. Many of the interventional studies have relied on a single measure of instructional effects, with a handful making use of two. The studies by Tateyama and her colleagues (Tateyama, 2001; Tateyama et al., 1997) were unique in their use of multiple measures. But there is more to this issue than quantity: far more attention needs to be paid to the development of outcome measures. The fact that most studies do not even mention test development, or discuss how validity and reliability were addressed, is a clear indicator of the need for more work in this area. A related issue here is the use of delayed posttests: only a handful of studies (Kubota, 1995; Liddicoat & Crozet, 2001; Lyster, 1994) report the use of delayed posttests, and for two of these the delay is only one month, whereas Liddicoat and Crozet (2001) conducted the delayed posttest one year after the end of the instruction period. Some studies indicate that a delayed posttest was planned, but not possible (Rose & Ng, 2001; Takahashi, 2001) due to institutional constraints or the unavailability of participants. Ideally, delayed posttests should be a standard design feature in interventional research because without their use it is not possible to determine whether the gains that students made through instruction are durable.

Yet another area relevant for the assessment of outcomes is the appeal to native-speaker norms, the prevailing practice that assessment of learner outcomes takes the form of comparison to some native-speaker "baseline." There are a number of problems with this approach. Determining such a norm is difficult because of the sociolinguistic variability in the language use of native speakers. Selecting the variety or varieties most relevant for a particular learner population in a principled manner is not a straightforward task for any target language; it is a particularly daunting task with respect to a language with a highly diverse native-speaker population such as English, the language most studied and taught worldwide. It is also unrealistic to posit an ideal communicatively competent native speaker as a target for L2 learners since communication among native speakers is regularly partial, ambiguous, and fraught with potential and manifest misunderstanding (Coupland, Giles, & Wiemann, 1991; House, Kasper, & Ross, 2003). And learners may not, for a range of reasons, aspire to L2 native-speaker pragmatics as their target, as we will discuss further in Chapter 8, nor may members of a speech community expect or even value complete convergence to their ways of speaking, as we have seen in Chapter 6. Since L2 learners are by definition multilingual speakers, a defensible standard against which their pragmatic ability is measured must be derived from successful multilingual speakers' interactions in activities relevant for a given learner population (House & Kasper, 2000). Establishing such a standard for language teaching and testing purposes is obviously a highly complex undertaking, requiring as input not only studies that examine pragmatic failure but, especially, research on divergent but successful nonnative-speaker communication.

Chapter Summary

This chapter has reviewed studies of the effects of instruction in second language pragmatics. We have discussed the learning targets, learner characteristics, learning contexts, and types of research issues represented in the small but growing body of interventional pragmatics studies published at the time of writing. These studies have addressed three main research questions: whether pragmatics is teachable, whether instruction in pragmatics produces results that outpace exposure alone, and whether explicit and implicit instruction yield different outcomes. Results of these studies strongly suggest that most aspects of L2 pragmatics are indeed teachable, that instructional intervention is more beneficial than no instruction specifically targeted on pragmatics, and that for the most part, explicit instruction combined with ample practice opportunities results in the greatest gains. There are, however, limits to the effects of instruction, particularly in cases where an insufficient control of processing is an issue. However, we have also noted that there is considerable room for improvement in the research methodology employed to examine the effects of instruction in pragmatics, as well as room for a wider range of theoretical orientations.

CHAPTER EIGHT

Individual Differences in L2 Pragmatic Development

Many aspects of pragmatics are inseparable not only from sociocultural practices and values but also from personal views, preferences, and style, which in turn may be related to learners' societal position and experience. Yet more often than not, in cross-cultural and interlanguage pragmatics research, individual variation is submerged in the aggregate. Whereas the study of individual differences (IDs) has long been a recognized subfield of second language acquisition research, with its own research traditions and a voluminous literature, the role of individual differences in the acquisition of L2 pragmatics has rarely been addressed. This is a remarkable lacuna, considering that L2 pragmatic practices may provoke affective responses in L2 learners that are unlikely to have counterparts in learners' responses to L2 grammar. Learners may well experience the English article, Chinese tones, and German word order as a nuisance to learn, but no research has shown any particular affective stance toward such formal properties of target languages, or how such a stance might influence the acquisition of the grammatical features. Pragmatics is a different sort of attitudinal object. Among nonnative speakers residing in the target speech community, L2 pragmatic practices are a favorite topic of conversation, together with other sociocultapturally distinct ways of doing things. People do not just register cross-cultural differences, they have opinions (often critical ones) about them. In a much-cited early paper, Thomas (1983)

275

commented that sociopragmatics (more so than pragmalinguistics) is closely related to people's cultural and personal beliefs and values, making it more of a personal value decision whether learners wish to converge to target practices—a speculation that does not hold up to empirical scrutiny, as the evidence cited in this chpater demonstrates. This chapter examines the relationship between IDs and the development of L2 pragmatics. First, we apply Ellis's typology for categorizing ID research to interlanguage pragmatic studies. Following this, we discuss a range of individual learner characteristics—age, gender, motivation, social and psychological distance, social identity—and their relationship to L2 pragmatic development.

A Framework for ID Research

In his review of literature on IDs in SLA, Ellis (1994) categorizes ID studies according to two dimensions, the role of theory and the research tradition. In hierarchical approaches (theory-then-research), a theory on IDs in L2 learning is adopted at the outset of the study and tested against data. Concatenative approaches (research-then-theory) are guided by research questions rather than by preexisting theory. They explore the relationship between ID factors, other variables, and (possibly) their differential impact on L2 learning and use. The main two research traditions are naturalistic, observing IDs between L2 learners in authentic contexts, and confirmatory, in which a research environment is specifically created for the purpose of the study. This dimension corresponds to our distinction between observational and interventional research (cf. Chapter 7). By combining the two dimensions, Ellis proposes four types of ID research: (a) hierarchical-naturalistic, (b) concatenative-naturalistic, (c) hierarchical-confirmatory, and (d) concatenative-confirmatory (p. 477). Although the body of research on IDs in L2 pragmatic development is small, it can usefully be framed in terms of Ellis's typology. A prime example of a hierarchical-naturalistic investigation is Schmidt's Wes study (1983), which was an explicit test of the acculturation model.

A hierarchical-confirmatory study was conducted by Takahashi (2000), who examined how motivation affected students' learning of request forms. Kim (2000) adopted a concatenative-confirmatory approach in her study on the impact of age of arrival, cultural identity, and input on learners' production of requests and apologies. The concatenative-naturalistic category is perhaps best illustrated by the ethnographic studies conducted by Siegal (1994, 1995, 1996), Iino (1996), and DuFon (1999), with the provision that these studies are all but theory-free. In keeping with the role of theory in ethnographic research, they are guided by explicit theoretical frameworks that help identify and interpret individual variation in the participants' learning of L2 pragmatics, but they are not designed as tests of a particular theory, as a hierarchical study would be.

The literature on IDs in second language acquisition commonly distinguishes such categories as age, gender, language aptitude, personality variables, and cognitive, social, and affective factors (Ellis, 1994, p. 472, for an overview). To the extent that interlanguage pragmatics research addresses IDs at all, it has considered all of these variables, with the exception of aptitude. However, the researchers' theoretical lens does not always permit sharp distinctions between these categories. In studies that fall into the "confirmatory" tradition in Ellis's model, either learner factors are conceptualized as causal variables that are believed to explain learner behavior (experimental research, "hierarchical"), or they are viewed as variables that pattern in particular ways—with other variables or with learner behavior—but no causality claims are made (correlational research, "concatenative"). Variables are neatly separated and, in the case of complex constructs, further broken down into more specific categories, such as different types of motivation. Typically, values of learner variables are understood to be stable and impervious to context variation. Views of individual differences in language learning as manifestations of measurable behaviors and constructs have a long tradition in SLA and are alive and well in contemporary research. Such views have been contested. In most of the "naturalistic" interlanguage pragmatic studies that have addressed individual differences, learners' efforts to learn the target language, their actions and attitudes are inseparable from who they are, where they are, in what activities they are engaged, and who they interact with. Isolating individual learner factors runs against the ontological assumption that language learning is always socially contextualized and often co-constructed. With the caveat in mind—that separating individual learner factors is not an unproblematic analytical undertaking with respect to holistic studies—we will examine how individual differences in developing L2 pragmatic ability may be related to age, gender, motivation, and sociocultural identity. As some factors have been addressed in only one study, and then not even as its central investigative concern, this review is probably best read as a strong invitation to research on individual differences in learning L2 pragmatics.

Age

In SLA, age has predominantly been treated as a neurological and neurolinguistic variable. The issue is whether age acts as a maturational constraint on the route and rate of second language development and on "ultimate attainment," that is, whether learners achieve native-speaker-like competence in the target language (Singleton, 2001, for review). Whereas the SLA literature on the topic is "quite enormous" (Ellis, 1994, p. 491), in interlanguage pragmatics, only one study has examined the effect of age thus far. In a "concatenative-confirmatory" study, Kim (2000) investigated whether the age at which Korean ESL learners arrived in the United States was related to their production of requests and apologies. The question was motivated by research on a critical period for second language acquisition. Unfortunately, Kim did not discuss how the outcomes of this research, which originally derived from the theory of an innate language acquisition device for *grammar*, might possibly be extended to pragmatics, for which no encapsulated module in the mind or brain has ever been postulated. Age of arrival correlated with ratings of pragmatic performance, showing that the younger the learners were when they came to the United States, the more native-like their requests and apologies were rated. Age of arrival interacted with input and cultural identity but did not independently predict the learners' request and apology production.

No other interlanguage pragmatics study has made the issue of age its focal concern, but several studies comment on it. These investigations conceptualize age not as a neuropsychological trait but as a social category. The question is how nonnative speakers' membership in a particular age bracket might affect their contacts with native speakers, the activities in which they participate, the input they receive, how they are expected to act and speak, and whether or not their L2 use is corrected. Two studies in very different L2 settings found that teenage learners returned from study abroad with a learner variety that was too colloquial, with little context differentiation between more or less formal styles. Marriott (1995) observed this phenomenon in high-school-aged Australian learners of Japanese (age 15–18), who overused the plain style. Regan (1995) noted a similar effect in college-aged Irish learners of French (age 19–21), who overextended the deletion of the *ne* particle in negations from informal to formal contexts. In both cases, the overuse of the informal variants appears to reflect age-graded input from peers, resulting in L2 use that is appropriate in casual teenage peer interaction but not in status-unequal and more formal encounters.

The status conferred to different age groups in the host society can have consequences for learners' opportunities to develop their L2 pragmatic ability. In Siegal's (1994) study of four Anglo European women's learning of Japanese, Mary was a participant in her mid-40s. In a society where higher age commands respect, Mary therefore enjoyed a superior status compared to the other participants, who were in their 20s. This proved to be a blessing and a curse. On the positive side, in service encounters, Mary received more polite, target-like input than the younger students. The downside was that her age status militated against opportunities for feedback. Mary's tutors were college students in their early 20s who did not correct her errors or intervene when they were unable to understand her. Siegal expressed concern that in the absence of corrective feedback, these interactions might in fact have been harmful to Mary's acquisition of Japanese (p. 200). Mary's age status, certainly together with other status factors, also appears to have influenced how she constructed her relationships with Japanese co-participants through her sociolinguistic and pragmatic choices. In a visit to her academic advisor's office, she constructed an equal-status relationship with the professor, a man in his mid-30s. She controlled the topic initiation and management, deployed *desu/masu* style instead of *sonkeigo*, the appropriate stylistic choice in interaction with her professor, and overused the epistemic modal auxiliary verb *deshoo* (Siegal, 1995, 1996). Partly, Mary may have made these status-incongruent linguistic choices because she did not have sufficient knowledge of honorific language, but they also appeared as an effort to position herself as a peer in the academic world (cf. Chapter 6 for more discussion).

Even though research on the effect of age in L2 pragmatic development is limited, it strongly suggests that when viewed as a social category, age may have an impact on the formality and politeness of native-speaker input, offers of corrective feedback, and learners' own pragmatic conduct. Because younger and older nonnative speakers engage in different activities and native-speaking peers are likely to model different target language varieties for them, at least in a naturalistic setting, the influence of age on pragmatic development deserves much further investigation.

Gender

In a review of the role of gender in first and second language learning and use, Ehrlich (1997) advises against asking "overly general [research] questions about women and men, girls and boys that ignore the social, cultural, and situational contexts in which second languages are acquired" (p. 427). The research evidence leads her to refute the myth of female superiority in L1 verbal ability and to conclude that there is no evidence for gender-based differences in language learning. Rather than isolating gender as a variable in SLA, she proposes a reconceptualization of gender as social practice, a perspective on the role of gender in language use and learning that has become influential in sociolinguistics. The main point of gender as social practice is that gender is understood as activity-mediated. In contexts where women and men use and learn language differently, they do so not because of some inherent traits but because they engage in different social activities; however, participation in activities may well be mediated by gender and other social category memberships such as class and race.

At this point, studies on the role of gender in interlanguage pragmatics mirror those in sociolinguistics and SLA on a drastically reduced scale. Two early studies on gender effects in ESL learners' pragmatic ability reported contrasting results. Rintell (1984) found no effect for gender on learners' perception of expressions of emotion by L2 speakers. On the other hand, in her study of assertiveness and supportiveness in NNS troubles talk, Kerekes (1992) found that as a group, female but not male ESL learners perceived qualifiers (e.g., *I think*, *sort of*) in the same way as NSs and high-proficiency learners (cf. also Chapter 4).

Undeniably, languages and the speech communities that (re)produce them emphasize social distinctions in different ways. Gender is a more salient distinction in Japanese than English. Even so, the social-practice approach to gender holds up. Siegal contends that in Japanese interaction, " 'women's language' is a stylistic domain that can be used strategically in certain situational contexts towards strategic goals" (1994, p. 111). Such strategic manipulation of linguistic choices was precisely what Mary did in interaction with her professor. For the younger participants in Siegal's study, what they perceived as Japanese women's style of speaking was not the kind of model they wished to emulate. Some of them were quite explicit in their critical comments, such as Sally, who described women in their early 20s and their enthusiastic speech style (*sugoi wa* "that's great MP," *kirei ne* "that's beautiful MP") as "silly and shallow" (Siegal, 1994, p. 334). Arina said about a friend and professor's wife: "I cannot stand the way she talks. She is so humble all the time. I don't want to be that humble. I am just going to stick with the *desu / masu* [polite form], it is polite and safe" (p. 340). This quote is revealing in several respects. It expresses Arina's distaste for a particular "feminine" way of speaking and thereby positions herself as different from women who speak in that style. It also points to two sociopragmatic misunderstandings about Japanese speech styles. As Siegal notes, using *sonkeigo*, or "humble" style, does not so much index the speaker as "humble" but is rather a refined style and indicator of social class (p. 341). It seems that Arina here falls in the trap of literal translation and of interpreting L2 contextualization cues in light of the indexical meanings that such cues may have in a different language and speech community. Her other misunderstanding is the alternative sociolinguistic choice she decided to make, that is, "sticking with *desu / masu*." This appears to be a common learner strategy, whether to facilitate the burden to decide between different speech levels in an interaction or as a sociolinguistically motivated choice. Both Arina's rejection of *sonkeigo* and option for *desu / masu* style as a one-size-fits-all solution show that she has not yet understood the "emic" social meanings of these styles in Japanese language use. Sally's alternative sociolinguistic choice was to (over)use plain style and the mitigator *to omoimasu* (I think) as a compensatory politeness strategy (p. 335). Like Arina, she too misunderstood the social meaning of her style of choice. Although she realized that men have greater license to use plain forms than women, and that polite forms are normative when speaking to older and higher-status interlocutors, she still used the plain form because it was "friendly" (p. 338). The participants in Siegal's study evaluated whether gendered sociolinguistic and pragmatic practices and the social meanings of these practices as they understand them were compatible with their view of themselves and how they wished to come across in interaction with Japanese native speakers. Siegal concludes that

> The learners created their own language system based on their perceptions of Japanese women's language and demeanor and their awareness of their position in Japanese society. This plays a part in their inadequate use of honorifics and sentence final pragmatic particles, and incorrect use of modality all of which are essential for developing proficiency in spoken Japanese. (1994, p. 344)

Although the learners actively constructed a counterdiscourse to Japanese "women's language," it is unlikely that the social meanings of their chosen styles had the desired effect on Japanese interlocutors. In fact, explicit corrections that Sally received on her use of the plain form (p. 338) testify to the contrary.

It remains to be seen whether L2 learners in other target communities develop the same keen awareness of gendered language use as Siegal's participants did. When gendered language is less salient and its use less normative, do learners notice it as readily and form just as strong opinions about it? Is the discursive construction of gender identity less of an effortful project when learners perceive the way women in the target community speak as compatible with their own sense of self and how they wish to relate to members of the host society? How does learners' perception of gendered language change over time? If it does, does their own language use follow suit, and into what direction does such change develop? These are some of the questions raised by the small but intriguing body of research on the role that gender as social practice may have in pragmatic development. We are looking forward to much future work on these issues.

Motivation

Motivation is a slippery notion. In SLA, the most influential theory of language learning motivation is Gardner's socioeducational model, which exists in different versions (e.g., Gardner, 1985; Gardner & MacIntyre, 1993). Although motivation according to Gardner is partly a set of individual difference variables with integrative motivation as its focal category, it also comprises such social-psychological factors as beliefs about intergroup relations between language communities, informal versus formal learning environment, and language learning success. The social dimension in motivation is also emphasized by Dörnyei (2001), who points out that motivation encompasses intrapsychological and interpsychological components. Schumann offers a neurobiological perspective, according to which motivation is understood as stimulus appraisal (Schumann, 1998) and (language) learning as a form of foraging (Schumann, 2001). A recent volume on motivation in second language learning bears testimony to the wide scope of constructs and investigative approaches to motivation, which are no longer limited to "quantitative" research but also include "qualitative" studies (Dörnyei & Schmidt, 2001).

In interlanguage pragmatics, some studies attribute differences in observed learner performance or knowledge displays to learners' motivation to learn the target language. Niezgoda and Röver (2001) reported that EFL students in the Czech Republic displayed high pragmatic awareness that surpassed that of EFL students in Hungary (Bardovi-Harlig & Dörnyei, 1998), a finding that the researchers partially attributed to the fact that the Czech students were enrolled in a competitive university EFL teacher preparation program and highly motivated to achieve native-like knowledge of the pragmatics of English. Cook (2001) found that students of Japanese as a foreign language, taught by the same instructor in parallel sections, differed considerably in their ability to distinguish polite from impolite speech styles in Japanese. Quite similar to the Czech students in Niezgoda and Röver's (2001) study, the students who successfully identified and interpreted the sociopragmatic significance of the different stylistic choices had specific investments in the target language, such as planning to work in a Japanese-speaking environment, studying in Japan, or (as heritage language students) desiring to communicate in Japanese with family in Japan. In her study on instruction of English request strategies to Japanese EFL students, Takahashi (2001) observed individual differences in participants' ability to notice the target request structures when the task did not direct student's attention to these forms. She suggested that motivation might be one factor to account for superior task performance.

Takahashi (2000) examined whether students' noticing of target request strategies was affected by their motivation rather than L2 proficiency and what subcomponents of a multidimensional motivation construct contributed to such an effect. Participants in this study were Japanese college students who majored in mechanical engineering, agriculture, and education. They had had EFL teaching in Japan for seven to eight years and had not spent more than two weeks in an English-speaking country. Data were collected by means of four instruments. Schmidt, Boraie, and Kassabgy's (1996) motivation questionnaire was adapted to fit the Japanese college students. L2 proficiency was measured by the Listening Comprehension and Reading Comprehension sections of the G-TELP (General Tests of English Language Proficiency). The treatment materials were transcripts of two dialogs in which a speaker makes a request to her next-door neighbor. In one of the dialogs, the neighbor was asked to stop her daughter's violin practice at night; in the other dialog, she was asked to fill out and return a questionnaire as soon as possible. Each dialog took place between native speakers of American English (NS-NS) and a nonnative requester and native-speaker requestee (NNS-NS). In both requests, the native speakers used bi-clausal request forms such as *I was wondering if you could VP* or *do you think you could VP*. In addition to the transcripts, students received an instruction sheet asking them to identify "native-(like) usage" in transcripts. The instruction did not direct students' attention to specific features of the dialogs. After the students completed the task, they responded to an awareness measure, a questionnaire including the target request strategies, discourse lubricants (*you know*, *maybe*), giving reasons for the request, and formulaic expressions. Students were asked to indicate on a seven-point scale to what extent they had noticed each of these pragmatic and discourse features and been "interested" in them. Based on the scores from the motivation and proficiency measures, students were divided into four groups: High Motivation/High EFL, High Motivation/ Low EFL, Low Motivation/High EFL, and Low Motivation/Low EFL. A three-way repeated measures ANOVA was conducted with "motivation" and "proficiency" as between- subjects factors and "noticing" as a within-subject factor. Results showed that the students attended more to the discourse features, such as discourse lubricants and request-related linguistic components. They indicated more interest in formulaic expressions than in the bi-clausal complex request forms.

The high noticeability of the idiomatic formulae suggests that L2-specific features may be more salient than pragmalinguistic forms that have L1 equivalents. The request structure *if you could VP* was the least noticed request form, but it was also the structure that was more noticed by the highly motivated than by the less motivated students. Takahashi explains that the shortened form might have been less salient or that the students did not understand the requestive meaning of the form. In addition, familiarity with this structure from Japanese can also have depressed noticeability as a "native English usage." One may speculate that students with a high motivation for L2 learning are in general more metalinguistically and metapragmatically aware and therefore more attuned to less salient forms and their pragmatic meanings. This would also explain why the extent to which students noticed the more salient forms *I wonder* and *Is it possible* was not influenced by motivation. Discourse lubricants, idiomatic expressions, and general discourse strategies were more noticed by the highly motivated students, who also indicated more interest in those features. The motivation profile of students who noticed these forms more included more subcomponents, such as intrinsic and extrinsic motivation, personal goals, and motivational strength. Furthermore, of the factors in the motivation construct, intrinsic motivation affected the extent to which students noticed the bi-clausal request forms *Is it possible* and *If you could VP*, idiomatic expressions, and discourse strategies, while motivational strength influenced how much students paid attention to the request form *Is it possible*, the discourse lubricants, and discourse strategies. Takahashi concludes that motivation, and in particular intrinsic motivation, is indeed involved in the extent to which students notice discourse features and complex request forms, as her earlier study suggested. Importantly, L2 proficiency did not influence students' attention to the discourse-pragmatic features in the input.

Takahashi's (2000) study is remarkable not only because it is the first to investigate the influence of motivation in L2 pragmatics but for the specific questions it addresses. Rather than asking how motivation may directly account for individual differences in students' learning of L2 pragmatics (Kim, 2000), the study examines how motivation affects students' attention in processing specific pragmalinguistic features. Conceptualized as a factor in attention allocation, Takahashi's notion of motivation is compatible with the neurobiological view of motivation as stimulus appraisal. It also sits well with a revised version of the socioeducational model, in which attention figures as one motivational behavior factor, a variable mediating between language attitudes, motivation, and achievement (Tremblay & Gardner, 1995). Motivation has been related to learners' use of cognitive and metacognitive learning strategies, many of which involve how learners allocate attentional resources in processing input (e.g., MacIntyre & Noels, 1996). Takahashi's findings are thus supported by research on the relationship of motivation and attention in the wider domain of L2 learning (Crookes & Schmidt, 1991; Schmidt, 2001). Furthermore, her study suggests that specific motivational factors and their strength are implicated in directing learners' attention to target pragmatic features. This finding bears further investigation, as does the intriguing possibility that different aspects of L2 pragmatics may be differentially noticeable to learners with different motivational profiles. Of course, generalizing from one carefully conducted study to different learner populations and contexts is unwarranted, but Takahashi gives us an excellent model for future studies on motivation as an individual difference variable in pragmatic learning.

Motivation appears to be linked to attention and noticing, but it also plays a role in subsequent learning and learners' own production. Japanese students at an international university in Japan indicated instrumental motivation to learn English and general willingness to accommodate to NS pragmatic practices, but their self-reports were not related to performance data (LoCastro, 2001). DuFon (1999) comments that all of the learners of Indonesian in her study noticed the different terms of address used by native speakers and themselves, that is, they "noticed the gap" (Schmidt & Frota, 1986). However, they differed individually in their efforts to close it. Three learners adopted the address term *anda* as a one-size-fits-all term, a form roughly equivalent to "you" in English but very restricted in native use and in fact a feature of foreigner talk (cf. Chapter 4). Other learners avoided *anda*, either using more target-like kinship (+ name) forms or avoiding address terms altogether. DuFon partially attributes these different solutions to learners' motivation to accommodate to native practices. Motivation may be one factor to explain the differences between noticing input, having knowledge of L2 pragmatic practices, and making productive use of this knowledge. But as we have discussed to some extent earlier in this chapter, learners' sense of who they are and desire to be in different situations of L2 learning and use can be a powerful factor in their decision whether to converge with target pragmatic practices.

Rather than being isolated from other learner factors, motivation has also been conceptualized as one of several variables that constitute (even) more complex composite constructs. One such construct is acculturation, which includes motivation as a psychological distance factor.

Social and Psychological Distance

As described in Chapter 2, the acculturation model (Schumann, 1978) is a social-psychological theory predicting that high acculturation to the target community results in successful acquisition of second language grammar. It is perhaps best characterized as an individual difference model of SLA, rather than a model of SLA, because it seeks to explain why some adult learners in naturalistic settings acquire the target language more successfully than others. Acculturation is conceptualized as low social and psychological distance, which in turn are composite constructs. Social distance to the target community subsumes a set of social variables, while psychological distance to target language speakers is composed of a set of affective variables. Low social and psychological distance is seen as equivalent to high acculturation, which predicts successful second language acquisition, and vice versa. Schumann (1986) suggested that "any learner can be placed on a continuum that ranges from social and psychological distance to social and psychological proximity with speakers of the TL, and . . . the learner will acquire the second language only to the degree that he acculturates" (p. 379). Extending the acculturation model to the acquisition of communicative competence, Schmidt (1983) established an acculturation profile for his participant Wes, which led to the predictions for Wes's interlanguage development listed in Table 8.1.

Only two factors predicted negatively or possibly negatively: the difference between Japanese and North American culture (albeit less pronounced in multiethnic Hawai'i, with its substantial Japanese influence), and Wes's minimal interest in studying English formally. As reported earlier in this book, Wes's low social and psychological distance to the host community did prove facilitative for his progress in discourse-pragmatic and strategic competence but not for his grammar. Wes's high interaction volume in diverse social contexts exposed him to large amounts of contextually varied input, and his high drive for communication, combined with low social inhibition, facilitated his active participation in social interaction, both professionally and interpersonally. Wes's positive attitude to the L2 group and low enclosure—his large and increasing circle of friends included more native speakers of English than members of the native Japanese-speaking community in Honolulu—appeared to have contributed to his gains in pragmatic and discourse ability as well. That affiliation with the

Table 8.1

Wes's Acculturation Profile and Predicted Acquisitional Effects

	Wes	Predicted Influence on SLA
Social Factors		
Communicative need	high, increasing	facilitative
Interaction, type & amount	varied, increasing	facilitative
Social dominance pattern	equal	facilitative
Social interaction pattern	adaptive	facilitative
Enclosure, cohesiveness	low	facilitative
Similarity of cultures	different	negative
Attitudes toward L2 group	positive	facilitative
Intended length of residence	indefinite/permanent	facilitative
Psychological Factors		
Culture shock	low	facilitative
Language shock	low	facilitative
Empathy, social outreach	high	facilitative
Inhibition, fear of appearing foolish	low	facilitative
Motivation type	integrative	facilitative
Motivation, drive for communication	very high	facilitative
Motivation for formal language study	very low	possibly negative
Preferred learning style	natural acquisition	facilitative

Note. From "Interaction, Acculturation and the Acquisition of Communicative Competence," by R. Schmidt, 1983, in N. Wolfson and E. Judd (Eds.), *Sociolinguistics and Second Language Acquisition,* p. 143. Rowley, MA: Newbury House.

L2 community may have positive effects on the acquisition of pragmatics was also reported by Kim (2000), who found that the more strongly Korean ESL learners identified themselves as "very American," the higher the ratings of their apology and request performance. For the most part, the strategy distribution for "very American" and "very Korean" learners was quite similar, with the "very American" learners approximating L2 native-speaker use more closely. It is difficult to explain how the "very Korean" learners' choices of individual apology and request strategies might be related to their Korean cultural identity, with two possible exceptions: they chose fewer alerters (greetings, terms of address) in their requests and fewer explanations in their apologies. Comparative data on Korean native-speaker request and apology production are not available, but negative pragmatic transfer might be at work in the learners' under-suppliance of alerters and explanations. This possibility raises an intriguing research issue: might learners with low affiliation to the target community, lower acculturation, or lower integrative motivation be more prone to negatively transfer L1 pragmatic practices into their interlanguage use? What social-psychological individual difference variables, if any, might be related to *foreign* language learners' pragmatic transfer?

It should be noted, however, that in Kim's study, cultural identity did not have an independent effect on learners' speech act performance but interacted with informal input (cf. Chapter 6) and age of arrival (cf. section on "Age" in this chapter). Furthermore, only the speech act strategy choices of learners who had rated their cultural identity close to the extremes of the "very Korean–very American" scale were selected for comparison. This methodological decision glosses over the fact that 48% of Kim's respondents had identified their cultural identity as "Korean-American," 32% had rated themselves as "very Korean," and only 10% identified as "very American" (p. 55). It would be particularly important to investigate in future research how learners who identify themselves as bi-cultural, or strive for a bi- (or multi-)cultural identity, make L2 pragmatic choices. Empirical evidence of multiculturality and multipragmaticality is provided in research documenting that multilingual speakers are not "two monolinguals in one person" (Grosjean, 1989; V. Cook, 1999), relying on two or more separate monolingual pragmatic competencies. Rather, research conducted in (among other places) Israel, Australia, Europe, and the United States suggests that multilingual groups and individual speakers tend to create "intercultural styles" (e.g., Blum-Kulka, 1991, 1997; Clyne, Ball, & Neil, 1991; Clyne, 1994; House & Kasper, 2000; Yoon, 1991), an embodiment of "third places" (Kramsch, 1993) that afford social, intellectual, and emotional spaces from which multilingual persons and groups position themselves somewhere between their historical place of origin and their new sociopolitical world, a place that affords them critical and ironic distance rather than naïve allegiance to either (Kramsch, 2003). Although not unconstrained, the multilingual person's agency in this process is at the heart of conceptualizations of identity and their relationship to pragmatic learning, the final issue we will take up in this chapter.

Beyond IDs: Social Identity in Learning L2 Pragmatics

Throughout this chapter, the reader will have sensed an uneasy tension between two fundamentally different ways of conceptualizing individual differences in pragmatic learning. Social and psychological distance as factors in the acculturation model, motivation, and cultural identity in the sense of Kim (2000) are treated as independent variables that predict or explain pragmatic choices (in the short term) and learning (in the long term). According to the ontological premises underlying the "positivist" view, individual-internal psychological traits are treated as static causal variables that determine unidirectionally whether, and in what shape and frequency, a particular "behavior" shows up. In the weaker case that is more common in variationist sociolinguistics, demographic factors such as geographical origin, social class, age cohort, and gender are correlated with variable linguistic choices in order to establish descriptive or predictive relationships between the two sets of variables. The received (social) psychological and variationist-sociolinguistic perspective on individual differences in language learning has been contested in recent discussions of social identity in multilingual settings and second language learning. We will briefly comment on some of the main theories of social identity and, to the extent it has happened, their adoption in accounts of individual differences in learning L2 pragmatics.

Social identity theory (e.g., Tajfel, 1978, 1981; Hogg & Abrams, 1988) is a social-psychological proposal that seeks to understand the subset of an individual's sense of self that derives from recognition of group membership and its attendant emotional meanings. Central to the theory is the emergence and practice of social categorization, including stereotype formation, in intergroup settings. The formation, maintenance, and change of social identity rely largely on social comparison of group members' own social group with others in the wider societal context. The theory recognizes social actors' memberships in multiple groups—Hoggs and Abrams (1988) refer to a repertoire of social identities, each of which may or may not become salient in different social contexts. Consistent with its social psychological origin, emphasis is placed on both individual cognition and the social dynamics of intergroup relations. In his recent defense of the theory, McNamara (1997b) therefore refutes post-structuralist complaints charging the theory with a monolithic, ahistorical and apolitical, and overly cognitive view of social identity, arguing that it continues to provide an insightful framework for understanding the role of social identity in second language learning, contextualized in inter- and intra-group relationships. While McNamara (1987a, 1987b) engaged social identity theory in his study of Hebrew-speaking Israeli immigrants to Australia, it has not been adopted in research on interlanguage pragmatic development.

Perhaps the best-known *social psychology of self* was elaborated in the work of Erving Goffman (1959, 1967, 1971, 1974), familiar in part to pragmaticians through Brown and Levinson's (1987) elaboration of Goffman's notion of face. While Goffman emphasized different aspects of self in his writings, he consistently proposed a nonessentialist construct of self, one that understands the self as a social product devoid of an underlying personal substratum. This is not to say that Goffman views the self as entirely determined by social structure; rather it encompasses both courses of action that follow societal scripts and manipulate situational resources to its advantage (Branaman, 1997). Engaging his famous theatrical metaphors, Goffman (1959) distinguishes the self as character from the self as performer. We quote a central passage here because it makes particularly clear the distinction between self as a preexisting individual trait and as an emerging outcome of social interaction.

> A correctly staged and performed character leads the audience to impute a self to a performed character, but this imputation—this self—is a *product* of a scene that comes off, and is not a *cause* of it. The self, then, as a performed character, is not an organic thing that has a specific location, whose fundamental fate is to be born, to mature, and to die; it is a dramatic effect arising diffusely from a scene that is presented, and the characteristic issue, the crucial concern, is whether it will be credited or discredited. (p. 244f., also in Branaman, 1997, p. xlix)

From Goffman's insistence on the societal derivation of the self, his much-cited definition of "face" is a logical extension.

> The term "face" may be defined as the positive social value a person effectively claims for himself by the line others assume he has taken during a particular contact. Face is an image of self delineated in terms of approved social attributes. . . . The person's face clearly is something not lodged in or on his body but rather something that is diffusely located in the flow of events in the encounter and becomes manifest only when these events are read and interpreted for the appraisals expressed in them. (Goffman, 1967, p. 5ff.)

Since face, then, is constantly established, maintained, enhanced, lost, and regained in social interaction, it is, just like the self, not entirely under the individual's sovereign control. While this is generally true (to the extent one follows Goffman's reasoning, of course), it is a particularly complex issue in contexts of individuals' nonmembership and (partial) incompetence, whether linguistic, pragmatic, or cultural. Much of the analysis that Siegal (1994, 1995, 1996) provides of the various interactions between the Anglo European women in her study and their

Japanese co-participants centers on this difficulty. Since what counts as approved lines of conduct and social attributes is variable across sociocultural contexts, learners may not know what the social expectations of appropriate conduct are, or they may not yet command the linguistic and other interactional resources necessary to fulfill such expectations, or they may not conform to societal expectations for reasons other than incompetence. To complicate matters further, as noted in several studies and discussed in Chapter 6, societal expectations of proper demeanor may not be the same for community members and outsiders (DuFon, 1999; Iino, 1996; Marriott, 1993; Siegal, 1994, 1995, 1996), and the kinds of conduct projected by community members as desirable for foreign learners may not coincide with the learners' own preferred presentation of self. Two examples for both cases are reported by Iino (1996) in his study of North American exchange students during a home stay in Kyoto. The formula *tsumaranai mono desu kedo douzo* (this is a useless thing, but please accept) is a polite formula that accompanies the presentation of a gift in native Japanese interaction. However, when the self-same formula was deployed by an American student upon presenting a gift to her hosts, her use of the expression was met with laughter because, in the host mother's comment on the event, "I thought there is no such custom in American's mentality as *tsumaranai mono*" (p. 220). Some students in Iino's study complained about being treated as "dolls," "babies," and "pets" in the home (p. 158), metaphors that index the exchange students' discontent with being cast in roles of incompetence in the host families. But very much in agreement with Goffman's emphasis on face as being in constant flux, learners also seized the opportunity to construct themselves as competent individuals who have valuable knowledge to impart, such as teaching the Japanese host mother a bit of American-English phonology (Iino, 1996, p. 160) or an Indonesian class of adult EFL students about gender relations in North America (DuFon, 1999, p. 481).

The issue of power looms large in post-structural theories of social identity. Norton's (2000) work on the role of identity in second language learning builds on prior theories addressing relations of material and symbolic power, different kinds of power relations, and their implications for social identity. Drawing on Bourdieu's (1977) economic metaphors, Norton (Peirce, 1995) reconceptualized the received construct of motivation as *investment,* referring to

> the socially and historically constructed relationship of learners to the target language, and their often ambivalent desire to learn and practice it. . . . If learners invest in a second language, they do so with the understanding that they will acquire a wider range of symbolic and material resources, which will in turn increase the value of their cultural capital. Learners expect or hope to have a good return on that investment—a return that will give them access to hitherto unattainable resources. (2000, p. 10)

Whereas Peirce (1995) linked the notion of investment with Bourdieu's (1977) point that competence includes "the right to speech" and "the power to impose reception" (Norton, 2000, p. 8), other writers have expanded the construct to comprise all modalities of language use and different types of discourse (McKay & Wong, 1996; Angelil-Carter, 1997). The discussion of investment is pertinent to the issue of social identity because the construct is tightly connected to Weedon's (1987) notion of *subjectivity.* Norton (2000) highlights three defining criteria of subjectivity: "the multiple, nonunitary nature of the subject; subjectivity as a site of struggle; and subjectivity as changing over time" (p. 8). On this view, language and subjectivity are dialectically related, as illustrated by Norton's (2000) analysis of self-reports provided by immigrant women to Canada. In this study, the only data of the learners' own language use were excerpts from self-report documents (diaries, notes from group sessions, interviews, and questionnaires), so that these sources, rather than observations of the women's interactional engagements, served as evidence of their language learning. The cited stories impress by their eloquence and linguistic sophistication, even granting that they were somewhat edited for readability. Intriguingly, the direct linguistic evidence that is presented strongly suggests that despite adverse experiences, different personal histories, and social positions in Canada, the women successfully developed a rather advanced command of written and spoken English (even though not all of them, by their reported self-assessment, saw it that way).

Siegal (1994, 1995, 1996), on the other hand, engaging subjectivity theory to interpret her participants' use and learning of Japanese, analyzed specifically occasioned speech events and genres in which the four women participated. While, as Siegal demonstrates, Goffman's notions of self, face, deference, and demeanor go a long way to get a conceptual handle on the identity-implicative aspects of the observed interactions, the conflictual demands experienced by the learners, their changing solutions to these conflicts over time, and their linguistic choices as "acts of identity" lend themselves particularly well to conceptualization within Weedon's subjectivity framework. Some of the observations cited above as illustrating the roles of age and gender in learners' pragmatic and sociolinguistic strategies can insightfully be understood in subjectivity-theoretical perspective. Two examples from Siegal (1995, 1996), involving two women of different ages in different activity types, will serve as illustrations. The first example is Mary's office visit with her academic advisor, to which we referred earlier in this chapter. Throughout the interaction, Mary pursued the strategy of initiating exchanges and exerting topic control. Against normative selections of speech level in this type of hierarchically structured encounter, she did not use honorifics, produced the modal verb *deshoo* (an epistemic marker that indexes, among other things, that the propositional information is known to recipient) as many as 10 times, and ventrilocated in the high-pitched voice affected by service girls. What appears as blatantly inappropriate against native Japanese standards can be understood, as Siegal suggests, as Mary's solution to conflicting pragmatic demands—the multiple situated self as a site of struggle, enacted as, and produced through, Mary's sociolinguistic and pragmatic choices. In Siegal's (1995) analysis:

Mary was confronted with a pragmatic conflict. To speak competently, she would have to use language that humbles her when she is speaking with her professor; yet, she also desires to maintain her face and position as a scholar. Indeed, she views herself as a competent researcher, not in need of mentoring or advice. Although it is not clear that she purposefully eschews honorific usage, it is clear that in lieu of honorifics she uses the verbal auxiliary modal *deshoo* to make her language polite and to maintain a polite demeanor. Because of the polysemy of *deshoo* her polite demeanor is, in a subtle way, sabotaged. (p. 240)

The second example refers to one of the younger women in Siegal's study, Arina, at 25 years of age a more typical foreign student with the additional "exotic" flair of being a Hungarian national. Several times throughout her stay in Hiroshima, Arina was invited to participate in a "foreigner-only" activity, that is, category-bound speech events in which the invited foreign guest is expected to deliver a formal speech. According to Japanese cultural conventions, it is understood that these speeches are treated as *keishiki toshite* (a matter of form) where the audience expects and values that the foreign speaker deliver a stylistically correct implementation of the genre rather than discussing substantive issues (Siegal, 1995, p. 235). The speech event as such serves a double act of identity in that it dialectically constructs the foreign speaker as the "other" and thereby reaffirms the sociocultural identity of the audience as a cohesive group of cultural members. Indeed, the foreigner-only speech event epitomizes Iino's (1996) notion of *gaijinization*. However, Siegal's report on Arina's handling of the various occasions where she made herself available as *gaijin* on display points to changes in Arina's views of the normative sociolinguistic conventions over time. Even though, compared to many speech events that reoccur on a daily basis, the special occasions for formal speech-making happened infrequently, they provided opportunities for pragmatic and sociolinguistic learning, and indeed, Arina's changing discursive practices in giving her speeches both displayed convergence and resistance to genre conventions. Such developments were particularly evident in Arina's use of honorifics and the topics she chose to address. Initially, Arina rejected using honorific and formulaic language as "too humble" and avoided using such forms. By the last recorded speech, she adopted *sonkeigo*, the normative formal and humble honorific speech level, and the formulaic phrases appropriate to the occasion. Through her sociolinguistic and pragmalinguistic choices, then, she displayed convergence—or successful socialization—to the social conventions associated with the formality of public speech-making. However, in her last speech, Arina also selected to make negative comments on aspects of Japanese society, such as bureaucratic inefficiency and racism. By giving her speech a critical and serious tone, she was thus bending a cultural genre that serves both entertainment and ritualistic affirmation, rather than questioning of the audience's and speaker's social identities. In subjectivity-theoretical terms, we see here a different solution to the conflicting identities of learners who desire to participate in the host society on their own terms, that is, initial resistance and partial accommodation that can be read to index the straddling of memberships in sociocultural groups with partially conflicting demands. Although the speech events that Siegal selected for analysis are quite different in Mary's and Arina's cases, the learners' courses of pragmatic and sociolinguistic action illustrate how their situated definition of selves in these activities comprised presentation of themselves as a competent researcher (Mary) and learner of Japanese and critical observer of the society (Arina) while striving to converge, with different degrees of success, to meet expectations of polite conduct in different types of social interaction.

From a *language socialization* perspective, Ochs (1993) argues for a close connection between language learning (first or second) and social identity, defined as "a cover term for a range of social personae, including social statuses, roles, positions, relationships, and institutional and other relevant community identities one may attempt to claim or assign in the course of social life" (p. 288). The role of language in claiming or assigning identity is that of enabling identity-relevant inferences through conventional associations of linguistic forms with social acts and stances. The challenge for the second language learner in this process is to identify the linguistic and interactional resources that conventionally serve to index acts and stances in the target community. As we saw, Mary's choice of the modal *deshoo* and high-pitched voice conveyed quite different identity claims than what she appeared to associate with these forms. Conversely, by using genre-specific stylistic conventions in her last *gaijin* speech, Arina displayed herself as a socially competent actor who, at least in part, had acquired the capacity to perform in public in accordance with the host community's cultural expectations.

While Ochs (1993) theorized the conventional links of linguistic forms with social acts and stances from a language socialization perspective, Gumperz (1982, 1996) proposed quite a similar association in his notion of *contextualization* conventions, whose situated use enables *conversational inferences*. Importantly, for both writers, the association between linguistic and other forms of conduct and their identity-implicative meanings are indexical and inferential rather than symbolic and referential. In order to examine how social identity and pragmatic development interrelate, it is critical to observe learners in social engagements and include the co-participants' situated actions in the analysis, as Siegal did in her study. The need for taking an interactional perspective on situated social identity is theorized in the concept of *co-construction,* defined by Jacoby and Ochs (1995) as "the joint creation of a form, interpretation, stance, action, activity, identity, institution, skill, ideology, emotion, or other culturally meaningful reality" (p. 171). Although *co*-construction emphasizes that some object or entity is constituted during and as the outcome of interaction (collaboration, coordination), the term is not biased toward affiliative interaction but refers to supportive and antagonistic socially situated processes alike.

Whereas theories of conversational inference particularly emphasize the role of contextualization cues in claims to and assignments of social identity, *conversation analysts* adopt a decidedly anti-mentalist perspective on the issue, focusing on identity and other social categories only to the extent that such identities are displayed, oriented to, made relevant, and treated as procedurally consequential by participants in the sequential organization of talk-in-interaction (Antaki & Widdicombe, 1998). As has been demonstrated in interactions between multilingual speakers, language choice can serve as a membership categorization device (Gafaranga, 2001). Examining the complex relations of pragmatic development and learners' social identities in a conversation-analytic framework is a promising and as yet under-explored line of investigation. Although the ethnomethodological/conversation-analytical perspective shares with subjectivity theory its post-structuralist orientation, subjectivity theory, especially in Norton's (2000) application, appears more compatible with what Silverman (2001) refers as an "emotionalist" research approach, which endeavors to unearth research participants' "authentic experience." While emotionalism differs from positivist approaches and their neat separation of independent and dependent variables, subject and object, text and context, identity and learning into fixed and discrete categories, emotionalism problematizes and goes some way to dissolve such oppositions. But as Silverman points out, by searching for the "authentic experience," which would include, relevant to this discussion, participants' "true" if multiple identities, the emotionalist pursuit aligns itself more with the positivist quest for "objective truth." Constructivist inquiry, by contrast, remains agnostic about truth claims and other essentialist matters, focusing instead on participants' displayed and procedurally consequential membership categorization in the sequential unfolding of talk-in-interaction.

As the research discussed in this chapter suggests, learners' development of pragmatic and, indeed, interactional competence interrelates with their own and their co-participants' situated identity constructions. Whereas these mutually constitutive processes can insightfully be explored through each of the perspectives on social identity discussed above, microanalytic constructivist approaches have the analytical advantage of enabling researchers to trace and document pragmatic learning and identity work in the details of talk exchanges. Surely, in order to advance our understanding of the connections between second language learning and social identity at a given moment and over time, it is critical to put the interactions in which learners participate, as well as the texts they produce, under the microscope. But as scholars such as DuFon, Iino, and Siegal have shown us, integrating microanalysis with theories that take a broader perspective on social, cultural, and political organization and processes can afford critical connections between micro and macro layers of social life that microanalysis alone may not achieve. One particularly successful example of such combinations is the linking of community of practice theory with the analysis of situated language use in sociolinguistic studies of sound change (Eckert, 2000) and gender-related language use (Holmes & Meyerhoff, 1999). While L2 pragmatic development and its relationship to social identity has yet to be examined in light of this analytical framework, interlanguage pragmaticians may want to explore its potential in future work.

Chapter Summary

We began this chapter by drawing on Ellis's (1994) four-way categorization of individual difference research in second language acquisition, noting that although little is known about individual differences in L2 pragmatic development, the small body of studies includes examples of each research type. We then considered, in turn, the factors age, gender, motivation, social and psychological distance, and social identity. Unsurprisingly, we noted that these factors have been addressed either from a "positivist" point of view, conceptualizing them as independent variables, or from various heterogeneous approaches that share a vaguely constructionist outlook but that, upon closer inspection, part company along the lines of emotionalism and constructivism (Silverman). Discussing such social-psychological approaches to identity as social identity theory (Tajfel) and Goffman's conceptualizations of self and self-presentation, we noted that Goffman's framework has been proven insightful in analyzing L2 pragmatic and sociolinguistic use and learning in the work of Iino and Siegal. Turning to Weedon's subjectivity theory, we pointed out that Norton and Siegal chose different methodological strategies for translating the theory into research approaches. In commenting on language socialization (Ochs) and co-construction (Jacoby & Ochs) as approaches to social identity and L2 learning, we noted strong affinity between the former and Gumperz's theory of contextualization and social inferencing. While conversation analysis recommends itself for the detailed examination of social identity and pragmatic learning in talk-in-interaction, frameworks that integrate (more) macro and micro levels of analysis may yield investigative gains that an exclusive focus on either layer may not achieve.

CHAPTER NINE

Epilogue

This book has considered theoretical and methodological issues in research on pragmatic development in a second language and discussed substantive findings from the research literature, grouped around six broad topics: acquisitional patterns over time, the relationship of pragmatic and grammatical development, the influence of different learning environments, the effect of planned instructional arrangements, and individual differences in L2 pragmatic learning. We will now briefly summarize these reviews and close by recommending three themes for investigation that we would like to see pursued in the years to come.

In our discussion of theories, we noted that much research in L2 developmental pragmatics has not been directly informed by theories of second language learning. Many studies have instead appealed to pragmatic and discourse theories in setting the target for analysis, theorizing the object—not the process—of pragmatic learning, often invoking theories as post hoc explanations of findings rather than as the impetus of the studies. Among the theoretical orientations that do address the learning process, we distinguished those with a primarily intra-psychological focus (the acculturation model and cognitive processing models) from social practice theories (sociocultural theory, language socialization theory, and approaches to interactional competence). Our review of studies drawing on these theoretical perspectives led us to conclude that research conducted from a cognitive-processing perspective as well as from different or combined social-practice approaches with an analytical focus on situated interactional engagements have demonstrated potential for explaining different facets of L2 pragmatic learning.

Moving from theories to research methods, we examined the main methodological approaches deployed in the L2 developmental pragmatics literature to date. We provided a condensed account of the methodological sources of research on developmental pragmatics from a range of social sciences and discussed the design requirements of developmental research. In order to review the diverse methods of data collection drawn on in the literature, we distinguished three major classes of data types: spoken discourse, questionnaires, and oral or written forms of self-report. Of these three classes of data, spoken discourse data are gathered by observation (typically, electronic recording), while the remaining two classes represent various forms of self-report. Within the broad class of oral discourse data, three types of interactions may be distinguished depending on how distant they seem from naturalistic activities: authentic discourse, elicited conversation (comprising sociolinguistic interviews and conversation tasks), and role play. The second class of data is collected by means of three different types of questionnaire: discourse completion, multiple-choice, and scaled-response questionnaires. A more heterogeneous class of self-report data includes interviews, which are interactive, oral, and, if not strictly prestructured by a schedule, narrative productions; verbal (concurrent or consecutive) protocols, which are oral and nonnarrative, at least in their classic cognitive-psychological versions; and diaries, which are narrative and either written or tape-recorded forms of self-reported text. We underscored the importance of appropriately matching research method to the task at hand, having a thorough understanding of what sort of information a particular approach can and cannot reasonably be expected to provide, and taking measures to critically explore the optimal implementation of whatever methods are chosen. Research adopting a multimethod approach, as a number of studies have, capitalizes on the different potential of various data-collection methods and provides a more complex and reliable view of pragmatic development.

Our discussion of the substantive findings of research on L2 pragmatic learning began with developmental patterns emerging from research on pragmatic comprehension, pragmatic and discourse ability, and speech acts. Cutting across the findings from these studies, we noted a tendency for beginning learners to rely on pregrammaticalized productions, routine formulae, and repetition, which gradually give way to an expansion of their pragmatic repertoire and overgeneralization of one form for a range of different functions. Even lower-proficiency learners are capable of controlling what might appear to be rather challenging aspects of target language pragmatics, and learners' pragmatic ability at a given stage in their development may not be accurately represented by their production in a particular setting or task. Particularly noteworthy are findings from studies of requests, which indicate that learners rely on pregrammaticalized utterances, direct strategies, and formulaic speech in the early stages of development, with a gradual move toward conventional indirectness, followed by the introduction of internal and external modification of requests as proficiency increases. These trends were summarized in a tentative five-stage developmental sequence for L2 request development. Concerning the sociopragmatics of request development, we noted that in the studies we reviewed, learning context plays a key role, with learners in second language settings generally demonstrating some measure of sociopragmatic development, and learners in foreign language contexts displaying far less. The chapter concluded with a discussion of the relationship between pragmatic transfer and development.

Researchers on pragmatic development often remark that learners' grammar constrains their L2 pragmatic comprehension and production but do not explore the relationship between grammatical and pragmatic development in detail. Endorsing Bardovi-Harlig's (1999) recommendation that research scrutinize how particular pragmalinguistic features emerge in relation to particular grammatical structures, we discussed two seemingly contradictory positions on adult learners' development of pragmatic and grammatical knowledge, namely, pragmatics precedes grammar, and grammar precedes pragmatics. In support of the first position, we proposed (adapting Ochs, 1996) a universal pragmatics principle, which specifies the discourse, pragmatic, and sociolinguistic competencies that adult learners bring to the task of acquiring the pragmatics of an additional language. For the second position (illustrated in the cases of more advanced learners who "have the grammar"), we considered three scenarios in which learners do not put to use their grammatical knowledge in ways that more expert language users would: (a) knowledge of the grammar without its concomitant use to express or modify illocutionary force; (b) knowledge of the grammar to express pragma linguistic functions that are not conventional in the target language; and (c) knowledge of grammar *and* its pragmalinguistic functions applied to non-target-like sociopragmatic use. Putting together the evidence on early and later acquisitional periods, it appears that learners at different stages of pragmalinguistic development face different learning tasks: Early learners have to acquire the L2 grammatical means to express already existing pragmatic categories, whereas later learners have to tease out the pragmatic meanings to which their now available L2 grammatical knowledge can be put.

Second language acquisition research acknowledges that opportunities for input and productive language use are necessary for L2 learning and finds that such opportunities are related to context and tasks. Therefore, we examined how pragmatic development is afforded by different learning environments, beginning with a review of early research that related pragmatic learning to length of stay in the target community. Later studies indicated that duration of residence is too coarse a factor to meaningfully explain pragmatic development, finding instead that the activities in which learners participate, and the occasions afforded learners for engagement as listeners and speakers, are relevantly related to pragmatic learning. Ethnographic studies of learners' interactions in noninstructional target contexts demonstrate vividly that the societal and local positioning of learners in the host community can both enable and constrain their learning of L2 pragmatics. Based on results gleaned from studies carried out in instructional settings, we called into question the poor reputation that language classrooms have as environments for learning L2 pragmatics, noting that the right question to ask is not *whether* pragmatics can be learned in the classroom but *how* classrooms can be arranged to most effectively support pragmatic development. We also considered studies comparing pragmatic learning in foreign and second language settings, paying particular attention to study-abroad research. According to this literature, the gains students make during study abroad are rather mixed, resulting in many cases in an overgeneralized informal speech style. This finding, together with others showing that students may actually develop parts of their interlanguage pragmatic ability away from target usage during residence abroad, suggests that students would benefit from instruction in pragmatics prior to and during their stay in the host community.

The mixed messages from research outcome on the opportunities for L2 pragmatic development *without* planned instruction in pragmatics call for examining how learners' pragmatic development fares when such instruction is provided. As a backdrop to the small but growing body of research on the effects of instruction in L2 pragmatics published to date, we discussed the learning targets, learner characteristics, learning contexts, and types of research issues represented in these studies. While a fairly wide range of learning targets has been covered in the studies done so far, this is decidedly not the case where learner characteristics and learning contexts are concerned—adult learners in university settings involving English and Japanese as native and target languages dominate the current literature. Research on the effect of instruction in pragmatics has addressed three main research questions: whether pragmatics is teachable, whether instruction in pragmatics produces results that outpace exposure in the classroom alone, and whether explicit and implicit instruction yield different outcomes. Results of these studies strongly suggest that most aspects of L2 pragmatics are indeed teachable, that instructional intervention is more beneficial than no instruction specifically targeted on pragmatics, and that for the most part, explicit instruction combined with ample practice opportunities results in the greatest gains. There are, however, limits to the effects of instruction, particularly in cases where an insufficient control of processing is an issue. Future studies will benefit from a wider range of theoretical orientations and improved research methodology to examine the effects of instruction in pragmatics.

Perhaps the most under-researched area addressed in this book is the relationship between individual learner differences and L2 pragmatic development. Drawing on Ellis's (1994) four-way categorization of approaches to individual differences in second language acquisition research, we considered age, gender, motivation, social and psychological distance, and social identity in their relation to L2 pragmatic learning. These factors have been addressed either from a "positivist" point of view, conceptualizing them as independent variables, or from various heterogeneous approaches that share a vaguely constructionist outlook but that, upon closer inspection, part company along the lines of emotionalism and constructivism. Discussing such social-psychological approaches to identity as social identity theory and Goffman's conceptualizations of self and self-presentation, we observed that Goffman's framework has proven insightful in analyzing L2 pragmatic and sociolinguistic use and learning. We also noted that in applying Weedon's subjectivity theory, researchers have chosen different strategies for translating the theory into research approaches, whereas studies that appeal to language socialization and co-construction as approaches to social identity and L2 learning have affinity with Gumperz's theory of contextualization and social inferencing. Finally, we commented that conversation analysis holds considerable promise for examining the interrelation between talk-in-interaction, social identity, and L2 pragmatic learning.

Throughout this book, we have pointed to issues and topics that merit future exploration. In closing, rather than suggesting specific research questions, we will delineate, in no particular order, three broad thematic areas for investigation.

First, with particular attention to social environments and individual differences, what is the development over time of learners' L2 pragmatic, discourse, and sociolinguistic ability in different sociocultural settings? Research in this area needs to draw on theories and methods that connect the micro level of situated interaction with macro levels of institutional, societal, and ideological dimensions of analysis.

Second, what is the comparative development over time of learners' pragmatics and grammar? This research needs to trace either how a particular pragmatic action (e.g., conveying a type of epistemic stance, doing a specific communicative act) is successively accomplished through different grammatical forms, or how a particular form, or set of forms, is increasingly put to various pragmatic uses. One particularly intriguing project is the emergence of grammar in and through interaction over time in microanalytical perspective, as it allows for the detailed exploration of the mutual constraints and affordances of interaction in different activities and the grammars of particular languages.

Third, future research needs to consider learners' acquisition of L2 pragmatics from different psychological perspectives, including cognitive theories and sociocultural theory. Especially in order to ground instruction in research and theory, it is critical to gain a more thorough, theoretically informed, and detailed understanding of what it takes to notice, understand, and develop control over pragmatic mappings of form, function, and context of use. Notions such as "implicit" and "explicit," whether applied to the learning or teaching of pragmatics, have been treated in a rather cavalier manner, without careful attention to their criterial features in cognitive psychology and consideration of how these cognitive constructs can be translated into instructional practice. Especially (but not only) in pragmatics, it may prove helpful, and in the long run necessary, to link cognitive with affective constructs such as motivation, because neuropsychological research indicates a strong connection between those domains.

While these topics bear great fascination in themselves, exploring them in carefully conducted studies will also bring eventual and perhaps even immediate benefits for educational practice.

References

Achiba, M. (2002). *Learning to request in a second language: Child interlanguage pragmatics*. Clevedon, England: Multilingual Matters.

Agar, M. H. (1994). *Language shock*. New York: William Morrow.

Ahrenholz, B. (2000). Modality and referential movement in instructional discourse: Comparing the production of Italian learners of German with native German and native Italian production. *Studies in Second Language Acquisition, 22*, 337–368.

American Council on the Teaching of Foreign Languages. (1986). *ACTFL proficiency guidelines*. Hastings-on-Hudson, NY: Author.

Angelil-Carter, S. (1997). Second language acquisition of spoken and written English: Acquiring the skeptron. *TESOL Quarterly, 31*, 263–287.

Antaki, C., & Widdicombe, S. (Eds.). (1998). *Identities in talk*. London: Sage.

Antón, M. (1999). The discourse of a learner-centered classroom: Sociocultural perspectives on teacher-learner interaction in the second-language classroom. *Modern Language Journal, 83*, 303–318.

Austin, J. L. (1962). *How to do things with words*. Oxford: Oxford University Press.

Babbie, E. (1990). *Survey research methods* (2nd ed.). Belmont, CA: Wadsworth.

Babbie, E. (1998). *The practice of social research* (8th ed.). Belmont, CA: Wadsworth.

Bailey, K. M. (1990). The use of diary studies in teacher education programs. In J. C. Richards & D. Nunan (Eds.), *Second language teacher education* (pp. 215–226). New York: Cambridge University Press.

Bailey, K. M., & Ochsner, R. (1983). A methodological review of the diary studies: Windmill tilting or social science? In K. M. Bailey, M. H. Long, & S. Peck (Eds.), *Second language acquisition studies* (pp. 188–198). Rowley, MA: Newbury House.

Baker, C. D. (2002). Ethnomethodological analyses of interviews. In J. F. Gubrium & J. A. Holstein (Eds.), *Handbook of interview research* (pp. 777–795). Thousand Oaks, CA: Sage.

Bakhtin, M. M. (1986). *Speech genres and other late essays*. (V. W. McGee, Trans.). Austin: University of Texas Press.

Bardovi-Harlig, K. (1999). Exploring the interlanguage of interlanguage pragmatics: A research agenda for acquisitional pragmatics. *Language Learning, 49*, 677–713.

Bardovi-Harlig, K. (2000). *Tense and aspect in second language acquisition: Form, meaning, and use.* Oxford: Blackwell.

Bardovi-Harlig, K. (2001). Empirical evidence of the need for instruction in pragmatics. In K. R. Rose & G. Kasper (Eds.), *Pragmatics in language teaching* (pp. 13–32). New York: Cambridge University Press.

Bardovi-Harlig, K., & Dörnyei, Z. (1998). Do language learners recognize pragmatic violations? Pragmatic vs. grammatical awareness in instructed L2 learning. *TESOL Quarterly, 32*, 233–259.

Bardovi-Harlig, K., & Hartford, B. (1990). Congruence in native and nonnative conversations: Status balance in the academic advising session. *Language Learning, 40*, 467–501.

Bardovi-Harlig, K., & Hartford, B. (1991). Saying "no" in English: Native and nonnative rejections. In L. F. Bouton & Y. Kachru (Eds.), *Pragmatics and language learning* (monograph series vol. 2, pp. 41–57). Urbana-Champaign, IL: Division of English as an International Language, University of Illinois, Urbana-Champaign.

Bardovi-Harlig, K., & Hartford, B. S. (1993a). Learning the rules of academic talk: A longitudinal study of pragmatic development. *Studies in Second Language Acquisition, 15*, 279–304.

Bardovi-Harlig, K., & Hartford, B. S. (1993b). Refining the DCT: Comparing open questionnaires and dialogue completion tasks. In L. F. Bouton & Y. Kachru (Eds.), *Pragmatics and language learning* (monograph series vol. 4, pp. 143–165). Urbana-Champaign, IL: Division of English as an International Language, University of Illinois, Urbana-Champaign.

Bardovi-Harlig, K., & Hartford, B. S. (1996). Input in an institutional setting. *Studies in Second Language Acquisition, 18*, 171–188.

Barron, A. (2002). *Acquisition in interlanguage pragmatics: Learning how to do things with words in a study abroad context.* Amsterdam: Benjamins.

Bartlett, F. C. (1932). *Remembering: An experimental and social study.* New York: Cambridge University Press.

Beebe, L. M. (1985). Input: Choosing the right stuff. In S. M. Gass & C. G. Madden (Eds.), *Input in second language acquisition* (pp. 404–414). Rowley, MA: Newbury House.

Beebe, L. M., & Cummings, M. C. (1996). Natural speech act data versus written questionnaire data: How data collection method affects speech act performance. In S. M. Gass & J. Neu (Eds.), *Speech acts across cultures: Challenges to communication in a second language* (pp. 65–86). Berlin: Mouton de Gruyter. (Original version 1985.)

Beebe, L. M., & Takahashi, T. (1989a). Do you have a bag? Social status and patterned variation in second language acquisition. In S. M. Gass, C. Madden, D. Preston, & L. Selinker (Eds.), *Variation in second language acquisition: Discourse and pragmatics* (pp. 103–128). Clevedon, England: Multilingual Matters.

Beebe, L. M., & Takahashi, T. (1989b). Sociolinguistic variation in face-threatening speech acts. In M. Eisenstein (Ed.), *The dynamic interlanguage* (pp. 199–218). New York: Plenum.

Behling, O., & Law, K. S. (2000). *Translating questionnaires and other research instruments*. Thousand Oaks, CA: Sage.

Bernard, H. (2000). *Social research methods: Qualitative and quantitative approaches*. Thousand Oaks, CA: Sage.

Bialystok, E. (1993). Symbolic representation and attentional control in pragmatic competence. In G. Kasper & S. Blum-Kulka (Eds.), *Interlanguage pragmatics* (pp. 43–59). New York: Oxford University Press.

Bialystok, E. (1994). Analysis and control in the development of second language proficiency. *Studies in Second Language Acquisition, 16,* 157–168.

Billmyer, K. (1990a). The effect of formal instruction on the development of sociolinguistic competence: The performance of compliments. (Doctoral dissertation, University of Pennsylvania, Philadelphia). *Dissertation Abstracts International, 51,* 1535.

Billmyer, K. (1990b). "I really like your lifestyle": ESL learners learning how to compliment. *Penn Working Papers in Educational Linguistics, 6,* 31–48.

Billmyer, K., & Varghese, M. (2000). Investigating instrument-based pragmatic variability: Effects of enhancing discourse completion tests. *Applied Linguistics, 21*(4), 517–552.

Blum-Kulka, S. (1987). Indirectness and politeness in requests: Same or different? *Journal of Pragmatics, 11,* 131–146.

Blum-Kulka, S. (1991). Interlanguage pragmatics: The case of requests. In R. Phillipson, E. Kellerman, L. Selinker, M. Sharwood Smith, & M. Swain (Eds.), *Foreign / second language pedagogy research* (pp. 255–272). Clevedon, Avon: Multilingual Matters.

Blum-Kulka, S. (1997). *Dinner talk*. Mahwah, NJ: Erlbaum.

Blum-Kulka, S., House, J., & Kasper, G. (Eds.). (1989). *Cross-cultural pragmatics: Requests and apologies*. Norwood, NJ: Ablex.

Blum-Kulka, S., & Olshtain, E. (1986). Too many words: Length of utterance and pragmatic failure. *Studies in Second Language Acquisition, 8,* 47–61.

Bonikowska, M. P. (1988). The choice of opting out. *Applied Linguistics, 9,* 69–181.

Bourdieu, P. (1977). The economics of linguistic exchanges. *Social Science Information, 16,* 645–668.

Bouton, L. F. (1988). A cross-cultural study of ability to interpret implicatures in English. *World Englishes, 17,* 183–196.

Bouton, L. F. (1992). Culture, pragmatics and implicature. *AFinLa Yearbook 1992,* 35–61.

Bouton, L. F. (1994a). Can NNS skill in interpreting implicatures in American English be improved through explicit instruction? A pilot study. In L. F. Bouton & Y. Kachru (Eds.), *Pragmatics and language learning* (monograph series vol. 5, pp. 88–109). Urbana-Champaign, IL: Division of English as an International Language, University of Illinois, Urbana-Champaign.

Bouton, L. F. (1994b). Conversational implicature in the second language: Learned slowly when not deliberately taught. *Journal of Pragmatics, 22,* 157–167.

Bouton, L. F. (1999). Developing nonnative speaker skills in interpreting conversational implicatures in English: Explicit teaching can ease the process. In E. Hinkel (Ed.), *Culture in second language teaching and learning* (pp. 47–70). Cambridge, UK: Cambridge University Press.

Branaman, A. (1997). Goffman's social theory: The production of self. In C. Lemert & A. Branaman (Eds.), *The Goffman reader* (pp. xlvii–liii). Oxford: Blackwell.

Bremer, K., Roberts, C., Vasseur, M.-T., Simonot, M., & Broeder, P. (1996). *Achieving understanding: Discourse in intercultural encounters.* London: Longman.

Briggs, C. L. (1986). *Learning how to ask.* New York: Cambridge University Press.

Brooks, F. B., Donato, R., & McGlone, J. V. (1997). When are they going to say "it" right? Understanding learner talk during pair-work activity. *Foreign Language Annals, 30,* 524–541.

Brown, P., & Levinson, S. D. (1987). *Politeness: Some universals in language usage.* New York: Cambridge University Press.

Bryman, A., & Cramer, D. (2001). *Quantitative data analysis with SPSS Release 10 for Windows.* London: Routledge.

Bühler, K. (1934). *Sprachtheorie* [Theory of language]. Jena: Fischer.

Canale, M. (1983). From communicative competence to language pedagogy. In J. Richards & R. Schmidt (Eds.), *Language and communication* (pp. 2–27). London: Longman.

Canale, M., & Swain, M. (1980). Theoretical bases of communicative approaches to second language teaching and testing. *Applied Linguistics, 1,* 1–47.

Carrell, P. (1981). Relative difficulty of request forms in L1/L2 comprehension. In M. Hines & W. Rutherford (Eds.), *On TESOL '81* (pp. 141–152). Washington, DC: TESOL.

Carroll, D. (2000). Precision timing in novice-to-novice L2 conversations. *Issues in Applied Linguistics, 11*(1), 67–110.

Chaudron, C. (1988). *Second language classrooms.* New York: Cambridge University Press.

Clancy, P. (1986). The acquisition of communicative style in Japanese. In B. Schieffelin & E. Ochs (Eds.), *Language socialization across cultures* (pp. 213–250). Cambridge: Cambridge University Press.

Clyne, M. (1994). *Intercultural communication at work.* Cambridge: Cambridge University Press.

Clyne, M., Ball, M., & Neil, D. (1991). Intercultural communication at work in Australia: Complaints and apologies in turns. *Multilingua, 10,* 251–273.

Cohen, A. D. (1996). Developing the ability to perform speech acts. *Studies in Second Language Acquisition, 18,* 253–267.

Cohen, A. D. (1997). Developing pragmatic ability: Insights from the accelerated study of Japanese. In H. M. Cook, K. Hijirida, & M. Tahara (Eds.), *New trends and issues in teaching Japanese language and culture* (Technical Report No. 15, pp. 133–159). Honolulu: University of Hawaiʻi, Second Language Teaching and Curriculum Center.

Cohen, A. D. (1998). *Strategies in learning and using a second language.* London: Longman.

Cohen, A. D., & Olshtain, E. (1993). The production of speech acts by EFL learners. *TESOL Quarterly, 27,* 33–56.

Cohen, L., Manion, L., & Morrison, K. (2000). *Research methods in education* (5th ed.). London: Routledge/Falmer.

Converse, J., & Presser, S. (1986). *Survey questions: Handcrafting the standardized questionnaire.* Newbury Park, CA: Sage.

Cook, H. M. (1992). Meanings of non-referential indexes: A case study of the Japanese sentence-final particle *ne. Text, 12,* 507–539.

Cook, H. M. (2001). Why can't learners of Japanese as a foreign language distinguish polite from impolite speech styles? In K. R. Rose & G. Kasper (Eds.), *Pragmatics in language teaching* (pp. 80–102). Cambridge: Cambridge University Press.

Cook, V. (1993). *Linguistics and second language acquisition.* New York: St. Martin's Press.

Cook, V. (1999). Going beyond the native speaker in language teaching. *TESOL Quarterly, 33,* 185–209.

Cooreman, A., & Kilborn, K. (1991). Functionalist linguistics: Discourse structure and language processing in second language acquisition. In C. Ferguson & T. Huebner (Eds.), *Crosscurrents in second language acquisition and linguistic theory* (pp. 195–224). Amsterdam: Benjamins.

Corder, S. P. (1967). The significance of learners' errors. *International Review of Applied Linguistics in Language Teaching, 5,* 161–170.

Coughlan, P., & Duff, P. A. (1994). Same task, different activities: Analysis of a SLA task from an activity theory perspective. In J. P. Lantolf & G. Appel (Eds.), *Vygotskyan approaches to second language research* (pp. 173–193). Norwood, NJ: Ablex.

Coulmas, F. (Ed.). (1981). *Conversational routine: Explorations in standardized communication situations and prepatterned speech.* The Hague: Mouton.

Coulmas, F. (1992). Linguistic etiquette in Japanese society. In R. J. Watts, S. Ide, & K. Ehlich (Eds.), *Politeness in language: Studies in its history, theory and practice* (pp. 299–323). Berlin: Mouton de Gruyter.

Crookall, D., & Saunders, D. (1989). *Communication and simulation.* Clevedon, England: Multilingual Matters.

Crookes, G., & Schmidt, R. (1991). Motivation: Reopening the research agenda. *Language Learning, 41,* 469–512.

Crystal, D. (Ed.). (1997). *The Cambridge encyclopedia of language* (2nd ed.). New York: Cambridge University Press.

Davis, K. A. (1995). Qualitative theory and methods in applied linguistics research. *TESOL Quarterly, 29,* 428–453.

Day, D. (1994). Tang's dilemma and other problems: Ethnification processes at some multicultural workplaces. *Pragmatics, 4,* 315–336.

DeCoo, W. (1996). The induction-deduction opposition: Ambiguities and complexities of the didactic reality. *International Review of Applied Linguistics, 34,* 95–118.

DeKeyser, R. (1995). Learning second language grammar rules: An experiment with a miniature linguistic system. *Studies in Second Language Acquisition, 17,* 379–410.

Denzin, N. K., & Lincoln, Y. S. (Eds.). (2000). *Handbook of qualitative research* (2nd ed.). Thousand Oaks, CA: Sage.

Dietrich, R. (1992). *Modalität im Deutschen. Zur Theorie der relativen Modalität* [Modality in German. On a theory of relative modality]. Opladen, Germany: Westdeutscher Verlag.

Dietrich, R., Klein, W., & Noyau, C. (1995). *The acquisition of temporality in a second language.* Amsterdam: Benjamins.

Dittmar, N. (1992). Grammaticalization in second language acquisition: An introduction. *Studies in Second Language Acquisition, 14,* 249–257.

Dittmar, N., & Ahrenholz, B. (1995). The acquisition of modal expressions and related grammatical means by an Italian learner of German in the course of 3 years of longitudinal observation. In A. Giacalone Ramat & G. Crocco Galèas (Eds.), *From pragmatics to syntax* (pp. 197–232). Tübingen, Germany: Narr.

Donato, R. (1994). Collective scaffolding in second language learning. In J. P. Lantolf & G. Appel (Eds.), *Vygotskyan approaches to second language research* (pp. 33–56). Norwood, NJ: Ablex.

Dörnyei, Z. (2001). *Teaching and researching motivation*. Harlow: Longman.

Dörnyei, Z., & Schmidt, R. (Eds.). (2001). *Motivation and second language acquisition* (Technical Report #23). Honolulu, Hawai'i: University of Hawai'i, Second Language Teaching & Curriculum Center.

Doughty, C. (2001). Cognitive underpinnings of focus on form. In P. Robinson (Ed.), *Cognition and second language instruction* (pp. 206–257). Cambridge: Cambridge University Press.

Doughty, C., & Williams, J. (1998). *Focus on form in classroom second language acquisition*. New York: Cambridge University Press.

Douglas, D., & Selinker, L. (1985). Principles for language tests within the "discourse domain" theory of interlanguage: Research, test construction, and interpretation. *Language Testing, 2,* 205–226.

Drew, P., & Heritage, J. (1992). Analyzing talk at work: An introduction. In P. Drew & J. Heritage (Eds.), *Talk at work: Interaction in institutional settings* (pp. 3–65). New York: Cambridge University Press.

Duff, P. A. (1995). An ethnography of communication in immersion classrooms in Hungary. *TESOL Quarterly, 29,* 505–537.

Duff, P. A. (1996). Different languages, different practices: Socialization of discourse competence in dual-language school classrooms in Hungary. In K. M. Bailey & D. Nunan (Eds.), *Voices from the classroom* (pp. 407–433). New York: Cambridge University Press.

DuFon, M. A. (1999). The acquisition of linguistic politeness in Indonesian as a second language by sojourners in a naturalistic context. (Doctoral dissertation, University of Hawai'i.) *Dissertation Abstracts International, 60,* 3985.

DuFon, M. A. (2000). The acquisition of negative responses to experience questions in Indonesian as a second language by sojourners in naturalistic interactions. In B. Swierzbin, F. Morris, M. Anderson, C. A. Klee, & E. Tarone (Eds.), *Social and cognitive factors in second language acquisition* (pp. 77–97). Somerville, MA: Cascadilla Press.

Dunn, W. E., & Lantolf, J. P. (1998). Vygotsky's zone of proximal development and Krashen's $i + 1$: Incommensurable constructs; incommensurable theories. *Language Learning, 48,* 411 442.

Duranti, A. (1997). *Linguistic anthropology*. Cambridge: Cambridge University Press.

Eckert, P. (2000). *Linguistic variation as social practice*. Oxford: Blackwell.

Edmondson, W., & House, J. (1991). Do learners talk too much? The waffle phenomenon in interlanguage pragmatics. In R. Phillipson, E. Kellerman, L. Selinker, M. Sharwood Smith, & M. Swain (Eds.), *Foreign / second language pedagogy research* (pp. 273–286). Clevedon, England: Multilingual Matters.

Ehrlich, S. (1997). Gender as social practice: Implications for second language acquisition. *Studies in Second Language Acquisition, 19*, 421–446.

Eisenstein, M., & Bodman, J. W. (1986). "I very appreciate": Expressions of gratitude by native and non-native speakers of American English. *Applied Linguistics, 7*, 167–185.

Eisenstein, M., & Bodman, J. W. (1993). Expressing gratitude in American English. In G. Kasper & S. Blum-Kulka (Eds.), *Interlanguage pragmatics* (pp. 64–81). New York: Oxford University Press.

Ellis, R. (1990). *Instructed second language acquisition*. Oxford: Blackwell.

Ellis, R. (1992). Learning to communicate in the classroom: A study of two learners' requests. *Studies in Second Language Acquisition, 14*, 1–23.

Ellis, R. (1994). *The study of second language acquisition*. Oxford: Oxford University Press.

Erickson, F. (1996). Ethnographic microanalysis. In S. L. McKay & N. H. Hornberger (Eds.), *Sociolinguistics and language teaching* (pp. 283–306). Cambridge, UK: Cambridge University Press.

Erickson, F., & Shultz, J. (1982). *The counselor as gatekeeper*. New York: Academic.

Ericsson, K. A., & Simon, H. A. (1993). *Protocol analysis*. Cambridge, MA: Bradford/MIT Press. (First edition 1984.)

Ericsson, K. A., & Simon, H. A. (1998). How to study thinking in everyday life: Contrasting think-aloud protocols with descriptions and explanations of thinking. *Mind, Culture, and Activity, 5*, 178–186.

Errington, J. (1988). *Structure and style in Javanese: A semiotic view of linguistic etiquette*. Philadelphia: University of Philadelphia Press.

Færch, C., & Kasper, G. (1982). Phatic, metalingual and metacommunicative functions in discourse: Gambits and repair. In N. E. Enkvist (Ed.), *Impromptu speech* (pp. 71–103). Åbo, Finland: Åbo Akademi University.

Falsgraf, C., & Majors, D. (1995). Implicit culture in Japanese immersion classroom discourse. *Journal of the Association of Teachers of Japanese, 29*(2), 1–21.

Ferguson, C. A. (1995). Foreword. In B. F. Freed (Ed.), *Second language acquisition in a study abroad context* (pp. xi–xv). Amsterdam: Benjamins.

Fielding, N. G., & Fielding, J. L. (1986). *Linking data*. Beverly Hills, CA: Sage.

Fiksdal, S. (1990). *The right time and pace: A microanalysis of cross-cultural gatekeeping interviews*. Norwood, NJ: Ablex.

Firth, A. (1996). The discursive accomplishment of "normality": On "lingua franca" English and conversation analysis. *Journal of Pragmatics, 26*, 237–259.

Fowler, F. (1995). *Improving survey questions: Design and evaluation.* Thousand Oaks, CA: Sage.

Fraser, B. (1990). Perspectives on politeness. *Journal of Pragmatics, 14,* 219–236.

Frawley, W., & Lantolf, J. P. (1984). Speaking and self-order: A critique of orthodox SLA research. *Studies in Second Language Acquisition, 6,* 143–159.

Fukushima, S. (2000). *Requests and culture.* Bern: Peter Lang.

Fukuya, Y., & Clark, M. (2001). A comparison of input enhancement and explicit instruction of mitigators. In L. F. Bouton (Ed.), *Pragmatics and language learning* (monograph series vol. 10, pp. 111–130). Urbana-Champaign, IL: Division of English as an International Language, University of Illinois, Urbana-Champaign.

Fukuya, Y., Reeve, M., Gisi, J., & Christianson, M. (1998). Does focus on form work for sociopragmatics? Paper presented at the 12th Annual International Conference on Pragmatics and Language Learning, University of Illinois, Urbana-Champaign, April.

Gafaranga, J. (2001). Linguistic identities in talk-in-interaction: Order in bilingual conversation. *Journal of Pragmatics, 33,* 1901–1925.

Gardner, R. C. (1985). *Social psychology and second language learning.* London. Arnold.

Gardner, R. C., & Lambert, W. E. (1972). *Attitudes and motivation in second-language learning.* Rowley, MA: Newbury House.

Gardner, R. C., & MacIntyre, P. (1993). A student's contribution to second language learning. Part II: Affective variables. *Language Teaching, 26,* 1–11.

Gass, S. M. (1997). *Input, interaction and the second language learner.* Mahwah, NJ: Erlbaum.

Gass, S. M., & Mackey, A. (2000). *Stimulated recall methodology in second language research.* Mahwah, NJ: Lawrence Erlbaum.

Giacalone Ramat, A. (1992). Grammaticalization processes in the area of temporal and modal relations. *Studies in Second Language Acquisition, 14,* 297–322.

Giacalone Ramat, A. (1995). Function and form of modality in learner Italian. In A. Giacalone Ramat & G. Crocco Galèas (Eds.), *From pragmatics to syntax* (pp. 269–293). Tübingen: Narr.

Giacalone Ramat, A., & Crocco Galèas, G. (Eds.). (1995). *From pragmatics to syntax. Modality in second language acquisition.* Tübingen, Germany: Narr.

Gibbs, R. W. (1994). *The poetics of the mind: Figurative thought, language, and understanding.* New York: Cambridge University Press.

Givón, T. (1979). *On understanding grammar.* New York: Academic Press.

Goffman, E. (1959). *The presentation of self in everyday life*. New York: Anchor Books.

Goffman, E. (1967). *Interaction ritual: Essays on face-to-face behavior*. New York: Anchor Books.

Goffman, E. (1971). *Relations in public*. Harmondsworth: Penguin.

Goffman, E. (1974). *Frame analysis*. New York: Harper and Row.

Goffman, E. (1981). *Forms of talk*. Oxford: Blackwell.

Grice, P. (1975). Logic and conversation. In P. Cole & J. Morgan (Eds.), Syntax and semantics. *Vol. 3: Speech acts* (pp. 41–58). New York: Academic Press.

Grosjean, F. (1989). Neurolinguists, beware! The bilingual is not two monolinguals in one person. *Brain and Language, 36*, 3–15.

Gubrium, J. F., & Holstein, J. A. (Eds.). (2002). *Handbook of interview research: Contexts and methods*. Thousand Oaks, CA: Sage.

Guiora, A. Z. (1972). Construct validity and transpositional research: Toward an empirical study of psychoanalytic concepts. *Comprehensive Psychiatry, 13*, 139–150.

Gumperz, J. J. (1982). *Discourse strategies*. Cambridge: Cambridge University Press.

Gumperz, J. J. (1992). Contextualization and understanding. In A. Duranti & C. Goodwin (Eds.), *Rethinking context* (pp. 229–252). Cambridge: Cambridge University Press.

Gumperz, J. J. (1996). The linguistic and cultural relativity of conversational inference. In J. J. Gumperz & S. Levinson (Eds.), *Rethinking linguistic relativity* (pp. 374–406). Cambridge: Cambridge University Press.

Gumperz, J. J., & Cook-Gumperz, J. (1982). Introduction: Language and the communication of social identity. In J. J. Gumperz (Ed.), *Language and social identity* (pp. 1–21). New York: Cambridge University Press.

Hall, J. K. (1993). The role of oral practices in the accomplishment of our everyday lives: The sociocultural dimension of interaction with implications for the learning of another language. *Applied Linguistics, 14*, 145–166.

Hall, J. K. (1995a). "Aw, man, where you goin'?": Classroom interaction and the development of L2 interactional competence. *Issues in Applied Linguistics, 6*, 37–62.

Hall, J. K. (1995b). (Re)creating our worlds with words: A sociohistorical perspective of face-to-face interaction. *Applied Linguistics, 16*, 206–232.

Hall, J. K. (1998). Differential teacher attention to student utterances: The construction of different opportunities for learning in the IRF. *Linguistics and Education, 9*, 287–311.

Hall, J. K. (1999). A prosaics of interaction: The development of interactional competence in another language. In E. Hinkel (Ed.), *Culture in second language teaching and learning* (pp. 137–151). Cambridge, UK: Cambridge University Press.

Hall, J. K., & Verplaetse, L. S. (Eds.). (2000). *Second and foreign language learning through classroom interaction*. Mahwah, NJ: Erlbaum.

Hartford, B., & Bardovi-Harlig, K. (1992). Experimental and observational data in the study of interlanguage pragmatics. In L. F. Bouton & Y. Kachru (Eds.), *Pragmatics and language learning* (monograph series vol. 3, pp. 33–52). Urbana-Champaign, IL: Division of English as an International Language, University of Illinois, Urbana-Champaign.

Hashimoto, H. (1993). Language acquisition of an exchange student within the homestay environment. *Journal of Asian Pacific Communication, 4*, 209–224.

Hassall, T. J. (1997). *Requests by Australian learners of Indonesian*. Unpublished doctoral dissertation, Australian National University, Canberra.

Hatch, E., & Lazaraton, A. (1991). *The research manual: Design and statistics for applied linguistics*. New York: Newbury House.

He, A. W. (1995). Co-constructing institutional identities: The case of student counselees. *Research on Language and Social Interaction, 28*, 213–231.

Heritage, J., & Atkinson, J. M. (1984). Introduction. In J. M. Atkinson & J. Heritage (Eds.), *Structures of social action* (pp. 1–15). New York: Cambridge University Press.

Hill, T. (1997). The development of pragmatic competence in an EFL context. (Doctoral dissertation, Temple University Japan.) *Dissertation Abstracts International, 58*, 3905.

Hinds, J. (1987). Reader versus writer responsibility. In U. Connor & R. Kaplan (Eds.), *Writing across languages* (pp. 141–152). Reading, MA: Addison-Wesley.

Hinkel, E. (1997). Appropriateness of advice: DCT and multiple choice data. *Applied Linguistics, 18*, 1–26.

Hoffman-Hicks, S. (1999). The longitudinal development of French foreign language pragmatic competence: Evidence from study abroad participants. (Doctoral dissertation, Indiana University.) *Dissertation Abstracts International, 61*, 591.

Hogg, M. A., & Abrams, D. (1988). *Social identifications: A social psychology of intergroup relations and processes*. London: Routledge.

Holmes, J., & Meyerhoff, M. (Ed.) (1999). Communities of practice in language and gender research [Special issue]. *Language in Society, 28*(2).

Holstein, J. A., & Gubrium, J. F. (1997). Active interviewing. In D. Silverman (Ed.), *Qualitative research* (pp. 113–129). London: Sage.

Houck, N., & Gass, S. M. (1996). Non-native refusal: A methodological perspective. In S. M. Gass & J. Neu (Eds.), *Speech acts across cultures:*

Challenges to communication in a second language (pp. 45–64). Berlin: Mouton de Gruyter.

House, J. (1986). Learning to talk: Talking to learn. An investigation of learner performance in two types of discourse. In G. Kasper (Ed.), *Learning, teaching and communication in the foreign language classroom* (pp. 43–57). Aarhus, Denmark: Aarhus University Press.

House, J. (1989). Politeness in English and German: The functions of *please* and *bitte*. In S. Blum-Kulka, J. House, & G. Kasper (Eds.), *Cross cultural pragmatics: Requests and apologies* (pp. 96–119). Norwood, NJ: Ablex.

House, J. (1996). Developing pragmatic fluency in English as a foreign language: Routines and metapragmatic awareness. *Studies in Second Language Acquisition, 18*, 225–252.

House, J., & Kasper, G. (2000). How to remain a nonnative speaker. In C. Riemer (Ed.), *Kognitive Aspekte des Lehrens und Lernens von Fremdsprachen* [Cognitive aspects of foreign language teaching and learning]. *Festschrift für Willis J. Edmondson zum 60. Geburtstag* [Festschrift for Willis J. Edmondson on the occasion of his 60th birthday] (pp. 101–118). Tübingen: Narr.

House, J., Kasper, G., & Ross, S. (Eds.) (2003). *Misunderstanding in social life*: *Discourse approaches to problematic talk*. Harlow, England: Longman/Pearson Education.

Hutchby, I., & Woofitt, R. (1998). *Conversation analysis*. Cambridge: Polity Press.

Hymes, D. (1972). On communicative competence. In J. Pride & J. Holmes (Eds.), *Sociolinguistics: Selected readings* (pp. 269–293). Harmondsworth, England: Penguin.

Iino, M. (1996). "Excellent Foreigner!": Gaijinization of Japanese language and culture in contact situations—An ethnographic study of dinner table conversations between Japanese host families and American students. (Doctoral dissertation, University of Pennsylvania, Philadelphia.) *Dissertation Abstracts International, 57*, 1451.

Jacoby, S., & Ochs, E. (1995). Co-construction: An introduction. *Research on Language and Social Interaction, 28*, 171–183.

Johnson, M. (2001). *The art of non-conversation. A reexamination of the validity of the Oral Proficiency Interview*. New Haven, CT & London: Yale University Press.

Johnston, B., Kasper, G., & Ross, S. (1998). The effect of rejoinders in production questionnaires. *Applied Linguistics, 19*, 157–182.

Kanagy, R. (1999a). Interactional routines as a mechanism for L2 acquisition and socialization in an immersion context. *Journal of Pragmatics, 31*, 1467–1492.

Kanagy, R. (Ed.). (1999b). Language socialization and affect in first and second language acquisition [Special issue]. *Journal of Pragmatics, 31*(11).

Kanagy, R., & Igarashi, K. (1997). Acquisition of pragmatics competence in a Japanese immersion kindergarten. In L. F. Bouton (Ed.), *Pragmatics and language learning* (monograph series vol. 8, pp. 243–265). Urbana-Champaign, IL: Division of English as an International Language, University of Illinois, Urbana-Champaign.

Kärkkäinen, E. (1992). Modality as a strategy in interaction: Epistemic modality in the language of native and non-native speakers of English. In L. F. Bouton & Y. Kachru (Eds.), *Pragmatics and language learning* (monograph series vol. 3, pp. 197–216). Urbana, IL: Division of English as an International Language, University of Illinois, Urbana-Champaign.

Kasper, G. (1981). *Pragmatische Aspekte in der Interimsprache* [Pragmatic aspects in interlanguage]. Tübingen, Germany: Narr.

Kasper, G. (1984). Pragmatic comprehension in learner-native speaker discourse. *Language Learning, 34,* 1–20.

Kasper, G. (1989). Interactive procedures in interlanguage discourse. In W. Olesky (Ed.), *Contrastive pragmatics* (pp. 189–229). Amsterdam: Benjamins.

Kasper, G. (1992). Pragmatic transfer. *Second Language Research, 8,* 203–231.

Kasper, G. (1997). 'A' stands for acquisition: A response to Firth and Wagner. *Modern Language Journal, 81,* 307–312.

Kasper, G. (2001). Classroom research on interlanguage pragmatics. In K. R. Rose & G. Kasper (Eds.), *Pragmatics in language teaching* (pp. 33–60). New York: Cambridge University Press.

Kasper, G., & Dahl, M. (1991). Research methods in interlanguage pragmatics. *Studies in Second Language Acquisition, 13,* 215–247.

Kasper, G., & Rose, K. R. (1999). Pragmatics and SLA. *Annual Review of Applied Linguistics, 19,* 81–104.

Kasper, G., & Rose, K. R. (Forthcoming). *Approaches to interlanguage pragmatics research.*

Kasper, G., & Schmidt, R. (1996). Developmental issues in interlanguage pragmatics. *Studies in Second Language Acquisition, 18,* 149–169.

Kerekes, J. (1992). *Development in nonnative speakers' use and perception of assertiveness and supportiveness in mixed-sex conversations* (Occasional Paper No. 21). Honolulu: University of Hawai'i at Mānoa, Department of English as a Second Language.

Kern, J. M. (1991). An evaluation of a novel role-play methodology: The standardized idiographic approach. *Behavior Therapy, 22,* 13–29.

Kim, I.-O. (2000). Relationship of onset age of ESL acquisition and extent of informal input to appropriateness and nativeness in performing four speech acts in English: A study of native Korean adult speakers of ESL.

(Doctoral dissertation, New York University.) *Dissertation Abstracts International, 61,* 1265.

Kipper, D. A. (1988). The differential effect of role-playing conditions on the accuracy of self-evaluation. *Journal of Group Therapy, Psychodrama, and Sociometry, 41,* 30–35.

Kitao, K. (1990). A study of Japanese and American perceptions of politeness in requests. *Doshida Studies in English, 50,* 178–210.

Klein, W., Dietrich, R., & Noyau, C. (1995). Conclusions. In R. Dietrich, W. Klein, & C. Noyau (Eds.), *The acquisition of temporality in a second language* (pp. 261–280). Amsterdam: Benjamins.

Knapp, M., Hopper, R., & Bell, R. (1984). Compliments: A descriptive taxonomy. *Journal of Communication, 34,* 19–31.

Koike, D. A. (1989). Pragmatic competence and adult L2 acquisition: Speech acts in interlanguage. *Modern Language Journal, 73,* 279–289.

Koike, D. A. (1996). Transfer of pragmatic competence and suggestions in Spanish foreign language learning. In S. M. Gass & J. Neu (Eds.), *Speech acts across cultures: Challenges to communication in a second language* (pp. 257–281). Berlin: Mouton de Gruyter.

Kondo, S. (1997a). Longitudinal study on the development of pragmatic competence in a natural learning context—Perception behind performance. *Proceedings of Sophia University Linguistic Society, 12,* 35–54.

Kondo, S. (1997b). The development of pragmatic competence by Japanese learners of English: Longitudinal study on interlanguage apologies. *Sophia Linguistica, 41,* 265–284.

Kramsch, C. (1986). From language proficiency to interactional competence. *Modern Language Journal, 70,* 366–372.

Kramsch, C. (1993). *Context and culture in language education.* Oxford: Oxford University Press.

Kramsch, C. (2003). Identity, role, and voice in cross-cultural (mis)communication. In J. House, G. Kasper, & S. Ross (Eds.), *Misunderstanding in social life. Discourse approaches to problematic talk* (pp. 129–153). Harlow, England: Longman/Pearson Education.

Kubota, M. (1995). Teachability of conversational implicature to Japanese EFL learners. *IRLT Bulletin, 9,* 35–67.

Kuha, M. (1997). The computer-assisted interactive DCT: A study in pragmatics research methodology. In L. F. Bouton (Ed.), *Pragmatics and language learning* (monograph series vol. 8). Urbana-Champaign, IL: Division of English as an International Language, University of Illinois, Urbana-Champaign.

Kvale, S. (1996). *InterViews.* Thousand Oaks, CA: Sage.

Labov, W. (1972). *Sociolinguistic patterns.* Philadelphia: University of Pennsylvania Press.

Labov, W. (1984). Field methods of the project on linguistic change and variation. In J. Baugh & J. Sherzer (Eds.), *Language in use* (pp. 28–53). Englewood Cliffs, NJ: Prentice-Hall.

Lantolf, J. P. (1994). Sociocultural theory and second language learning. *Modern Language Journal*, *78*, 418–420.

Lantolf, J. P. (2000a). Introducing sociocultural theory. In J. P. Lantolf (Ed.), *Sociocultural theory and second language learning* (pp. 1–26). Oxford: Oxford University Press.

Lantolf, J. P. (Ed.). (2000b). *Sociocultural theory and second language learning*. Oxford: Oxford University Press.

Lantolf, J. P., & Appel, G. (1994a). Theoretical framework: An introduction to Vygotskyan perspectives on second language research. In J. P. Lantolf & G. Appel (Eds.), *Vygotskyan approaches to second language research* (pp. 1–32). Norwood, NJ: Ablex.

Lantolf, J. P., & Appel, G. (Eds.). (1994b). *Vygotskyan approaches to second language research*. Norwood, NJ: Ablex.

Larsen-Freeman, D., & Long, M. H. (1991). *An introduction to second language acquisition*. London: Longman.

Lave, J., & Wenger, E. (1991). Situated learning: Legitimate peripheral participation. New York: Cambridge University Press.

Lazaraton, A. (1995). Qualitative research in applied linguistics: A progress report. *TESOL Quarterly*, *29*, 455–472.

Lebra, T. (1976). *Japanese patterns of behavior*. Honolulu: University of Hawai'i Press.

Leech, G. (1983). *Principles of pragmatics*. London: Longman.

Leont'ev, A. N. (1981). The problem of activity in psychology. In J. V. Wertsch (Ed.), *The concept of activity in Soviet psychology* (pp. 37–71). Armonk, NY: M. E. Sharpe.

Levinson, S. (1979). Activity types and language. *Linguistics*, *17*, 365–399.

Levinson, S. (1983). *Pragmatics*. New York: Cambridge University Press.

Liddicoat, A., & Crozet, C. (2001). Acquiring French interactional norms through instruction. In K. R. Rose & G. Kasper (Eds.), *Pragmatics in language teaching* (pp. 125–144). New York: Cambridge University Press.

Lim, D. S. J. (1996). *Cross-cultural instruction and classroom discourse: A study of the foreign language classroom culture*. Unpublished master's thesis, University of Hawai'i at Mānoa, Department of East Asian Languages and Literatures.

LoCastro, V. (1997). Pedagogical intervention and pragmatic competence development. *Applied Language Learning*, *8*, 75–109.

LoCastro, V. (1998). *Learner subjectivity and pragmatic competence development*. Paper presented at the conference of the American Association of Applied Linguistics, Seattle, WA, March.

LoCastro, V. (2001). Individual differences in second language acquisition: Attitudes, learner subjectivity, and pragmatic norms. *System, 29*, 69–89.

LoCastro, V., & Netsu, M. (1997). *Point of view and opinion-giving in discussion tasks.* Paper presented at the conference of the American Association of Applied Linguistics, Orlando, FL, March.

Long, M. H. (1983). Does second language instruction make a difference? A review of the research. *TESOL Quarterly, 17*, 359–382.

Long, M. H. (1996). The role of the linguistic environment in second language acquisition. In W. C. Ritchie & T. K. Bhatia (Eds.), *Handbook of second language acquisition* (pp. 413–468). San Diego: Academic Press.

Long, M. H., Adams, L., McLean, M., & Castaños, F. (1976). Doing things with words: Verbal interaction in lockstep and small group classroom situations. In J. Fanselow & R. Crymes (Eds.), *On TESOL '76* (pp. 137–153). Washington, DC: Teachers of English to Speakers of Other Languages.

Long, M. H., & Robinson, P. (1998). Focus on form: Theory, research, and practice. In C. Doughty & J. Williams (Eds.), *Focus on form in classroom second language acquisition* (pp. 15–41). Cambridge: Cambridge University Press.

Lörscher, W. (1986). Conversational structures in the foreign language classroom. In G. Kasper (Ed.), *Learning, teaching and communication in the foreign language classroom* (pp. 11–22). Aarhus, Denmark: Aarhus University Press.

Lörscher, W., & Schulze, R. (1988). On polite speaking and foreign language classroom discourse. *International Review of Applied Linguistics in Language Teaching, 26*, 183–199.

Lyster, R. (1994). The effect of functional-analytic teaching on aspects of French immersion students' sociolinguistic competence. *Applied Linguistics, 15*, 263–287.

MacIntyre, P., & Noels, K. A. (1996). Using social-psychological variables to predict the use of language learning strategies. *Foreign Language Annals, 29*, 373–386.

Maeshiba, N., Yoshinaga, N., Kasper, G., & Ross, S. (1996). Transfer and proficiency in interlanguage apologizing. In S. M. Gass & J. Neu (Eds.), *Speech acts across cultures: Challenges to communication in a second language* (pp. 155–187). Berlin: Mouton de Gruyter.

Manes, J., & Wolfson, N. (1981). The compliment formula. In F. Coulmas (Ed.), *Conversational routine: Explorations in standardized communication situations and prepatterned speech* (pp. 115–132). The Hague: Mouton.

Margalef-Boada, T. (1993). Research methods in interlanguage pragmatics: An inquiry into data collection procedures. (Doctoral dissertation, Indiana University.) *Dissertation Abstracts International, 55*, 233.

Markee, N. (2000). *Conversation analysis.* Mahwah, NJ: Erlbaum.

Marriott, H. (1993). Acquiring sociolinguistic competence: Australian secondary students in Japan. *Journal of Asian Pacific Communication, 4,* 167–192.

Marriott, H. (1995). The acquisition of politeness patterns by exchange students in Japan. In B. F. Freed (Ed.), *Second language acquisition in a study abroad context* (pp. 197–224). Amsterdam: Benjamins.

Matsumura, S. (2001). Learning the rules for offering advice: A quantitative approach to second language socialization. *Language Learning, 51,* 635–679.

McKay, S. L., & Wong, S. C. (1996). Multiple discourses, multiple identities: Investment and agency in second language learning among Chinese adolescent immigrant students. *Harvard Educational Review, 3,* 577–608.

McMeekin, A. (In progress). *Negotiation of meaning in home stay and school environments during study abroad in Japan.* Unpublished doctoral dissertation, University of Hawai'i.

McNamara, T. (1987a). Language and social identity: Israelis abroad. *Journal of Language and Social Psychology, 6,* 215–228.

McNamara, T. (1987b). Language and social identity: Some Australian studies. *Australian Review of Applied Linguistics, 10,* 33–58.

McNamara, T. (1997a). "Interaction" in second language performance assessment: Whose performance? *Applied Linguistics, 18,* 446–466.

McNamara, T. (1997b). What do we mean by social identity? Competing frameworks, competing discourses. *TESOL Quarterly, 31,* 561–566.

Mey, J. L. (1993). *Pragmatics: An introduction.* Oxford: Blackwell.

Miles, P. (1994). Compliments and gender. *University of Hawai'i Occasional Papers Series, 26,* 85–137.

Miller, D. C., & Salkind, N. J. (Eds.). (2002). *Handbook of research design and social measurement* (6th ed.). Thousand Oaks, CA: Sage.

Miller, L. (1994). Japanese and American indirectness. *Journal of Asian Pacific Communication, 5,* 37–55.

Mitchell, R., & Myles, F. (1998). *Second language learning theories.* London: Arnold.

Mori, J. (2002). Task design, plan, and development of talk-in-interaction: An analysis of a small group activity in a Japanese language classroom. *Applied Linguistics, 23,* 323–347.

Morita, N. (2000). Discourse socialization through oral classroom activities in a TESOL graduate program. *TESOL Quarterly, 34,* 279–310.

Morris, C. (1938). Foundations of the theory of signs. In O. Neurath, C. Carnap, & C. Morris (Eds.), *International encyclopedia of unified science* (pp. 77–138). Chicago: University of Chicago Press.

Nattinger, J. R., & DeCarrico, J. S. (1992). *Lexical phrases and language teaching.* Oxford: Oxford University Press.

Niezgoda, K., & Röver, C. (2001). Pragmatic and grammatical awareness: A function of learning environment? In K. R. Rose & G. Kasper (Eds.), *Pragmatics in language teaching* (pp. 63–79). New York: Cambridge University Press.

Norris, J., & Ortega, L. (2000). Effectiveness of L2 instruction: A research synthesis and quantitative meta-analysis. *Language Learning, 50,* 417–528.

Norton, B. (2000). *Identity and language learning.* Harlow, England: Pearson.

Ochs, E. (1986). *Culture and language acquisition: Acquiring communicative competence in a Samoan village.* New York: Cambridge University Press.

Ochs, E. (1993). Constructing social identity: A language socialization perspective. *Research on Language and Social Interaction, 26,* 287–306.

Ochs, E. (1996). Linguistic resources for socializing humanity. In J. J. Gumperz & S. L. Levinson (Eds.), *Rethinking linguistic relativity* (pp. 407–437). New York: Cambridge University Press.

Ochs, E., Schegloff, E. A., & Thompson, S. A. (Eds.). (1996). *Interaction and grammar.* Cambridge: Cambridge University Press.

Ohta, A. S. (1994). Socializing the expression of affect: An overview of affective particle use in the Japanese as a foreign language classroom. *Issues in Applied Linguistics, 5,* 303–326.

Ohta, A. S. (1995). Applying sociocultural theory to an analysis of learner discourse: Learner-learner collaborative interaction in the zone of proximal development. *Issues in Applied Linguistics, 6,* 93–121.

Ohta, A. S. (1997). The development of pragmatic competence in learner-learner classroom interaction. In L. F. Bouton (Ed.), *Pragmatics and language learning* (monograph series vol. 8, pp. 223–242). Urbana-Champaign, IL: Division of English as an International Language, University of Illinois, Urbana-Champaign.

Ohta, A. S. (1999). Interactional routines and the socialization of interactional style in adult learners of Japanese. *Journal of Pragmatics, 31,* 1493–1512.

Ohta, A. S. (2001a). A longitudinal study of the development of expression of alignment in Japanese as a foreign language. In K. R. Rose & G. Kasper (Eds.), *Pragmatics in language teaching* (pp. 103–120). New York: Cambridge University Press.

Ohta, A. S. (2001b). *Second language acquisition processes in the classroom: Learning Japanese.* Mahwah, NJ: Lawrence Erlbaum.

Olshtain, E. (1983). Sociocultural competence and language transfer: The case of apology. In S. Gass & L. Selinker (Eds.), *Language transfer in language learning* (pp. 232–249). Rowley, MA: Newbury House.

Olshtain, E., & Blum-Kulka, S. (1985). Degree of approximation: Nonnative reactions to native speech act behavior. In S. M. Gass & C. Madden (Eds.),

Input in second language acquisition (pp. 303–325). Rowley, MA: Newbury House.

Olshtain, E., & Cohen, A. D. (1990). The learning of complex speech act behavior. *TESL Canada Journal, 7*, 45–65.

Omar, A. (1991). How learners greet in Kiswahili: A cross-sectional survey. In L. F. Bouton & Y. Kachru (Eds.), *Pragmatics and language learning* (monograph series vol. 2, pp. 59–73). Urbana-Champaign, IL: Division of English as an International Language, University of Illinois, Urbana-Champaign.

Pallotti, G. (2001). External appropriations as a strategy for participating in intercultural multi-party conversations. In A. Di Luzio, S. Günthner, & F. Orletti (Eds.), *Culture in communication* (pp. 295–334). Amsterdam: Benjamins.

Pearson, R. W., Ross, M., & Daws, R. M. (1992). Personal recall and the limits of retrospective questions in surveys. In J. M. Tanur (Ed.), *Questions about questions* (pp. 65–94). New York: Russell Sage Foundation.

Peirce, B. N. (1994). Using diaries in second language research and teaching. *English Quarterly, 26*, 22–29.

Peirce, B. N. (1995). Social identity, investment, and language learning. *TESOL Quarterly, 29*, 9–31.

Peräkylä, A. (1997). Reliability and validity in research based on transcripts. In D. Silverman (Ed.), *Qualitative research* (pp. 201–220). London: Sage.

Perdue, C. (1993). *Adult language acquisition: Cross-linguistic perspectives.* New York: Cambridge University Press.

Perdue, C. (Ed.). (2000). The structure of learner varieties [Special issue]. *Studies in Second Language Acquisition, 22*(4).

Pienemann, M. (1998). *Language processing and second language development.* Amsterdam: Benjamins.

Pomerantz, A. (1978). Compliment responses: Notes on the co-operation of multiple constraints. In J. Schenkein (Ed.), *Studies in the organization of conversational interaction* (pp. 79–112). New York: Academic Press.

Poole, D. (1992). Language socialization in the second language classroom. *Language Learning, 42*, 593–616.

Porter, P. A. (1986). How learners talk to each other: Input and interaction in task-centered discussions. In R. R. Day (Ed.), *Talking to learn: Conversation in second language acquisition* (pp. 200–222). Rowley, MA: Newbury House.

Psathas, G. (1990). Introduction: Methodological issues and recent developments in the study of naturally occurring interaction. In G. Psathas (Ed.), *Interaction competence* (pp. 1–30). Washington, DC: University Press of America.

Rampton, B. (1990). Displacing the "native speaker": Expertise, affiliation, and inheritance. *ELT Journal*, *44*, 97–101.

Rampton, B. (1995). *Crossing: Language and ethnicity among adolescents.* London: Longman.

Regan, V. (1995). The acquisition of sociolinguistic native speaker norms: Effects of a year abroad on second language learners of French. In B. F. Freed (Ed.), *Second language acquisition in a study abroad context* (pp. 245–267). Amsterdam: Benjamins.

Regan, V. (1996). Variation in French interlanguage: A longitudinal study of sociolinguistic competence. In R. Bayley & D. R. Preston (Eds.), *Second language acquisition and linguistic variation* (pp. 177–201). Amsterdam: Benjamins.

Rintell, E. (1984). But how did you feel about that? The learners perception of emotion in speech. *Applied Linguistics, 5*, 255–264.

Rintell, E., & Mitchell, C. J. (1989). Studying requests and apologies: An inquiry into method. In S. Blum-Kulka, J. House, & G. Kasper (Eds.), *Cross-cultural pragmatics* (pp. 248–272). Norwood, NJ: Ablex.

Roberts, C., Davies, E. & Jupp, T. (1992). *Language and discrimination.* London: Longman.

Robinson, M. (1992). Introspective methodology in interlanguage pragmatics research. In G. Kasper (Ed.), *Pragmatics of Japanese as native and target language* (Technical Report No. 3, pp. 27–82). Honolulu: University of Hawai'i at Manoa, Second Language Teaching and Curriculum Center.

Rodriguez, S. (2001). *The perception of requests in Spanish by instructed learners of Spanish in the second- and foreign-language contexts: A longitudinal study of acquisition patterns.* Unpublished doctoral dissertation, Indiana University, Bloomington, IN.

Rogoff, B. (1990). *Apprenticeship in thinking: Cognitive development in social context.* New York: Oxford University Press.

Rose, K. R. (1992). Speech acts and questionnaires: The effect of hearer response. *Journal of Pragmatics, 17*, 49–62.

Rose, K. R. (1994). On the validity of discourse completion tests in non-Western contexts. *Applied Linguistics*, *15*, 1–14.

Rose, K. R. (1996). Japanese, American English, and directness: More than stereotypes. *JALT Journal, 18*, 67–80.

Rose, K. R. (2000). An exploratory cross-sectional study of interlanguage pragmatic development. *Studies in Second Language Acquisition, 22*, 27–67.

Rose, K. R., & Kasper, G. (Eds.). (2001). *Pragmatics in language teaching.* New York: Cambridge University Press.

Rose, K. R., & Ng, C. (2001). Inductive and deductive teaching of compliments and compliment responses. In K. R. Rose & G. Kasper (Eds.), *Pragmatics in language teaching* (pp. 145–170). New York: Cambridge University Press.

Rose, K. R., & Ono, R. (1995). Eliciting speech act data in Japanese: The effect of questionnaire type. *Language Learning, 45,* 191–223.

Rost-Roth, M. (1999). Der Erwerb der Modalpartikeln. Eine Fallstudie zum Partikelerwerb einer italienischen Deutschlernerin im Vergleich mit anderen Lernervarietäten [The acquisition of modal particles. A case study of the particle acquisition by an Italian learner of German in comparison with other learner varieties]. In N. Dittmar & A. Giacalone Ramat (Eds.), *Grammatik und Diskurs / Grammatica e discorso. Studi sull'acquisizione dell'italiano e del tedescho / Studien zum Erwerb des Deutschen und des Italienischen* [Grammar and discourse. Studies of the acquisition of German and Italian] (pp. 165–209). Tübingen, Germany: Stauffenburg.

Roever, C. (2001). A web-based test of interlanguage pragmalinguistic knowledge: Speech acts, routines, implicatures. (Doctoral dissertation, University of Hawai'i.) *Dissertation Abstracts International, 62,* 2095.

Röver, C. (1996). *Linguistische Routinen: Systematische, psycholinguistische und fremdsprachendidaktische Überlegungen* [Linguistic routines: Systematic, psycholinguistic, and pedagogical considerations]. *Fremdsprachen und Hochschule, 46,* 43–60.

Salsbury, T., & Bardovi-Harlig, K. (2000). Oppositional talk and the acquisition of modality in L2 English. In B. Swierzbin, F. Morris, M. Anderson, C. A. Klee, & E. Tarone (Eds.), *Social and cognitive factors in second language acquisition* (pp. 56–76). Somerville, MA: Cascadilla Press.

Salsbury, T., & Bardovi-Harlig, K. (2001). "I know your mean, but I don't think so": Disagreements in L2 English. In L. F. Bouton (Ed.), *Pragmatics and language learning* (monograph series vol. 10, pp. 131–151). Urbana-Champaign, IL: Division of English as an International Language, University of Illinois, Urbana-Champaign.

Sasaki, M. (1998). Investigating EFL students' production of speech acts: A comparison of production questionnaires and role plays. *Journal of Pragmatics, 30,* 457–484.

Sawyer, M. (1992). The development of pragmatics in Japanese as a second language: The sentence-final particle *ne.* In G. Kasper (Ed.), *Pragmatics of Japanese as a native and foreign language* (Technical Report No. 3, pp. 83–125). Honolulu: University of Hawai'i at Mānoa, Second Language Teaching & Curriculum Center.

Scarcella, R. (1979). On speaking politely in a second language. In C. A. Yorio, K. Peters, & J. Schachter (Eds.), *On TESOL '79: The learner in focus* (pp. 275–287). Washington, DC: Teachers of English to Speakers of Other Languages.

Scarcella, R. (1983). Discourse accent in second language performance. In S. M. Gass & L. Selinker (Eds.), *Language transfer in language learning* (pp. 306–326). Rowley, MA: Newbury House.

Schegloff, E. (1992). On talk and its institutional occasions. In P. Drew & J. Heritage (Eds.), *Talk at work* (pp. 101–134). New York: Cambridge University Press.

Schegloff, E., & Sacks, H. (1973). Opening up closings. *Semiotica, 8,* 289–327.

Schieffelin, B. B. (1990). *The give and take of everyday life: Language socialization of Kaluli children.* New York: Cambridge University Press.

Schieffelin, B. B., & Ochs, E. (1986). Language socialization. *Annual Review of Anthropology, 15,* 163–191.

Schiffrin, D. (1987). *Discourse markers.* New York: Cambridge University Press.

Schlieben-Lange, B. (1974). *Linguistische Pragmatik* [Linguistic pragmatics]. Stuttgart: Kohlhammer.

Schmidt, R. (1983). Interaction, acculturation and the acquisition of communicative competence. In N. Wolfson & E. Judd (Eds.), *Sociolinguistics and second language acquisition* (pp. 137–174). Rowley, MA: Newbury House.

Schmidt, R. (1993). Consciousness, learning and interlanguage pragmatics. In G. Kasper & S. Blum-Kulka (Eds.), *Interlanguage pragmatics* (pp. 21–42). Oxford: Oxford University Press.

Schmidt, R. (1995). Consciousness and foreign language learning: A tutorial on the role of attention and awareness in learning. In R. Schmidt (Ed.), *Attention and awareness in foreign language learning* (pp. 1–63). Honolulu: University of Hawai'i, Second Language Teaching & Curriculum Center.

Schmidt, R. (2001). Attention. In P. Robinson (Ed.), *Cognition and second language instruction* (pp. 3–33). New York: Cambridge University Press.

Schmidt, R., Boraie, D., & Kassabgy, O. (1996). Foreign language motivation: Internal structure and external connections. In R. L. Oxford (Ed.), *Language learning motivation: Pathways to the new century* (Technical Report No., 11, pp. 9–70). Honolulu: University of Hawai'i, Second Language Teaching & Curriculum Center.

Schmidt, R., & Frota, S. N. (1986). Developing basic conversational ability in a second language: A case study of an adult learner of Portuguese. In R. Day (Ed.), *Talking to learn* (pp. 237–326). Rowley, MA: Newbury House.

Schumann, J. H. (1978). The acculturation model for second language acquisition. In R. C. Gringas (Ed.), *Second language acquisition and foreign language teaching.* Arlington, VA: Center for Applied Linguistics.

Schumann, J. H. (1986). Research on the acculturation model for second language acquisition. *Journal of Multilingual and Multicultural Development, 7,* 379–392.

Schumann, J. H. (1998). *The neurobiology of affect in language.* Oxford: Blackwell.

Schumann, J. H. (2001). Learning as foraging. In Z. Dörnyei & R. Schmidt (Eds.), *Motivation and second language acquisition* (Technical Report No. 23, pp. 21–28). Honolulu: University of Hawai'i, Second Language Teaching & Curriculum Center.

Schwarz, N., & Hippler, H.-J. (1991). Response alternatives: The impact of their choice and presentation order. In P. P. Biemer, R. M. Groves, L. E. Lyberg, N. A. Mathiowetz, & S. Sudman (Eds.), *Measurement errors in surveys* (pp. 41–56). New York: Wiley.

Schwarz, N., & Sudman, S. (1996). *Answering questions: Methodology for determining cognitive and communicative processes in survey research.* San Francisco, CA: Jossey-Bass.

Searle, J. (1969). *Speech acts: An essay in the philosophy of language.* Cambridge, UK: Cambridge University Press.

Searle, J. (1975). Indirect speech acts. In P. Cole & J. Morgan (Eds.), *Syntax and semantics: Vol. 3. Speech acts* (pp. 59–82). New York: Academic Press.

Searle, J. (1976). A classification of illocutionary acts. *Language in Society, 5,* 1–23.

Selting, M., & Couper-Kuhlen, E. (Eds.) (2001). *Studies in interactional linguistics.* Amsterdam: Benjamins.

Sharwood Smith, M. (1993). Input enhancement in instructed SLA: Theoretical bases. *Studies in Second Language Acquisition, 15,* 165–179.

Shea, D. P. (1994). Perspective and production: Structuring conversational participation across cultural borders. *Pragmatics, 4,* 357–389.

Shimamura, K. (1993). *Judgment of request strategies and contextual factors by American and Japanese EFL learners* (Occasional Paper No. 25). Honolulu: University of Hawai'i at Manoa, Department of English as a Second Language.

Siegal, M. (1994). Learning Japanese as a second language in Japan and the interaction of race, gender and social context. (Doctoral dissertation, University of California-Berkeley.) *Dissertation Abstracts International, 56,* 1692.

Siegal, M. (1995). Individual differences and study abroad: Women learning Japanese in Japan. In B. F. Freed (Ed.), *Second language acquisition in a study abroad context* (pp. 225–244). Amsterdam: Benjamins.

Siegal, M. (1996). The role of learner subjectivity in second language sociolinguistic competency: Western women learning Japanese. *Applied Linguistics, 17,* 356–382.

Silverman, D. (2001). *Interpreting qualitative data* (2nd ed.). London: Sage.

Sinclair, J., & Coulthard, R. (1975). *Towards an analysis of discourse.* Oxford: Oxford University Press.

Singleton, D. (2001). Age and second language acquisition. *Annual Review of Applied Linguistics, 21*, 77–89.

Skiba, R., & Dittmar, N. (1992). Pragmatic, semantic, and syntactic constraints and grammaticalization: A longitudinal perspective. *Studies in Second Language Acquisition, 14*, 323–349.

Smagorinsky, P. (1998). Thinking and speech and protocol analysis. *Mind, Culture, and Activity, 5*, 157–177.

Smagorinsky, P. (2001). Rethinking protocol analysis from a cultural perspective. *Annual Review of Applied Linguistics, 21*, 233–245.

Spradley, J. P. (1979). *The ethnographic interview*. New York: Holt, Rinehart & Winston.

Stauble, A.-M. (1978). The process of decreolization: A model for second language acquisition. *Language Learning, 28*, 29–54.

Stemmer, B. (1981). Kohäsion im gesprochenen Diskurs deutscher Lerner des Englischen. *Manuskripte zur Sprachlehrforschung, 18*. Bochum, Germany: Ruhr-Universität.

Stengal, E. (1939). On learning a new language. *International Journal of Psychoanalysis, 20*, 471–479.

Svanes, B. (1992). *Utviklingen av realisasjonsmønsteret for språkhandlingen 'å be noen om å gjøre noe' hos utenlandske studenter I løpet av 3 år i Norge* [Development of realization patterns of the speech act "asking someone to do something" by foreign students during three years in Norway]. *Norsk Lingvistisk Tidsskift, 1*, 1–50.

Swain, M. (1996). Three functions of output in second language learning. In G. Cook & B. Seidlhofer (Eds.), *Principle and practice in applied linguistics* (pp. 245–256). Oxford: Oxford University Press.

Swain, M. (2001). Examining dialogue: Another approach to content specification and to validating inferences drawn from test scores. *Language Testing, 18*, 275–302.

Tajfel, H. (1978). *Differentiation between social groups: Studies in the social psychology of group relations*. London: Academic Press.

Tajfel, H. (1981). *Human groups and social categories*. Cambridge: Cambridge University Press.

Takahashi, S. (1995). Pragmatic transferability of L1 indirect request strategies perceived by Japanese learners of English. (Doctoral dissertation, University of Hawai'i.) *Dissertation Abstracts International, 56*, 1758.

Takahashi, S. (1996). Pragmatic transferability. *Studies in Second Language Acquisition, 18*, 189–223.

Takahashi, S. (2000). *The effects of motivation and proficiency on the awareness of pragmatic strategies in implicit foreign language learning*. Unpublished manuscript.

Takahashi, S. (2001). The role of input enhancement in developing pragmatic competence. In K. R. Rose & G. Kasper (Eds.), *Pragmatics in language teaching* (pp. 171–199). New York: Cambridge University Press.

Takahashi, T., & Beebe, L. M. (1987). The development of pragmatic competence by Japanese learners of English. *JALT Journal, 8*, 131–155.

Tao, H., & Thompson, S. A. (1991). English backchannels in Mandarin conversation: A case study of superstratum pragmatic "interference." *Journal of Pragmatics, 16*, 209–223.

Tateyama, Y. (2001). Explicit and implicit teaching of pragmatic routines: Japanese *sumimasen*. In K. R. Rose & G. Kasper (Eds.), *Pragmatics in language teaching* (pp. 200–222). New York: Cambridge University Press.

Tateyama, Y., Kasper, G., Mui, L., Tay, H., & Thananart, O. (1997). Explicit and implicit teaching of pragmatic routines. In L. F. Bouton (Ed.), *Pragmatics and language learning* (monograph series vol. 8, pp. 163–178). Urbana-Champaign, IL: Division of English as an International Language, University of Illinois, Urbana-Champaign.

Thomas, J. (1983). Cross-cultural pragmatic failure. *Applied Linguistics, 4*, 91–112.

Thomas, J. (1995). *Meaning in interaction. An introduction to pragmatics.* London: Longman.

Tomlin, R., & Villa, V. (1994). Attention in cognitive science and second language acquisition. *Studies in Second Language Acquisition, 16*, 183–203.

Traugott, E. C., & Heine, B. (Eds.). (1991). *Approaches to grammaticalization.* Amsterdam: Benjamins.

Tremblay, P. F., & Gardner, R. C. (1995). Expanding the motivation construct in language learning. *Modern Language Journal, 79*, 505–520.

Trosborg, A. (1987). Apology strategies in natives/nonnatives. *Journal of Pragmatics, 11*, 147–167.

Trosborg, A. (1995). *Interlanguage pragmatics.* Berlin: Mouton de Gruyter.

Truscott, J. (1998). Noticing in second language acquisition: A critical review. *Second Language Research, 14*, 103–135.

Turnbull, W. (2001). An appraisal of pragmatic elicitation techniques for the social psychological study of talk: The case of request refusals. *Pragmatics, 11*(1), 31–61.

Tyler, A. (1995). The co-construction of cross-cultural miscommunication. *Studies in Second Language Acquisition, 17*, 129–152.

Tyler, A., & Davies, C. (1990). Cross-linguistic communication missteps. *Text, 10*, 385–411.

Verschueren, J. (1987). *Pragmatics as a theory of linguistic adaptation* (Working Documents No. 1). Antwerp: International Pragmatics Association.

Vygotsky, L. S. (1964). *Denken und Sprechen* [Thinking and speaking]. Berlin: Akademie-Verlag. West-German license edition: Stuttgart: S. Fischer (1969).

Vygotsky, L. S. (1978). *Mind in society: The development of higher psychological processes.* Cambridge, MA: Harvard University Press.

Vygotsky, L. S. (1981). The genesis of higher mental functions. In J. V. Wertsch (Ed.), *The concept of activity in Soviet psychology* (pp. 144–188). Armonk, NY: M. E. Sharpe.

Wagner, J., & Firth, A. (1997). Communication strategies at work. In G. Kasper & E. Kellerman (Eds.), *Communication strategies: Psycholinguistic and sociolinguistic perspectives* (pp. 323–344). London: Longman.

Walters, J. (1980). Grammar, meaning, and sociological appropriateness in second language acquisition. *Canadian Journal of Psychology—Revue Canadienne de Psychologie, 34,* 337–345.

Watson-Gegeo, K. A. (1992). Thick explanation in the ethnographic study of child socialization: A longitudinal study of the problem of schooling for Kwara'ae (Solomon Islands) children. In W. Corsaro & P. J. Miller (Eds.), *Interpretive approaches to children's socialization* (pp. 51–66). San Francisco: Jossey-Bass.

Watson-Gegeo, K. A., & Gegeo, D. W. (1986). Calling-out and repeating routines in Kwara'ae children's language socialization. In B. B. Schieffelin & E. Ochs (Eds.), *Language socialization across cultures* (pp. 17–50). New York: Cambridge University Press.

Watson-Gegeo, K. A., & Nielsen, S. (In press). Language socialization in SLA. In C. Doughty & M. Long (Eds.), *Handbook of second language acquisition.* Oxford: Blackwell.

Weedon, C. (1987). *Feminist practice and poststructuralist theory.* Oxford: Blackwell.

Wenger, E. (1998). *Communities of practice: Learning, meaning, and identity.* New York: Cambridge University Press.

Wertsch, J. V. (Ed.). (1981a). *The concept of activity in Soviet psychology.* Armonk, NY: M. E. Sharpe.

Wertsch, J. V. (1981b). The concept of activity in Soviet psychology: An introduction. In J. V. Wertsch (Ed.), *The concept of activity in Soviet psychology* (pp. 3–36). Armonk, NY: M. E. Sharpe.

Wertsch, J. V., & Stone, C. A. (1978). Microgenesis as a tool for developmental analysis. *Quarterly Newsletter of the Laboratory of Comparative Human Cognition* (Center for Human Information Processing, University of California, San Diego), *1*(1).

White, S. (1989). Backchannels across cultures: A study of Americans and Japanese. *Language in Society, 18,* 59–76.

Widjaja, C. S. (1997). A study of data refusal: Taiwanese vs. American females. *University of Hawai'i Working Papers in ESL, 15*(2), 1–43.

Wildner-Bassett, M. (1984). *Improving pragmatic aspects of learners' interlanguage.* Tübingen, Germany: Narr.

Wildner-Bassett, M. (1986). Teaching and learning "polite noises": Improving pragmatic aspects of advanced adult learners' interlanguage. In G. Kasper (Ed.), *Learning, teaching and communication in the foreign language classroom* (pp. 163–178). Aarhus, Denmark: Aarhus University Press.

Wilkes-Gibbs, D. (1997). Studying language use as collaboration. In G. Kasper & E. Kellerman (Eds.), *Communication strategies: Psycholinguistic and sociolinguistic perspectives* (pp. 238–274). London: Longman.

Willet, J. (1995). Becoming first graders in L2: An ethnographic study of language socialization. *TESOL Quarterly, 29*, 473–503.

Wishnoff, J. (2000). Hedging your bets: L2 learners' acquisition of pragmatic devices in academic writing and computer-mediated discourse. *Second Language Studies: Working Papers of the Department of Second Language Studies, University of Hawai'i, 19*, 119–157.

Wolfson, N. (1976). Speech events and natural speech: Some implications for sociolinguistic methodology. *Language in Society, 5*, 189–209.

Wolfson, N. (1989). *Perspectives: Sociolinguistics and TESOL.* Rowley, MA: Newbury House.

Wray, A. (2002). *Formulaic language and the lexicon.* New York: Cambridge University Press.

Yoon, K. K. (1991). Bilingual pragmatic transfer to speech acts: Bi-directional responses to a compliment. In L. F. Bouton & Y. Kachru (Eds.), *Pragmatics and language learning* (Vol. 2, pp. 75–100). Urbana, IL: Division of English as an International Language, University of Illinois at Urbana-Champaign.

Yoshimi, D. (1999). L1 socialization as a variable in the use of *ne* by L2 learners of Japanese. *Journal of Pragmatics, 31*, 1513–1525.

Yoshimi, D. R. (2001). Explicit instruction and JFL learners' use of interactional discourse markers. In K. R. Rose & G. Kasper (Eds.), *Pragmatics in language teaching* (pp. 223–244). New York: Cambridge University Press.

Young, R. (1999). Sociolinguistic approaches to SLA. *Annual Review of Applied Linguistics, 19*, 105–132.

Young, R. (2002). Discourse approaches to oral language assessment. *Annual Review of Applied Linguistics, 22*, 243–262.

Young, R., & He, A. W. (Eds.). (1998). *Talking and testing: Discourse approaches to the assessment of oral proficiency.* Amsterdam: Benjamins.

INDEX

A

accommodation theory, 31
acculturation model, 16–20
  affective variables, 17–18
  as an individual difference model, 288–9
  as a causal model, 20, 58
  communicative competence and, 19
  "high" acculturation, 18
  intra-psychological focus of, 7, 61, 305
  "low" acculturation, 18
  and pidginization, 16–17
  pragmatic development, as explanation of, 58–9
  Schmidt's Wes study, 18–20, 276, 299
  of Schumann, 16–17, 18
  social and psychological distance and, 288–9, 292
  social variables, 17, 18
acknowledgement, 130
"act of communication," 4–5
activity, 3, 4, 28–9, 31, 34–6, 38–9, 44, 47, 50, 56, 60, 68, 86–7, 105, 107, 112, 145, 188, 199, 208, 214–16, 233–4, 281, 297–8, 300
activity theory, 34–6
address terms
  choice of, 25, 45; noticing hypothesis, 29–30; two-dimensional model, 23–4
  Indonesian, 24, 25–6, 28–30, 50, 53, 126, 133, 134, 232
advice, 84, 147, 226, 228, 298
age, 14, 43, 69, 197–9, 203, 230–1, 244–5, 270, 276–80, 291–2, 297–8, 302, 310
age of arrival, 197–9, 277–9, 291
agreement/disagreement, 105, 154, 165, 169, 173, 175, 212–15, 240, 250, 264

alignment, 14, 41, 60, 76, 125, 129–31, 211
apology, 14, 87, 91, 99, 101, 103, 110, 144–5, 154–5, 192–3, 195, 197, 201, 223–5, 241, 251, 253, 261, 279, 290–1
aspect(s), 1, 9–10, 34, 43–4, 48, 52, 60, 67, 83–7, 89, 93, 114, 118, 133–4, 145, 157, 159, 164, 180, 187, 200, 204, 206, 210, 212, 217, 223, 226–7, 230, 234, 240, 250–1, 253, 255, 258, 267, 273, 275, 287, 293, 297, 299, 307, 310
attention, 5, 7, 21–4, 26–7, 29–33, 40, 44, 47, 49, 56, 60, 66–7, 72–3, 98, 105, 111, 117, 123, 129, 133, 160, 163, 211, 213, 215, 219, 233, 243, 249, 255, 259, 263, 266, 271, 285–8, 309, 311
audio, 66, 80–3, 115, 271
authentic discourse, 7, 63, 79–80, 80–3, 82, 87, 92–3, 105, 116, 306
awareness, 21, 25, 27, 49, 52, 57, 133, 145, 151, 161–2, 218–19, 233, 248, 283–5

B

backchannel, 29
"bracketing," 65
Brazilian Portuguese, 126–8, 132

C

Cantonese, 141, 244
CCSARP DCT, 91
Chinese, 85, 94, 151
"choice"/"constraint" tension, 3
closed role play, 87, 92
cognitive processing, ix, 5, 7, 15, 20–32, 33, 58, 60–1, 305
  address terms, choice of, 23–4, 29–30
  attention role of, 31

341

Made in the USA
Middletown, DE
24 March 2016